Mucho Corazón

This book is part of the Peter Lang Regional Studies list.
Every volume is peer reviewed and meets
the highest quality standards for content and production.

PETER LANG
New York • Bern • Berlin
Brussels • Vienna • Oxford • Warsaw

Alicia Chavira-Prado

Mucho Corazón

Stages in the Life of a Pioneer Female Mariachi

PETER LANG
New York • Bern • Berlin
Brussels • Vienna • Oxford • Warsaw

Library of Congress Cataloging-in-Publication Data

Names: Chavira-Prado, Alicia, author.
Title: Mucho corazón: stages in the life of a pioneer female mariachi / Alicia Chavira-Prado.
Description: [1.] | New York: Peter Lang, 2022.
Includes bibliographical references and index.
Identifiers: LCCN 2021058464 (print) | LCCN 2021058465 (ebook)
ISBN 978-1-4331-9056-8 (paperback)
ISBN 978-1-4331-9057-5 (ebook pdf) | ISBN 978-1-4331-9058-2 (epub)
Subjects: LCSH: Prado Pastrano, Aurora. | Las Generalas. | Mariachi musicians—Mexico—Biography. | Mariachi musicians—United States—Biography. | Mexican American musicians—Biography. | Women musicians—Mexico—Biography. | Women musicians—United States—Biography. | Mariachi—United States—20th century—History and criticism. | LCGFT: Biographies. | Ethnographies. Autoethnographies.
Classification: LCC ML420.P886 C43 2022 (print) | LCC ML420.P886 (ebook) | DDC 782.42164092 [B]—dc23
LC record available at https://lccn.loc.gov/2021058464
LC ebook record available at https://lccn.loc.gov/2021058465
DOI 10.3726/b18633

Bibliographic information published by **Die Deutsche Nationalbibliothek**.
Die Deutsche Nationalbibliothek lists this publication in the "Deutsche Nationalbibliografie"; detailed bibliographic data are available on the Internet at http://dnb.d-nb.de/.

© 2022 Peter Lang Publishing, Inc., New York
80 Broad Street, 5th floor, New York, NY 10004
www.peterlang.com

All rights reserved.
Reprint or reproduction, even partially, in all forms such as microfilm, xerography, microfiche, microcard, and offset strictly prohibited.

John, my eternal love. To you, Babe, I dedicate this book, with all of my heart.

Table of Contents

List of Photos ix
Acknowledgments xiii

Chapter One: Introduction: Mucho Corazón 1
Chapter Two: *Sin un Amor*: Life and Music in El Chamizal 13
Chapter Three: *Llorarás, Llorarás*: Life and Music in Juárez 33
Chapter Four: Mexican Education, the Golden Age of Cinema,
and National Identity 57
Chapter Five: Naa, Na, Na, Na, Naa: The Chicano Movement and the
Birth of the East Side Sound 75
Chapter Six: La Estrella de la Canción Romántica 95
Chapter Seven: Volver, Volver: Mariachi Music and Performance 119
Chapter Eight: My Participation in Mariachi Las Generalas: En Primera Voz 133
Chapter Nine: Mariachi Las Generalas 145
Epilogue: Fallaste Corazón: Legacies, Closures, and Failings of the Heart 163

Appendix A: Misa Panamericana/Order of Mass as Played by Mariachi Las
Generalas 175
Appendix B: Aurora Prado Pastrano's Collection of Old Popular Song Titles 177
Appendix C: Selected Song Lyrics 189

Index 221

List of Photos

Front cover photo: Aurora P. Pastrano with guitarrón, in mariachi regalia during her years with Mariachi Las Generalas, 1970s.
Back cover photo: Aurora Prado Pastrano and author. From the private photo collection of the author.
Photo 3.1: Aurora Prado, 1950s. From the author's private collection. 42
Photo 3.2: Aurora Prado, c1955. From the author's private photo collection. 43
Photo 5.1: Promotional photo of Amalia Mendoza's performance at Teatro California, Los Angeles. From the private archives of Aurora Prado Pastrano, c1965. 77
Photo 5.2: The Big Beats. Joe Chavira, second from the left. At Millie's Lounge in East Los Angeles, 1962. Provided to the author by Joe Chavira, from his private collection. 90
Photo 6.1: Aurora Prado, 1968. From her private collection. 96
Photo 6.2: Promotion of *La Estrella*, 1968. From the private archives of Aurora Prado Pastrano. 98
Photos 6.3 a, b: From the private archives of Aurora Prado Pastrano. 1968. 100

Photos 6.4 a, b:	Aurora Prado, performing at a fundraising event supporting candidacy of Bobby Kennedy (photo background). At the State Ballroom, Los Angeles, April 27, 1968.	102
Photo 6.5:	Conjunto Papaloápan album cover. From the private record collection of Aurora Prado Pastrano.	103
Photo 6.6:	Promotional poster of Mother's Day event sponsored by Thrift Furniture Co. Aurora Prado was among the performers on the program.	111
Photo 6.7:	Promotional poster of performance program on Catalina Island, 1968. Aurora Prado, among the featured artists. From the private archives of Aurora Prado Pastrano.	112
Photo 7.1:	Poster purchased by the author, of the International Mariachi Conference in Tucson, 2006. From the author's private archives.	125
Photo 7.2:	Program from the Mariachi Festival X (10th) Anniversary, June 19 & 20, 1999, at the Hollywood Bowl. From the author's private archive collection.	126
Photo 8.1a:	Aurora Prado Pastrano, performing as part of duo *Las Golondrinas*, at Azteca Restaurant, Los Angeles, c1985.	139
Photo 8.1b:	Aurora Pastrano and Lupe Rodriguez, performing with their teacher, Maestro Larios, 1988.	140
Photo 8.2a, b:	(a): Aurora Pastrano with Saulo Sedan (requintista), Los Diamantes. La Costa Restaurant. March 6, 1988. (b): Aurora Pastrano with Eduardo Novelo (lead vocals), Trio Montejo. La Costa Restaurant. March 06, 1988.	141
Photo 8.3:	Aurora Pastrano and Lupe Rodriguez, performing as duo Las Golondrinas, La Costa Restaurant. May 1988.	142
Photo 9.1:	Mariachi Las Generalas, late 1970s. From the author's private photo collection.	146
Photo 9.2:	Mariachi Las Generalas, with instruments, c1970s. From the author's private photo collection.	147
Photo 9.3:	Poster of event in Bakersfield in which Las Generalas were to accompany famous singer Pepe Infante. November 19, 1982. From the private archives of Aurora Prado Pastrano.	151

LIST OF PHOTOS | XI

Photo 9.4:	Promotional poster of event featuring Mariachi Las Generalas. c1983. From the private archive collection of Aurora Prado Pastrano.	154
Photo 9.5:	Promotional poster of event featuring *Mariachi Las Generalas* as guests of honor. January 28, 1983. From the private archive collection of Aurora Prado Pastrano.	157
Photo 9.6:	Aurora Prado Pastrano, in Mariachi *traje*, 1994. From the private photo collection of the author.	161
Photo E.1:	Aurora Prado Pastrano, examining her guitarrón. December 2020. From the private photo collection of the author.	168
Photo E.2:	Aurora Prado Pastrano, up late playing the piano. December 2020. From the private photo collection of the author.	168
Photo E.3:	Some of the Cancioneros in Aurora Prado Pastrano's private collection.	169
Photo E.4:	Aurora Prado Pastrano with David Chanes, in Yucaipa, CA. May 12, 2017. From the private photo collection of the author.	171
Photo E.5:	Aurora Prado Pastrano, May 14, 2015. From the private photo collection of the author.	173

Acknowledgments

I am grateful to several people whose encouragement to carry out this project brought it to fruition. I am most grateful for, and to, the man with whom I shared most of my life. Thank you, for the loving eyes that gleamed along with the crooked, knowing smile when I was happy, when I sang, when I got my way. By always believing in me, you helped me to believe in myself, to know that whatever I endeavored was worthwhile because it was my passion. Fate separated us from each other in our earthly existence in the last weeks of the book's completion, ripping you away from me along with my heart and my soul. Even at your deathbed, you cheered me on to finish this project. Though our love is eternal, I know that until we meet again, I shall never again know such love, but part of its legacy is represented in this book.

I am deeply grateful to my mom, Aurora, for never letting life's obstacles stop her from sharing her music with everyone around her. Through her love of music and performance she infused me with a sense of cultural knowing and belonging through which I experienced a world that I might never have known or appreciated otherwise. That music lives in my heart, my mind, my body and my *sentimientos*, feelings and understandings, that still help me make sense of an otherwise chaotic world. I am thankful to her also because, in spite of her aloofness toward being recognized in history for her musical contributions, she provided me important information for the documenting of her artistic life, and for allowing me to relate some of the most painful, private, but very relevant and enlightening parts of her life in this biography.

I owe a great debt of gratitude to the reviewers of the first draft of the manuscript, for their analytic insights in seeing the value of this project. Their critiques and generous comments were invaluable in helping me to focus my objectives and organize around them, and to reshape the earlier version into one that is far more worthy of the story it tells. While the work benefited significantly from their reviews, I take full responsibility for any shortcomings in this project.

I wish to thank also other persons whose voices helped enrich the breadth and meaning of this biographical/ethnographic account by allowing me to include interviews and conversations I had with them in telling this story. They include, Lupe and Sylvestre Rodriguez and their family, Eddie Chavira, Joe (Pepe) Chavira, David Chanes, and Ozzie Reinoso.

I also wish to thank my wonderful, loving, children, Miguela and Sahuaro. While going through our grief, they unselfishly poured their love and support to help me reach the final steps of this book. Thank you also, kids, for critiquing those segments I shared with you from the first draft.

Finally, but never least, I thank my acquiring editor at Peter Lang Publishing, Laurence Pagacz, for seeing merit in my original manuscript submission, for his kind assistance with all my queries, and for his support and understanding in getting me through the final steps to publication.

CHAPTER ONE

Introduction: Mucho Corazón

Juárez, Chihuahua, Mexico, late 1950s. Hearing her singing over the loud speaker at the church fair made my stomach cringe with anxiety. *Mona, esa es tu mamá, la oyes?* My friend came running to tell me while I played tag with a group of friends on the street in front of the church near our house. My friend was making sure I knew it was my mother singing on that platform stage, as if I had not already recognized her voice. I knew she had likely volunteered or asked the band to let her come up and sing a song with them. She would do this at different occasions and places, and even though I was only six or seven years old, I was embarrassed by her boldness. Maybe I felt that being an amateur left her open to possible ridicule. As children often do, I feared becoming the social casualty of my mother's exposure to public criticism. To my relief, her listeners were always attentive and seemingly impressed, perhaps by her talent and her beauty or they were intrigued by her audacity. Still, I had hoped that the size of the fair's crowd and the dimming light of dusk might keep the other kids from noticing it was my mother up there. More than dreading that my friends might tease me about my mother, I was afraid knowing that if my father found out about her singing on that stage, it would unleash his brutality. I cowered for her at the thought. She was well aware of his prohibitions: No going outside the house but for church service, marketing, and other necessities. No contact or unnecessary conversations with strangers, especially men. Her singing in public would fall well outside of his rules, if he ever found out. At home we mostly abided by his rules, and my mother seemed timid and submissive. But my mother never let him, nor any other obstacle, stop her from pursuing her love of music and performance. Her voice coming through the microphone at the fair betrayed no concern with potential consequences. What I heard was the love of music in her singing, in her blending of melody and lyrics like the music that we heard on the radio. This was one of those moments in which my mother's singing, wrapped in her public performance, signified resistance, defiance and self-expression.

This is the story of Aurora Prado Pastrano, of the stages of her life and the stages of her public performance as a music artist. In the late 1960s' East Los Angeles nightclub circuit, she became a bolero interpreter, known as *La Estrella de la Canción Romántica*, the "Star of the Romantic Song." In performance, she was a self-representation of cultural identity and gendered subjectivity. In that stage of her artistic career, referring here to both a developmental period and performative site, she would develop an aesthetic that would ultimately help shape her stage persona as a pioneer female mariachi.

Aurora Prado Pastrano was the first professional female mariachi *guitarrón* player, and original member of arguably the first, all-female mariachi group in the United States, known as *Las Generalas*. In 1976, this grassroots group of women in East Los Angeles, the mariachi capitol outside of Mexico City, broke a cultural tradition that had defined mariachi performance strictly as a male domain. As trailblazers, they faced disapproval by their own families, disdain from male mariachis, and resistance from audiences accustomed to the male image, yet they ushered in a new era in Mexican American cultural history. They helped re-create the mariachi art into one that encompasses all genders in a more inclusive, diverse representation of our Mexican American identity and experience in what I call, our *cultural music*.

By our *cultural music* I mean those musical sounds, rhythms, lyrics, and instrumentations that represent our cultural identity and community, that relate to our shared values, experiences, traditions, and history, and evoke and reaffirm our sense of belonging. I conceive of that term similarly to what Deborah Vargas describes as *la onda:* "an umbrella term for Mexican American/Chicano/Tejano music … the ways the broader public and Chicanas/os have claimed music as 'our own'".[1] However, I use the term *cultural music* in a more specific yet internationally inclusive sense, as the compilation of sounds that people who identify themselves as members of a cultural tradition, regardless of their geographical location, nationality, or trans-national social experience, love as their own and recognize as a symbol of their cultural belonging, in this case, of their Mexican and Latino heritage.

As the first female professional guitarrón player in the United States, Aurora Prado Pastrano personified a unique defiance of the gender ideology that defined the mariachi tradition as the hyper-heterosexual masculine ideal. The *guitarrón* is prominent in mariachi music because as the base instrument, it leads the tempo that anchors the music produced by the other instruments. It is a stringed, big-bodied acoustic bass, shaped like a big, round-backed guitar. Its exaggerated size and weight demand greater bodily strength and stamina in its player compared to the other instruments used in mariachi music. As Pérez notes, the *guitarrón's* large profile becomes associated with masculine virility, a perception assisted by the way the instrument conceals the torso section of the player's body, and in the case of a woman instrumentalist, hiding the most anatomically distinct aspects of her femininity, while also revealing the lower part of her ankle-length mariachi skirt, the part of her *traje de charra* (performance wear) that affirms her female identity to her audience.[2] This contradictory gender dichotomy would challenge the gender binary and macho ideological construction of mariachi in the public imagination, especially when *Las Generalas* represented a new social phenomenon, when they appeared as the first all-women mariachi group on the stage. At about 5 ft. 4 inches tall and roughly 135 pounds, Aurora's command of the *guitarrón* became a portrait of embodied innovation in mariachi artistry.

The *Bolero* is a musical style defined by its lyrics of heartbreak, passion and romance embedded in innuendo. It is either abstractive in sexually identifying the protagonist or the protagonist is female.[3] In the bolero, "the main melody is performed by solo voice, allowing for more individual expression than is possible in the *son*".[4] Its slow-tempo music and narrative evoke sensuality and dramatize it especially in the female performer.[5] A *bolerista* is measured especially by the artist's ability to interpret vocally, the drama of the lyrics, with the requisite sensibility, eloquence and sophistication that are supposed to set the bolero apart from other Mexican genres such as the *ranchera or corrido*,[6] that are also standard musical styles in mariachi music. In interpreting the bolero, with its female and gender-neutral aesthetic tradition, as a female mariachi, Aurora further pushed her audience's cultural dissonance and tested their acceptance of women in mariachi performance. In so doing, she advanced the deconstruction of the machismo that had framed the mariachi tradition by embodying a musical contradiction to the normative gendering of mariachi.

Mariachi has been a topic of academic inquiry for decades, and although it has been socially viewed as a male musical performance, historians and ethnomusicologists generally ignored the significance of gender and the absence of female mariachis.[7] In addition, music artists, especially female, typically receive historical recognition only if they reached national fame[8] and such recognition always tends to focus on young performers, or on the youthful beginnings of famed celebrities, creating the misconception that public performers always start out young.

Las Generalas were not young by comparison to most beginning artists. They were wives, mothers, and grandmothers, perceivably in their mid-life years, which disassociated them from the typical image of the young rising artist. They also were not trained through either academic musical education, nor through the individual mariachi apprenticeship that traditionally was available to boys and young men. Mariachi musicianship became offered to all genders as part of public education, in community centers, and conservatories, especially in the Southwest, after groups like *Las Generalas,* and changes stimulated by the Chicano Movement and its cultural Renaissance, helped bring it about. Also, the all-female groups that have emerged since *Las Generalas* have been young, so that newer groups have not faced the same barriers as their predecessors. Unfortunately, their lack of formal training, combined with their gender and age, have worked to obscure *Las Generalas* from historic recognition. Credit for being "the first" all-female mariachi group has been incorrectly assigned[9] and some uncertainty exists about whether earlier groups preceded them.[10] As Reifler Flores notes:

> The first all-female mariachi Show group of international stature in the United States, *Mariachi Reyna de Los Angeles*, debuted in 1994 in Los Angeles. This group was made up of women who had very dissimilar backgrounds and musical training, but all had previous experience playing in mixed gender mariachis … .In sharp contrast to this, in 1976 the first all-female mariachi was formed in the United States, a group called *Las Generalas* … Located in Los Angeles.[11]

While the primacy of the all-female group name can be debated, based on group size and instrumentation, *Las Generalas* were the first to be comprised of eight members and to include the *guitarrón*, and thus to be what could be defined as a complete (fully equipped) mariachi musical ensemble. To date, they also remain the only known professional mariachi group composed of "older" women in mariachi in United States history.[12]

Why an Autoethnographic Biography

For years I tried to write the story of Aurora Prado Pastrano's life as a bolero artist and pioneer female mariachi. I first conceived of the project as a way to historicize her contributions as *La Estrella de la Canción Romántica* and as a member of *Las Generalas* in our Mexican American music history, by documenting a factual record of her artistic trajectory. In the intermittent years, I came to realize that the raw facts or mechanisms of her performance are not the most important aspects of a public artist's history; rather, it is the story of the life and contexts that formed the musical artist, the challenges she met along the way, and the ways in which her musical performance represents and expresses the sentiments, traditions, and other forms of cultural identity that she shares with her audience. This is why I partly titled this book "Stages in the Life," because I concentrate on her childhood, family, education, social environment, and mostly, the music that gave meaning to her life experiences because they are all fundamental aspects of her personal life and relate to her public life as a musical stage performer. Through a close look at the life that formed the artist, I try to uncover the person who performed on that stage as *La Estrella de la Canción Romántica* and the pioneer female mariachi and, in that way, assist a clearer and more comprehensive understanding of the meaning and true contributions of her artistic career to our cultural music history.

My initial intent was to write this story in my mother's own words. She met this idea with the same aloofness with which she always met the obstacles she confronted as a performing artist. Then I switched to asking her to collaborate on this writing, which took many years of patience on my part, as her usual response was: *Pues como ya te dije. ¿Que mas te puedo decir?* [Well, as I've already told you, what else can I tell you?] My attempts to conduct focused interviews with her usually got me an earnest, *¡Pos qué quieres que te diga, hombre, ya!* [Well, what do you want me to say, already?!], dismissing my enthusiasm with the feistiness she uses to insult doctors who annoy her or to scoff at their unfavorable diagnoses. My mature adult status has not transformed the mother-child relationship enough to make dealing with her unique temperament any easier. Time has served only to fuel her strong and feisty will. When she did answer my interview questions, often the information she provided was trite, lacking the original richness that I had heard in our casual conversations and her accounts over the years and which I hope to convey here.

What had been my effort to secure Aurora Prado Pastrano's rightful place in music history and do honor to her artistic contributions, was to her, irrelevant, inconsequential and unnecessary. My mother has never objected to my writing about her, but her attitude toward it has made it clear that it does not matter to her. After all these years, I understand why: Fame and glory never compelled her artistic pursuits or achievements; she did not enter into public performance with that or any other agenda. Like her ad hoc performances that caused me such consternation as a child, her professional performances were never about seeking public adulation. Admiration was not meaningless to her; she appreciated having a pleased audience, but that did not determine her continued pursuit of and her love for music and performance. She has never cared if her past as an artist became memorialized or revered. For her, her musical past is not reducible to an evaluation of her merits or achievements. Music to her is not something she achieves, but something with which she has a relationship. As expressed in the song she has always loved to interpret, which I believe has been her true favorite among the many songs she loves, the sole reason why she has performed music, is that musical performance has always been the love of her life, it is what fills and to what she always gave her very big heart. This is the difference between artists who strive to reach stardom through their music, and those who, having no expectation of historical acknowledgments, give us the music they love, from the heart, as Aurora said in performing *Mucho Corazón*:

> *Di si encontraste*
> *en mi pasado*
> *una razón para quererme*
> *o para olvidarme/*
> *Pides cariño, pides ternura*
> *si te conviene,*
> *no llames corazón*
> *lo que tu tienes/*
> *De mi pasado*
> *preguntas todo*
> *que como fue*
> *si antes de amar*
> *debe tenerse fe/*
> *Dar por un querer*
> *la vida misma*
> *sin morir*
> *eso es cariño*
> *no lo que hay en ti/*
> *Yo para querer*
> *no necesito una razón*
> *me sobra mucho*
> *pero mucho corazón.*[13]
> [Tell, did you find
> in my past
> a reason to love me
> or to forget me? /
> You ask for love
> you ask for tenderness
> if it benefits you
> don't call what you have, a "heart." /

> About my past
> you ask, what was it all like?
> Well, before we love
> we must have faith in it/
> To give for what we love
> life itself, without dying
> that is what love is,
> and that is not what is in you/
> I, to love
> I need no reason
> I have much
> too much, heart.] (Translation my own)

Although my mother is a native Tex-Mex, she never performed with or was particularly interested in the *conjunto norteño*, which has been defined as the music of the Tex-Mex experience.[14] Nor have her interests aligned with *bandas*, which have produced popular borderland and border-crossing *corridos*. The singing icons of the *canción ranchera* of the 1940s–1950s period were lasting inspirations to her, but her main inspirations were not the Mexican American divas of the Texas border region, such as Lydia Mendoza. Instead, Aurora's muses included Mexican iconic artists Amalia Mendoza (aka *La Tariácuri*), Lola Beltrán, Pedro Infante, Jorge Negrete, José Alfredo Jiménez, Miguel Aceves Mejía, and Cuco Sánchez. Equally prominent in the formation of, and most influential to her musical identity, were the bolero trios of Mexico, such as Los Tres Aces, Los Dandys, and Los Panchos, and Mexico's most famous composers,[15] among them, Ema Elena Valdelamar, composer of *Los Mil Besos* and *Mucho Corazón*.

As a young child, I would practice singing *boleros, rancheras, corridos, tangos*, and more with my mother, sitting on the edge of the bed at bedtime, or at the kitchen table. My lullabies were popular *boleros* my mother sang to me, especially *Muñequita Linda* (aka *Te Quiero, Dijiste*), and *Consentida*. At times, she would tell me to use my ears to listen to songs, to pay attention to the vocal notes and pitch; at others, while we sang together, she had me keep tempo by tapping my finger. Sometimes she would have me sing solo. Many times, we would sing in harmony, with me singing the lead, *primera voz*, while she sang harmony, s*egunda*. The truth is, I sang lead because I could not harmonize. My lead or solo singing also never reached public display quality. Or I never developed the same confidence and audacity that drove my mother to perform in public. Whatever the case, by comparison to my ability to sing harmony, singing solo in private was my big accomplishment. I was never able to do *segunda*, even as my mother tried to guide my voice, signaling me to go a note higher or lower. Regardless of my musical limitations, I did learn one lesson that she taught me well: The first and most important requirement to produce beautiful music, is that you have to sing with a lot of heart: *Ándale, hija, échale, con mucho corazón!*

It is that full-hearted spirit that I metaphorically use in telling this story, as I try to follow with text, what my mother taught me about music. Simulating our singing in harmony, I lead most of this narrative in first voice. I cede to her accounts where only her voice can give true and complete meaning. I include both our voices wherever possible and where I consider them appropriate or needed for amplification or clarification. Unlike my musical failure to learn the art of *segunda*, my mother's own narratives are in her own, *primera voz*, and I switch from *primera* to *segunda* as I translate or otherwise elaborate, following her voice with text. I do not presume to deal with the methods, nuances, or merits of the music or genres referred to here. Like my mother, I am musically illiterate. I do not understand musical notation, structure, or any other aspect involved in the academic approach to the production of music. My intention is to tell the story of how this musical artist was formed, how her life, her family, her personal history, and the contexts of her experiences produced the identity and subjectivity contained in her musical performance.

Most of the book's content comes from observing my mother's life, the insights that my own immersion in it provided me, and from our many conversations and times I heard my mother's story, our family's oral history as I learned it from her and from relatives, and generally what I came to experience and understand from living with my mother as her only child. It is thus both a biography and an autoethnography, because looking at her life through the lens of my own gave me a unique vantage point from which I interpret her story. The information on her performances is from what I witnessed, what I learned from notes she wrote and shared with me, from interviews I conducted with her, and the stories she told me through the years. I include printed articles on *La Estrella* and photos of her performance promotions, images of promotional posters, which I obtained from her archives, of some show engagements of *Las Generalas*, and which, to my knowledge, have not been previously historicized. The group portraits, which appear in the websites mentioned above, were commissioned by the group for their own promotion and remain the sole published images of their professional years.

I hope that this book serves as a resource and expands the existing knowledge about the music of Mexican Americans. The music that my mother grew up with, learned from, and performed, in many ways shaped her as an artist; therefore, I also include a number of songs and as much information about them as the scope of this project allowed me to do. I conceive of this project as an illustration of how our public artists, especially our grassroots, local ones, represent our own experiences through their public performances; therefore, I also hope that this book promotes continued academic inquiry and general interest in the contributions of our grassroots cultural workers, to advance their historical recognition and documentation in the production, evolution, and continuation of our cultural music.

Chapter Overview

Chapter Two begins the biographical account of the Prado family, our cultural origins and family history set in the context of a developing United States southwest and El Chamizal district of El Paso, Texas. It tells of the life of Aurora Alicia Prado as a Mexican American child growing up devoid of love and of opportunities to nurture her early musical interests, the music that surrounded Mexican Americans like her, and the racialized environment that affected my mother's sense of ethnic identity, belonging, nationalism, and cultural citizenship, all of which contributed to her personal and artistic formation.

Chapter Three, Llorarás, Llorarás, was the most evocative in the writing of this book, because I relate the intimate, disturbing, and pivotal events and experiences of my mother's life, and by association, of my own childhood. For years I questioned whether I should include in this project, details that victims of abuse often hide in order to avoid re-living the trauma and humiliation, the stigma that often accompanies such experiences. The now former White House occupant, Donald Trump, called Mexican men "rapists" and otherwise denigrated brown-skinned people and their countries of origin, and I feared writing something that might feed the mischaracterization of my own cultural group and Mexican nation. Racist slander aside, I decided that the story is of utmost importance because my mother raises her own voice to tell that part of her own story, and I buttress her voice against the wrong that was done her. This is fundamental to understanding Aurora Prado Pastrano the artist, who, through her music and the power of her musical performance, convicted the guilty, claimed the love owed her, and thus vanquished the grim realities of her life. The chapter also covers the twenty-year period of my mother's life in Mexico during most of her adolescent life and her painful marriage while coming of age and coming to terms with the major challenges of her life.

In Chapter Four, I describe some of the public education I experienced and shared with my mother, and how the Golden Age of Cinema incorporated music, because both were major influences in shaping the country's Mexican national identity. Films of the era effectively defined Mexican society, culture, race, class, gender, sexuality, religion, foods, regionalism, indigenous peoples, geography, the Revolution, politics, dance, and introduced and popularized music, so effectively as to become perhaps the most influential media to the Mexican masses. I elaborate on films and music of that era in the chapter's endnotes. Like much of the rest of the country, my mother absorbed a Mexican cultural identity as defined through film and the music it promoted, something she conveyed artistically in her stage performance.

Chapter Five is my autoethnographic account of adolescent life in East Los Angeles in the midst of the Chicano Civil Rights Movement and the birth of what was known as the West Coast East Side Sound. I detail some of the social and political events as the context of our lives and describe the music that defined the times. An era of social change, the Movement revitalized our Mexican legacy in the arts, literature, and music in the cultural Renaissance of the 1960s–1970s, in which artists like *La Estrella de la Canción Romántica* and the group *Las Generalas* emerged. As I discuss in the chapter, however, a Chicano political consciousness was not uniform among all Mexican Americans, including my mother.

Chapter Six focuses on *La Estrella de la Canción Romántica*, the music, aesthetics, and personal trajectory of Aurora Prado in becoming a recognized local artist of *bolero*. It shows the effects of her musical career on her family and other personal relationships, and how she became part of the local music circuit. It revisits an active nightlife set in East Los Angeles in the late 1960s and 1970s, where live bolero music played, Mexican American artists were made, and music became the bridge connecting culturally Mexican people of all generations, across geographic and temporal space.

Chapter Seven is an overview of Mariachi music and performance, which I intend mostly for readers unfamiliar with the origins, symbolisms, and music of the mariachi tradition. I review the cultural characteristics of mariachi performance and some of its most popular music and artists, general history, instruments, diverse regional origins and the styles of music it encompasses, and some of its adaptations in performance in the United States. I review the characteristics of *rancheras*, *corridos*, and *boleros*, some of the music most associated with mariachi performance, to assist an unfamiliar reader's understanding of how it presented specific gendered issues that *Las Generalas* confronted as artistic interpreters, specifically as female mariachis. I also give a description of the characteristic Mariachi interactions with its audience. My attention to gender is intentional and necessary for a holistic understanding of mariachi tradition and performance.

Chapter Eight is an autobiographical narrative of the making of a female mariachi. It is included here as written by my mother, in *primera voz*, in the form of a letter she wrote me, in which she narrates how she came to be one of *Las Generalas*, her experiences and relationships with her group members, and other aspects of her life as a mariachi. After leaving *Las Generalas*, she and fellow mariachi, Lupe Rodriguez, became a singing duo, which she also describes in the letter.

Chapter Nine is a biography of *Las Generalas*. I expound upon the limited existing published information on the group, to historicize how they achieved a competitive and legitimate artistic status as a female group in a male musical public arena, some of their performing experiences and relationships with their audiences, and obstacles they encountered and navigated, especially related to gender, age, and musical training. The chapter also shows the importance of family and family attitudes toward the women's development from grassroots artists into pioneer professional female mariachis.

I borrow the title of the Epilogue from a song title, *Fallaste Corazón*, [You Failed, Heart], using it here to mean the opposite of the book's opening and to mark the closing of the book. The chapter looks at the legacies of *La Estrella de la Canción Romántica* and of the pioneer mariachi and the group of women known as *Las Generalas*, who, along with other groups and artists, left us a gift to history, our cultural music. The imprint of a musical past is represented in groups like Suavé The Band, and other music players and artists whose music today continues to celebrate our Mexican/Chicano/Latino heritage, evidencing the value of artists too often forgotten or unrecognized by history.

Appendix A contains the Order of Mass as played by *Las Generalas* during their performing years. Appendix B is a list of some of the titles of songs known to my mother, including selected songs she performed in public as *La Estrella*, in *Las Generalas*, or in other public performances. Appendix C includes the lyrics to selected songs mentioned in the chapters or the endnotes, if the lyrics are not already included in the main text.

Notes

1. Deborah Vargas 2012, p. x.
2. Pérez, 2015.
3. Pedelty, 1999.
4. Pearlman, 1984, p. 4.
5. Vargas, 2008.
6. Peña, 1985.
7. Reifler Flores, 2015.
8. Koegel, 2005; Vargas, 2012.
9. Hernandez, 2016; Buzzell & Massie, 2007.
10. Sobrino and Pérez were the first to recognize *Las Generalas* as a pioneer all-female mariachi group in the U.S; in the website, A History of Women in Mariachi Music-1970s Muñoz reports

that a group named *Las Rancheritas* formed around 1964; and Perez and Reyna (2015) noted that *Las Generalas* began in 1976, and therefore list them as the second such group in the country.
11. Reifler Flores 2015, n.p.
12. Mariachi Publishing Co. and Pérez, 2005.
13. Song title, Mucho Corazón, Ema Elena Valdelamar, composer. As sung by Amalia Mendoza.
14. Peña, 1985.
15. Epecially Consuelo Velásquez, Maria Grever, and Agustín Lara.

References

Buzzell, M., & Massie, E. (Directors). (2007). *Compañeras* [Motion Picture].
Hernandez, J. (2016). *Mariachi Reyna de los Angeles*. Retrieved from http://reynadelosangelesmusic.com/
Koegel, J. (2005). Review: Mexican American Music. *American Music, 23*(2), 257–274.
Mariachi Publishing Co., & Pérez, X. (2005). *Women in Mariachi History*. Retrieved from http://www.sobrino.net/mpc/womenmariachi/
Pearlman, S. R. (1984). Standarization and Innovation in Mariachi Music Performance in Los Angeles. *Pacific Review of Ethnomusicology, 1*, 1–12.
Pedelty, M. (1999). The Bolero: The Birth, Life, and Decline of Mexican Modernity. *Latin American Music Review / Revista de Música Latinoamericana, 20*(1), 30–58.
Peña, M. (1985). *The Texas-Mexican Conjunto: History of a Working-Class Music*. Austin: University of Texas Press.
Perez, L. a. (2015). The Women of Mariachi: Breaking Barriers in a Machismo Culture. *She Shreds, 19*, n.p.
Reifler Flores, C. (2015). Las Generalas: Origins of Women's Participation in Mariachi and the Cultural and Transnational Implications. *Karpa, 8*, n.p.
Vargas, (2008). Borderlands Bolerista: The Lycentious Lyricism of Chelo Silva. *Feminist Studies, 34*(1/2), 178–197.
Vargas, D. (2012). *Dissonant Divas in Chicana Music: The Limits of La Onda*. Minneapolis: University of Minnesota Press.

CHAPTER TWO

Sin Un Amor:[1] Life and Music in El Chamizal

In the 1800s, Anglos migrated illegally into Texas, which was then part of Mexico ... and gradually drove the *Tejanos* (native Texans of Mexican descent) from their lands, committing all manner of atrocities against them. Their illegal invasion forced Mexico to fight a war to keep its Texas territory ... The border fence that divides the Mexican people was born on February 2, 1848 with the signing of the Treaty of Guadalupe-Hidalgo. It left 100,000 Mexican citizens on this side, annexed by conquest along with the land. The land established by the treaty as belonging to Mexicans was soon swindled away from its owners. The treaty was never honored and restitution, to this day, has never been made.[2]

After the annexation of the Mexican territory and starting around 1870, the United States began to develop major industries that profoundly influenced Mexican immigration, shaping the southwest and the history of Mexican Americans. The industries included mining, construction and agriculture, as well as minerals, lumber, cotton, corn, cattle, sheep, fruits and vegetables, all of which depended on labor to:

> ... work the beet fields of Colorado, the gardens and groves of California, the railroads of the entire West, the copper mines of Arizona, the cotton fields of Texas, even the iron works of Chicago and the coal mines of West Virginia.[3]

The development of the railway system was of paramount importance to transport the products and connect enterprises between the east and the west. A labor force was required for this development, to build the railroad and work in the industries that depended upon it. But labor was unavailable from the east and insufficient in the Southwest, so recruitment of Mexican immigrant labor began.

By the late 1800s, up to 90% of the railway workers of the Southern Pacific and Santa Fe railroads were Mexican. The railroad companies paid Mexican workers less than Anglos for the same work and never raised their salaries. Such labor practices kept Mexican railroad workers and their families isolated and impoverished in labor camps that developed around the railway lines. Those labor camps formed into permanent settlements and eventually became urban communities characterized by poverty, a process Vélez-Ibáñez called *Barrioization*,[4] in southwestern cities like El Paso, Texas. Among those barrios was *El Chamizal*, a strip of land on the north side of and adjacent to the U.S.-Mexico border.[5] That is the geo-historical context in which the Mexican American part of our family history began.

The Prado Family

Our family's history is based on oral tradition, the transference of information through story-telling from one generation to another. Our collective memory begins in a political era, the Mexican Revolution of 1910–1917, when the peasantry rose against Porfirio Díaz's thirty-six-year dictatorship in Mexico. Families like ours, who came from that Indian and peasant population, lacked civil registry records that would document the lives of our ancestors. Most of Mexico's population was rural, children were born at home, and births, deaths, marriages, causes of death and other genealogical or personal information, especially about Indians and rural Mestizos like us, went unrecorded. The memory-bound stories that my great-grandmother, called *Abuelita Juanita*, was able or willing to share with her descendants, and which my mother's generation passed on to mine, have been the means of learning about and affirming our family's origins.

Sometime before 1917, Juanita migrated from Mexico to El Paso as a young widow with four children, including my grandfather, Esteban. Most Mexican immigrants of that era fled to the United States due to the Mexican Revolution. Most were peasants who had suffered virtual enslavement in Mexico's hacienda system.[6] Others fled to avoid the political unrest brought on by the Revolution, when both of the opposing forces, the federal army and the revolutionaries, claimed young recruits, tearing apart families and property alike. Juanita's oldest child, Ricardo, just a boy fighting under the command of General Orozco in

Pancho Villa's rebel army, was killed, presumably in battle. My mother recalls a trip with her siblings and grandmother years later to visit relatives, to a *rancho* named Rubio. Most family accounts concur that Juanita and her children came from a region near San Antonio de los Arenales[7] (later renamed Cuauhtémoc), in the Chihuahua section of the Sierra Madre Occidental, the mountainous homeland to the Rarámuri Indians of northern Mexico. Spanish invaders and missionaries referred to the Rarámuri as Tarahumara, as they became more commonly known.

Since the Spanish conquest, people identified as Indians have faced enslavement, genocide and a continuing racism, in Mexico as well as in the United States:

> To be publicly identified as a Yaqui (or any other tribal affiliation) in the nineteenth- or early twentieth-century Americas was an almost instant death warrant. Native forms of worship and celebration were forced to the underground of *disimulo* (camouflage). Even the United States did not pass the Freedom of Religion Act until 1978. Until then, Native American spirituality (hence culture) was outlawed .... On both sides of the border, to be indigenous is to be displaced, hunted, sold, relocated, fleeing, or hiding behind 'Mexicanness.'[8]

The Tarahumara, who today continue to suffer the ongoing racism, managed to maintain their cultural heritage in part perhaps because they tended to hide rather than fight.[9] My mother remembers hearing her *abuelita Juanita* claim her Indian origins but doing so only privately, at home: *Yo soy pura Tarahumara,* and scold the children at home in her non-Spanish native language. As far as anyone remembers, however, she never elaborated on this or any other part of her past.

Either as a Tarahumara or as a young Mestiza peasant widow, Juanita and her children would have been especially vulnerable to the lawlessness unleashed by the Revolution. Hiding her Indian identity and assimilating into the *Mestizaje,* the hybrid, majority population by learning their Spanish language and assuming the cloak of Catholicism, would have been her strategy to insure her own and her family's survival. This would explain why she insisted that her children and grandchildren learn both the Spanish language and the practice of Catholicism well, and why she never seemed to offer much information about her background even to her descendants. Among the stories she did relate, is how she left her homeland by taking advantage of a single opportunity to board a northbound train, averting *los federales* who would sweep the countryside for goods and recruits among the Indians and peasantry, and escaped with her three younger children to protect them from the same fate that befell her oldest son, Ricardo. Afraid of also losing Esteban to the war, she convinced him to flee as well. He either preceded or followed her but they rejoined in Texas. He walked across a border that was unmarked and unguarded at the time, and eventually became a United States citizen.

Years later, Esteban met and married Texas-born Susana Apodaca in El Paso. Susana's Texan family had deep Mexican roots that would have pre-dated the annexation of the northern Mexican territory by the United States. As a young man, Esteban became a laborer for the Southern Pacific Railroad, from which he ultimately retired. It was during that employment that, like other railroad workers, he purchased a small plot of land and built the family's first adobe house next to *Las Pompas*, the city's water pumps and alongside the railroad tracks. He later sold it and bought another plot of land a block or so away, where he built another adobe house, both in the city section that later became known as *El Segundo Barrio*. This would be the Prado family's home, located within *El Chamizal*, the most Mexican-identified and poorest section of El Paso, Texas, and adjacent to the U.S.-Mexico border. Today *El Segundo Barrio* is historically recognized as the oldest Mexican American settlement and has been called "the heart of the Mexican diaspora."[10]

Aurora Alicia Prado was the fifth of eight children, all born in the four-room adobe house built by their father in El Chamizal. At the base of the Great Depression and at the age of four years, she lost her mother to poverty. Susana died at home of a post-partum hemorrhage three days after giving birth to her eighth child, because the family was unable to raise the money to pay the doctors who evaded Esteban's plea for help. Subsequently, Esteban kept busy pursuing work and women, leaving most of the raising of his eight children to his mother, Juanita, who moved in, along with her unmarried adult daughter, Kika, to help manage the family. Afflicted with a rheumatism that hunched her back and numbed her legs, the old woman struggled daily to care for her grandchildren. In spite of her vigilance, pneumonia killed Roberto nine months after the death of his mother, while Celia, the family's next youngest, increasingly deteriorated with a health condition that caused her seizures of an unspecified nature.

The family subsisted on the government-rationed supply of oatmeal and flour, but all the children had to help provide food for the family. The older ones took over the kitchen chores while Juanita trimmed produce for the bodega grocers in downtown El Paso and the younger children scrubbed the grocers' floors:

> *Teníamos que ayudarle a mi abuelita desde chiquitos. Las grandes ayudaban en la cocina y los chicos a limpiar los pisos de las bodegas. Mientras que ella les cortaba lo pudrido a las verduras, nosotros tallabamos los pisos.*
>
> [We had to help my grandmother since we were little. The older ones helped in the kitchen and the younger ones cleaned the floors of the bodegas. While she trimmed away the rotted parts of the produce, we scrubbed the floors.]

They were collectively compensated with the leftover boxes of partially spoiled produce. They scavenged the railroad tracks in front of their house for the charcoal and produce that sometimes dropped off the cars. Finding no wood meant having no kindling for the wood stove or heat for the house, and the same was true about food, especially in winter: *En el invierno nos mandaba a buscar madera para la estufa porque si no, no había comida o manera de calentar la casa.* [In the winter she would send us to look for wood kindling for the stove because if not, there wouldn't be any food or way to heat the house.]

My mother remembers the hunger that worsened the cutting chill of the cold winter mornings when she and her siblings, Maria and Arturo, were sent to church and school with their stomachs empty because there was no food in the house:

> *Hacía tanto frío en el invierno cuándo nos mandaban a Misa antes de irnos a la escuela a veces sin comer, porque no había comida. ¡Íbamos con un hambre! A veces nos robábamos la leche que entregaban a la tiendita que se llamaba 'La Palestina' cuándo se descuidaba el lechero y nos la tomábamos en la iglesia, a veces con las Hostias que nos robábamos de la sacristía.*

The children would conspire to steal milk from the delivery truck at a neighborhood grocery store named *La Palestina*, when the driver was distracted. During Mass, they would sneak up to the church balcony to fill their stomachs with the milk and the fistful of communion wafers they pilfered from the sacristy. Thus, the children knew cold, work, hunger, illness and death. Like her siblings, Aurora Alicia grew up materially deprived and emotionally needy, yet like her grandmother, also determined to survive.

Her siblings balked at the very idea of braving the cold weather to attend Mass, but Aurora secretly welcomed it as an opportunity to sneak into the balcony and play on the church organ when the church emptied out. She would play the keys with her index finger and figure out the melodies of popular songs. Too small to reach both the foot pedals and the keys simultaneously, she would switch back-and-forth, delighted in her discoveries. In the belfry she loved swinging on the ropes to make the bells ring:

> *Me encantaba subirme al balcón de la iglesia a escondidas. Cuándo se iva la gente, me ponía a tocar el órgano, con un sólo dedo, le sacaba sonido y luego jugaba con los pedales. También me gustaba columpiarme en los lazos de las campanas.*
>
> [I loved to climb up to the church balcony, hiding. When people left, I took to playing the organ, with one finger, I would get it to play a sound and then I played with the pedals. I also liked to swing on the ropes of the bells.]

More than once such activities caused her to be plucked by the scruff of the neck by the elderly sacristan, Salvador, and thrown out of the church. On one occasion, little Aurora became so absorbed in her antics up in the balcony that she absentmindedly interrupted an ongoing Mass with a full congregation, by playing and singing *Amor Chiquito* a popular polka. Filled with dismay, the angry sacristan promptly climbed up, dragged her down the church stairs, and thrust her onto the sidewalk on her backside.

From their grandmother's iron hand, my mother and her siblings learned *buenas costumbres*, the values and customs of a respectable Mexican upbringing. To Juanita, those values included a strong work ethic, responsibility to family, and a demonstrated respect for God, neighbor and authority. Juanita was neither truly religious nor literate, markers of her Indianness and peasant past. Still, she inculcated in her grandchildren both the practice of Catholicism and a rich Mexican cultural knowledge grounded in the Spanish language. For this, she required that before they went to school each day, the children attend daily Mass, at El Sagrado Corazón de Jesus, located near their neighborhood, where all services were held in Spanish because everyone there was Mexican: *Toda la gente era Mexicana, así que la iglesia así se llamaba y las Misas y todo era en español*. They also learned catechism in Spanish from their aunt, Kika. Juanita attended Mass only on Sundays. She also required the children to read the Spanish newspaper out loud, although she herself could not read. Her survival skills had given her a keen ear to the sound of the printed word, and she corrected and scolded the children if she heard them stumble on the words.

Juanita dealt with mischief or disobedience swiftly and with harsh physical punishment that either she handled or passed to Esteban. (My mother still remembers the sting of the shaving strap her father used to hit her with when she was only eight years old). As the matriarch, her grandmother's demand for obedience to her authority also applied to her own adult daughter and son. Esteban was aloof toward his children, never demonstrating affection or tenderness toward them, but if he questioned his mother's governance of the children, she would threaten to leave it entirely to him, meaning he would lose the principal caretaker of his family, and/or his relative freedom from parenting, which she knew he wished to secure:

> *A mi papá le convenía que ella se hiciera cargo de nosotros. Así que si el se metía cuándo mi abuelita nos golpeaba, ella se le enojaba y le decía, '¡si no te gusta, hazte cargo de ellos tú solo, si es que puedes. ¡A ver si eso sí te gusta!'*

> [My father benefited from her caring for us children, so if he interfered when my grandmother hit us, she would get angry with him and tell him, 'If you don't like it, then you take charge of them yourself, if you can. Let's see if you like that!']

That draconian upbringing was the grandmother's way of compensating for her grandchildren's lack of maternal affection and guidance. The ideals she instilled gave meaning and value to the life of poverty that the family knew, but her teachings also provided no comfort from the painful discrimination that the children encountered at school, or the stigma they suffered as motherless children in a community that epitomized motherhood as central to family life.

At the same time that she held authority over her son, *abuelita Juanita* expected the children to obey and be deferential to their father. She privileged Esteban as the principal provider, despite his obvious susceptibility to the economic conditions of that era and regardless of her own, Kika's, and the children's contributions to the survival of the family. Esteban had been laid off his job from the Southern Pacific Railroad during the Depression. When he could not find other employment, he resorted to selling vegetables or making and selling ice cream and Mexican sweet bread out of his old pick-up truck: *No sé de dónde, pero mi papá tenía una troquita en ése tiempo. Sabía hacer nieve y empanadas para vender o a veces vendía verduras.* [I don't know from where, but my father had a little truck at that time. He knew how to make ice cream and *empanadas* to sell or sometimes he sold vegetables.]

Juanita would serve him before anyone else at the table, the best and biggest portions. On the rare occasions when meat was available, she reserved it for him while the children, salivating with anticipation, got the leftover bones: *Cuando llegaba a haber carne, mi abuelita se la servía a mi papá y a nosotros se nos hacía agua la boca. Nomás nos tocaban los huesitos que dejaba.*

By exaggerating Esteban's importance while exercising her own matriarchal power over him and the family, Juanita sent her grandchildren a mixed message about the myth of men as principal providers, the importance of male dominance, and the power of women to wield their own control over it.[11]

Legacies of Discrimination

Institutionalized discrimination against working-class Mexicans and Mexican culture is historical. It began with the brutality toward Mexicans by the Texas Rangers following the annexation of the Mexican territory and continued with the lynching of Mexican Americans who protested unfair treatment by the Justice system. Mexican Americans were refused entry and service in business establishments, and segregation and discrimination in housing, employment, and education became systematic.[12] The prohibition on speaking Spanish in schools prevented schoolchildren from speaking their native language. Mexican Americans in Texas thus suffered what has been called "The Tejano Jim Crow Experience":

> The flood of Mexican immigration in the 1910s and 1920s gave rise to the so called Mexican problem. During these decades many Americans viewed Mexican immigrants

ambivalently, as a sort of necessary evil. Some Americans wanted Mexicans as a source of cheap labor; others resented them as economic competitors or despised them as potential despoilers of the social fabric. On the one hand, rapid capitalist development in Texas made Mexicans highly prized workers, especially in the agricultural, mining, and railroad industries ... Mexican immigrants-and by association, Mexican American citizens-were both wanted and resented.[13]

The economic downfall of the 1930s produced a mass unemployment that many whites blamed on Mexican immigrants. The dependency of past decades on Mexican labor turned to angry scapegoating:

Once the Great Depression hit and unemployment surged among Whites, though, not even Mexicans who spoke fluent English escaped the anti-immigrant hysteria. More than 500,000 were forcibly deported during the 1930s, among them many who were U.S. citizens.[14]

My mother remembers seeing her grandmother's alarm when Anglo vigilantes in pick-up trucks were rounding up people in El Paso believed to "look Mexican" and deporting them to Mexico. My grandfather, who had been out looking for work on one of those occasions, somehow avoided being among those picked up and deported.

Racism in Education

The educational system was a major instrument of Anglo domination since the 1870s, when Mexican children in the U.S. began to be taught in public schools that they could only be good Americans if they rejected their native culture.[15] Spanish-language use and a Spanish-accented English became signs of inferior status and Anglos equated the culture of Mexican working-class people with ignorance, poverty, laziness, lack of hygiene, hypersexuality and deficient morality.[16] The imposition of English and the subordination of Spanish in schools were means of "shaping the consciousness of students to accept the social and material conditions of inequality ... to perpetuate the social relations of dominance and subordination."[17]

Like all Mexican American children, as a schoolgirl, my mother was forbidden by her teachers and school officials to speak Spanish: *No nos dejaban hablar Español. They would tell us to stop it.* In a community where all the children came from working-class and Spanish-speaking homes, my mother learned an Anglo-imposed English at a functional level, heavily punctuated with Spanish forms of pronunciation and modified by a hybrid vocabulary that marked her Tex-Mex social status. Her spoken and written English still carries the classism, racism and cultural domination with which she was taught, including, until recently, the "yes/no m'am/sir" appendage when addressing an Anglo person or a person with the authority of one acting in an official capacity. Her struggle with English shows the language of a subordinated speaker, an English truncated behind a level of sophistication that would otherwise facilitate discourses of contestation. Even now, it is not the language that my mother speaks easily, nor is comfortable with, even though she has acquired a linguistic skill that enables her growing tendency to insult doctors and others who do not attend well to her needs. Members of my family (my husband, children, and I), recognize the socioeconomic and sociopolitical disadvantages that my mother endured, and admire how she confronts her linguistic challenges daily. English grammar and vocabulary engage her in an audible struggle that endears their Nana to her bilingual grandchildren:

> The weather is so *cole* today, I think I'll cook some chicken *thigs*.

> The door is not *lock*.

> Yes, *Mijo*, I got your *meshash*.

> I like Japanese food, but I don't like *Soochee*.

From birth, my mother and her siblings learned to speak, read and write Spanish at a native level of proficiency, as their grandmother expected of them. It was their daily language at home, in their community, in their religious practices, and in the music they heard. Aurora's native level of understanding and use of Spanish is most evident in her singing and musical compositions. Yet, her daily practice of Spanish still carries in my mother the mark of a Mexican child Americanized by the school system in the form and to the degree to which she was subjected and in which, regardless of the fact that she was a United States–born citizen, she was treated as a "foreigner."[18]

Race and Class Differences

El Chamizal was an incipient Mexican American urban community in the 1930s. Economic constraints on its residents reduced opportunities for local entrepreneurs and consequently Mexican businesses such as restaurants, *panaderías*, (Mexican bakeries), *tortillerías* (tortilla factories), *hierberías* (shops specializing in traditional plants, herbs, potions, and home remedies) and other shops characteristic in today's Mexican American barrios, were absent or few. Mexican ethnic families like my mother's frequented businesses across the border, in Juárez, to obtain their

Mexican foodstuffs, avoid the limitations set by government rations, and optimize their dollar.

Though characterized by poverty, economic levels varied among the households. Some families were better off than others, a sign of the emerging class differences among working-class urban Mexican Communities throughout the southwestern United States at the time.[19] Economic levels depended not only on the ability to secure employment among household members, or on household economic strategies, but also on the country's economic climate. The railroad tracks that ran along the front and across the street from the Prado family's house marked the home as within the poorest area of the city. The house was equipped with a wood-burning stove used for cooking and heating, and water was hand–pumped at the small kitchen sink. The toilet was located in a detached outhouse, as it was for some, though not all, residences in the neighborhood. Prior to 1929, Esteban's employment with the Southern Pacific Railroad provided the family's basic needs and even some excesses. He was able to purchase a Ford Model T automobile and a piano, and family anecdotes recall entertaining guests on Sundays, for whom Susana prepared a generous table. The Great Depression changed all that. As did many other employees, Esteban lost his job with the Southern Pacific Railroad and subsequently resorted to whatever daily employment, if any, he could find. The car was replaced with the old pick-up truck from which he sold vegetables throughout El Paso.

The social position of a family in the community had a lot to do with the presence of a mother. A mother was supposed to help optimize the family's socially perceived economic achievement as, for example, in the appearance of the family's home, and the upbringing, appearance and behavior of the children; hence, lacking a mother was viewed as a social deficit.

My mother's uncle, Tío Juan, and his family lived on the other side of the railroad tracks, in a bigger house near the small Mexican American business sector that included the church, a grocery store, and a bakery, in El Chamizal. Juan and Felipa's house had modest but well-polished furnishings ornamented with doylies and figurines that seemed to be a source of Felipa's pride. She was as meticulous about the grooming of her children's appearance and behavior, as she was about the tidiness of the home. During Aurora's family's infrequent visits to that house, Felipa would look at my mother and her siblings disdainfully, and would not permit them to sit or touch anything, nor invite them to partake in any meal:

> Mi tío Juan era muy bueno con nosotros, pero mi tía Felipa no nos quería. No quería ni que nos sentáramos, ni que tocáramos nada. A veces estaban cocinando y olía tan sabroso, pero no nos ofrecía.

[My uncle Juan was very kind to us, but my aunt Felipa did not like us. She didn't even want us to sit, or to touch anything. Sometimes they would be cooking, and it smelled so delicious, but she would not offer us.]

Felipa's attitude toward my mother and her siblings signaled the significance of missing a mother and rendered my mother's family as socially inferior. Other families, including neighbors, treated my mother's family similarly, regarding the motherless children as dirty urchins and thereby reproducing and reinforcing the class and race relations the children experienced at school:

Pórque eramos huérfanos, la gente hasta del mismo barrio nos veía y nos trataba como si fuéramos unos mugrosos. [Because we were orphans, even people from our own neighborhood saw us and treated us as if we were dirty.]

My mother so internalized the social value of motherhood within the family that she still refers to her siblings and herself as having been *huérfanos,* a word suggesting the loss of both parents in childhood, in spite of having had their father present in their lives. Motherhood, and the consequential stigma of a motherless life, was a constant and sorrowful theme that has run through my mother's life as it did through those of her siblings, especially in the case of her sister, Maria.

Maria became pregnant at about fourteen years of age. The details are uncertain, and the child's father remains unknown, but she left home as a consequence of her pregnancy. No one knows the circumstances of her life while she was away. Weeks or months later, as my grandfather was walking by an old tenement, he recognized the figure that was leaning against the doorway. Alarmed by his daughter's bedraggled and emaciated appearance, Esteban ordered her to come home with him: *¿¡Pos qué carájos estás haciendo aquí, muchacha?! ¡Mira nomás cómo estás! ¡Ándale, vámonos para la casa!* [Well, what the … are you doing here, girl? Just look at you! Come on, let's go home!]

Maria was subsequently installed in a home for unwed mothers, where she was made to work for her keep. My mother, about eleven years old then, remembers sneaking away one day to visit her sister. Peeking into a courtyard through a porthole, she saw Maria hanging laundry on a clothesline, as was presumably her job, appearing tired, thin, dark circles around her eyes, hollowed cheekbones, chiseled nose, and a heavy, overgrown belly: *¡Se veía tan cansada! Cómo me dio lástima de ver a mi hermana así; de ver cómo la tenían trabajando, y con su pancita tan grande que apenas podía alcanzar el tendedero. Pobrecita.* [She looked so tired! How sorry I felt seeing my sister like that; seeing how they had her working, and with her little belly so big that she could hardly reach the clothesline. Poor thing.]

While telling me this story many years later, tears fell from my mother's eyes and her chin trembled with the memory and the pity she remembered feeling at seeing her sister so thin and tired and so big with child that she was barely able to reach the clothesline. Maria was forced to give up her newborn daughter to adoptive parents whose identities she would never know. She lived with a female housemate for years during her short adult life, producing speculations about her sexuality. She would spend the rest of her life searching for the child that was taken from her and die tragically twelve years later while avoiding another.

My grandmother Susana's mother had nine children, the products of several marriages or *novios* (boyfriends). Her family disapproved of her having many relationships. My mother remembers that she and her siblings rarely were taken to visit their maternal grandmother's house, and the whispers at the mention of that grandmother's name. One of her marriages was to a black man surnamed Williams, who spoke only Spanish, as far as my mother and her family knew. The couple had two children, who grew up speaking Spanish at home, like their half-siblings and their parents. Much information about my grandmother Susana and our Williams kin remains lost. Whether this was consciously or unconsciously, the result was that it covered up some of my great-grandmother's non-conforming lifestyle. Sadly, it also caused our families to disassociate from each other's Mexican and black identity respectively, and the wealth of family sharing that could have been ours otherwise.

Emphasizing racial distance by identifying themselves as different from blacks and from Indians, was an effort of my Mexican American family to deny their own inferior status in a white-dominated system. The denial between the families was mutual, and reflected the pervasive racism affecting both blacks and Mexicans in Texas. The wounds of that history created an uneasiness between Blacks and Latinos that centered on the need felt by each group to preserve their cultural integrity. In a context of historically racist policies and practices that assigned "social value of the most negative sort"[20] based on phenotypic categorizations, Mexican Americans perceived the negative value of blackness, as they did the value of Indianness. Even in my own childhood, I remember, for example, hearing my aunt Josefina telling my mother once, with a tone of alarm, how she had used a public restroom before noticing the sign designating it as "Black Only." The discussion between Jorge Klor de Alva and Cornel West, "The Uneasiness between Blacks and Latinos" helps to understand how racism left wounds on many families like my mother's. According to West:

> People identify themselves in certain ways in order to protect their bodies, their labor, their communities, their way of life; in order to be associated with people who ascribe value to them, who take them seriously, who respect them; and for purposes of recognition, to be acknowledged, to feel as if one actually belongs to a group, a class, a

tribe, a community. So that any time we talk about the identity of a particular group over time and space, we have to be very specific about what the credible options are for them at any given moment.[21]

It was not until the year 2000, in a family reunion that my mother's first cousin, George Williams, convened, that the Apodaca–Williams families met or re-acquainted with each other. I had the opportunity to meet that side of my family and introduce them to my own. Generations had passed, memories had blurred but some remained intact, and precious new relationships would be short–lived, as George passed away not long after that event. In the recollections and conversations through which family history and lore were shared, I learned and gained valuable insight about the foundations of my mother's social, political, and family views. Twenty years later, in the midst of the Trump administration's reaction to the Black Lives Matter Movement, those views would sadly come more into focus.

Music in El Chamizal

Aurora has no memory of her family's better economic times; she only remembers the piano that remained in her home until she was about six years old, when it was either sold or traded due to financial need. While it was still in her home, she was forbidden to touch it. The neighbors on one side of her house had a piano and provided music lessons to their own child, something Aurora would never have. The closeness of the neighbor's window allowed my mother to eavesdrop. When her family members were too occupied to prevent it, she would listen to the instructor next door and quickly run to try it on the piano keys, using her index finger. If she got caught, it usually meant getting a swift spanking. One day, when she was about five years old, her grandmother surprised her by calling her to play for company. As Aurora began to play with her finger, Juanita took the child's wrists, placed her small hands brusquely on the keyboard and demanded that she use both hands: *"¡Con las dos manos! ¡Así!"* Thus, Aurora was forcibly introduced to the use of both hands and all her digits to produce a greater spectrum of combined musical sounds.

Aurora loved to listen to the music on the radio, and even though the family owned one, *Abuelita Juanita* would often keep it off to ensure industriousness in her grandchildren, believing that deriving too much enthusiasm from the music might encourage idleness in the them. Aurora found that the family's toilet facility was the answer, because she could hear the popular Mexican music coming through the walls from the other neighbor's radio:

¡No nos dejaba oír el radio! Se le hacía que con eso íbamos a estar dioquis. Así que yo me metía allí para que creyeran que estaba usando el escusado. Así podía oír la música del radio de los vecinos, muy a gusto, hasta que mi abuelita me descubrió y me gritaba que me saliera de allí.

[She wouldn't let us listen to the radio! She believed that it would make us idle. So, I would go into the bathroom so they would think I was using the toilet. That way I could hear the music from the neighbor's radio, very comfortable, until my grandmother discovered me, and she would yell at me to get out of there.]

Having been discovered for hiding in the outhouse to hear music, Aurora devised another plan:

Después empecé a llevar la bacinilla de mi abuelita al baño en las noches, para poder oír el radio de los vecinos. Pero en una de esas, mi abuelita notó que me estaba dilatando mucho y me fue a buscar cuando yo ya venía. Nos encontramos en una esquina de la pared y nos asustamos tanto que las dos gritamos, y en eso levanté la bacinilla y sin pensar le di con ella a mi abuelita en la mera frente.

At night, she would volunteer to take her grandmother's chamber pot to empty it out at the toilet, where she would linger long enough to hear whatever was playing on the neighbor's radio. On one of those times her delay caused her grandmother to go check on her just as Aurora was rounding the corner on her way back. Running into each other in the dark, they both let out a startled yell as Aurora raised the chamber pot, landing it squarely on her grandmother's forehead.

In spite of the obstacles, Aurora grew up hearing the sounds of music that represented her *Mexicanidad*. She heard the music belonging to her Mexican heritage and to the contemporary musical compositions, instrumentations, songs, and singers with which Mexicans on both sides of the binational border identified culturally. In spite of Juanita's objections to radio music during her grandchildren's chore-times, my mother remembers the beautiful voice in her grandmother's singing:

Le gustaba cantar. ¡Y tenía tan bonita voz! Cantaba rancheras, corridos, música de la revolución. También cantaba en su idioma de ella. Se oía muy bonito, aunque nosotros no le entendíamos.

Desde niña me gustó cantar. Con mi abuelita, todos cantábamos. Yo fui la única que seguí. Las canciones en ese tiempo, no me acuerdo, los últimos de los treintas. La preferida de mi abuelita era "La Adelita" y "El Barrilito" era una polca. Se hizo internacional esa pieza. Cantábamos muchas canciones. Sometimes como boleros y a mi me gustaba hacer la tercera voz. Berta y Carolina cantaban y yo les hacía tercera. María Grever, Agustín Lara, Guti Cárdenas, siempre en Español.

[She loved to sing, and she had such a beautiful voice! She sang *rancheras, corridos*, music of the Revolution. Also, she sang in her own language. It sounded very pretty even though we did not understand her.

Ever since I was a child, I enjoyed singing. With my grandmother we all sang. I was the only one who continued. The songs of the times, I can't remember, it was the late 1930s. My grandmother's favorite was *La Adelita* and *El Barrilito*, it was a polka. It became an international hit. We sang many songs. Sometimes like *boleros* and I liked to sing third voice harmony. Berta and Carolina sang, and I did third voice. Maria Grever, Agustin Lara, Guti Cárdenas, always in Spanish.[22]]

The guitar was prominent in the music heard in El Chamizal. It was a primary instrument in the music and accompaniment of most of Mexico's traditional folk music and songs, especially the *rancheras, corridos,* and later the *boleros*. Fundamentally, the instrument's sound showcased the singer's (or singers') voice(s), a reason why it would later become intimately tied to my mother's musical development.

Mexican music surrounded the family's Texan Mexican community of El Chamizal during my mother's childhood. Solo artists and *duetos* (duos) of rancheras, corridos, boleros, and other Mexican music were popular both in Mexico and throughout the U.S. southwest. For example, Las Hermanas Padilla, who sang to guitar accompaniment, and the Tejana icon, Lydia Mendoza, who sang and accompanied herself with the guitar, as well as Lydia's three brothers. As my mother recalls, however, it was not until she was already living away from El Chamizal that she became aware of Mendoza's fame. Radio stations from both Texas and Ciudad Juárez filled the border area's airwaves and the households with *rancheras, corridos, valses, boleros, polkas, pasodobles,* and even the schottische, which was adopted from its cross-cultural German and Scottish roots.[23]

Although Conjuntos Tejanos and *música norteña*, with its characteristic accordion, had begun to form by the late 1920s and constituted a musical style by the 1930s, they did not influence my mother musically like the traditional music of Mexico, or the emerging bolero. Studies of Texas-Mexican conjunto music and their pioneer artists suggest they grew out of a northward influence from the Mexican state of Monterrey, thus becoming closely associated geographically with the Rio Grande Valley part of Texas, and as having reached its musical stronghold among Mexican Americans throughout Texas in the post-World War II era of the 1940s and 1950s.[24] Conjunto Tejano music may not have been as popular or influential in the El Paso border region during my mother's childhood and early adolescence, although it certainly was present in her life later, when she was married and living in Juárez. I have heard my mother refer to the percussive *tambora*, to *el tololoche*, and to other instruments identified with Tex-Mex music styles of earlier and later periods. Similarly, *Música de Orquesta*, while part of the music familiar to her community, was distanced by socioeconomic barriers. Live performances were limited to the *bailes* (dances) or events that only the affluent or economically able could afford, although, more humble versions of it, such as by *grupos*, may have spread the music otherwise associated with *orquestas*.

As an element of the elite, classical music became familiar to Aurora by chance. She was introduced to samples of it through the next-door neighbor's piano lessons. She recalls listening to the neighbor's instructor playing musical pieces and referring to Schubert. Perhaps it was there that her profound appreciation for his composition, Ave Maria! was born. That has been the only euro-religious song Aurora ever loved to sing professionally or in public. Otherwise, neither religious nor classical music per se interested my mother, beyond that youthful curiosity that helped introduce her to the piano. To my knowledge, she has never collected the recordings of, or even attempted to play Beethoven's, Chopin's, or any other euro-classical composer's music. Her interest in the Mexican or Latin American "light classics," some of which are classified also as boleros, which she has played most on the piano include, *Marta*, written by Cuban operetta composer, pianist, and jazz bandleader, Moisés Simón (aka Simons) Rodríguez,[25] *Nochecita* by Mexican composer Ernesto Cortázar, and my favorite, by Mexican composer Alberto Ramírez, *Perfidia*; however, among her greatest inspirations for the piano was Cole Porter's *Begin the Beguine*, first recorded in 1935.[26] She was 8–9 years old at the time, and by then the family had no musical instruments. It is therefore noteworthy that she somehow taught herself to play this musical piece, which she still plays skillfully at age 94. Her piano repertory also includes melodies of rancheras, such as José Alfredo Jiménez's *Tu Olvido*, which she plays as a waltz, and many *boleros*. These outstanding compositions and their genres are the music that would move her interest in and exploration of the piano from her childhood in El Chamizal, into her adult life.

Born to Run

When my mother was ten years old, she suffered an accident that would haunt her for life. One morning, she tried telling her grandmother that it was a holiday and schools were closed, but her older sister, Maria, and younger brother, Arturo, had concocted a lie so they could spend a chore-free day playing. They convinced their grandmother that Aurora was lying to get out of attending school. *Abuelita* Juanita regarded this as laziness and scolded Aurora and ordered her to go to school. Later that day, Aurora was playing on the rooftop of a two-story building. She leaned over to answer Arturo, who was calling up to her from the sidewalk below, when suddenly:

> *Me fui de cabeza, pero no sé como fue que Arturo extendió los brazos, tratando de agarrarme y así fue como me volteó. Si no hubiera sido por eso, hubiera caído de cabeza y me hubiera matado.*

As she leaned over, she recalls falling head-first as Arturo's arms reflexively extended to catch her. She believes it was his effort to break her fall that upended her because somehow, she landed on her feet. Hitting the cement head-first surely would have killed her. Her legs immediately began to give out as she tried to focus on her brother's face and on the sound of his voice as both began fading away. She recalls a tearful, fearful, eight-year-old child pleading lovingly to his sister to stand and be well: *Hermanita, Hermanita, por favor, párate. Estás bien, estás bien, Hermanita. Por Favor.* [Sister, sister, please stand up. You're okay, you're okay, sister. Please.] Someone called an ambulance and Aurora was taken to the hospital. A saddened and worried Doña Juanita arrived later. She looked tearfully, lovingly at the granddaughter she had disbelieved earlier that morning. The granddaughter saw a tenderness she had never seen before in the old eyes looking back at her. The doctors sent Aurora home a day or so later. The diagnosis was tragic: She would never walk again. She did not know it then, but she also would never have children.

Abuelita Juanita was not prepared to accept the medical diagnosis doctors made about her granddaughter. She deployed her own Indigenous cultural knowledge in her treatment of Aurora's affliction at home beginning the next day. She soaked Aurora's immobile legs in a *tina* (washtub) of hot water that she heated on her woodburning stove and treated it with her medicinal Indian potions, obtained from the *hierberías*, the botanical medicine shops that were located in Juárez. Juanita held stubbornly and faithfully to her ritual, not dissuaded by the passing of time that seemed to bring no apparent change. One morning, about six months later, Aurora got up from the bed and walked into the kitchen, to her grandmother's and her family's profound joy and relief, but not to Juanita's surprise; she had already predicted that Aurora was, like her Tarahumara kindred, Born to Run.[27]

Notes

1. Song title. Trio Los Panchos.
2. Anzaldúa, 1999, p. 28.
3. Sánchez, 1997, p. 121.
4. Ibáñez, 1996, pp. 118–119.

5. El Chamizal was part of the Mexican territory that was annexed by the United States after the Treaty of Guadalupe Hidalgo in 1848. Dispute over the land strip continued until President Kennedy returned part of it to Mexico in 1962. Family and social ties among peoples across the region pre-dated the annexation and the creation of the political border. Transnational relationships continued to characterize the region as shown by massive back-and-forth daily movement of people and goods across the border and the composition of what became known as "cross-border households" among both the Mexican and the Mexican American communities (Márquez & Romo, 2008; Segura & Zavella, 2007; Vélez-Ibañez, 1996; Updike, 2001).
6. Año Nuevo Kerr, 1990.
7. My mother believes Esteban may have been born in the state of Guerrero; however, she and her sister Berta also remember that they once visited relatives in San Antonio de Los Arenales with their grandmother. It was the only visit they ever made to close relatives and one that our family members believe was a return to the homeland.
8. Broyles-González, 2002, pp. 120–121; italics in original.
9. McDougall, 2009.
10. Chávez Leyva, 2011.
11. Del Castillo, 1993.
12. In the 1950s, the great Mexican American folklorist, Américo Paredes, one of only a handful of non-White professors at the University of Texas at Austin, was unable to get a haircut in a barbershop across the street from the campus because the barbershop refused to serve "Meskins" (Nájera-Ramírez, 2012, p. 73).
13. Treviño, 2003, p. 141.
14. Gonzalez, 2011, p. 103.
15. Vélez-Ibáñez, 1996.
16. Gonzalez, 1997.
17. Darder, 1997, p. xi.
18. Gonzalez, 1997, p. 163.
19. Peña 1985, p. 4.
20. Velez-Ibanez 1996, p. 219.
21. Klor de Alva, 1998, p. 181.
22. Interview with my mother, January 16, 1993.
23. Hartman, 2003.
24. Peña, 1985; Hartman, 2003.
25. Moises Simons Rodriguez, 2020.
26. Songfacts, 2020.
27. McDougall, 2009.

References

Año Nuevo Kerr, L. (1990). Chicanas in the Great Depression. In A. R. Castillo (Ed.), *Between Borders: Essays on Mexicana/Chicana History* (pp. 257–268). Encino: Floricanto Press.

Anzaldúa, G. (1999). *Borderlands: La Frontera.* San Francisco: Aunt Lute Books.

Broyles-González, Y. (2002). Indianizing Catholicism: Chicana/India/Mexicana Indigenous Spiritual Practices in Our Image. In N. E.-R. Cantú, & N. E.-R. Cantú (Ed.), *Chicana Traditions* (pp. 117–132). Urbana and Chicago: University of Illinois Press.

Chávez Leyva, Y. (2011, May 27). *Segundo Barrio: A 'living history' Lesson*. Retrieved from Borderzine: Reporting Across Fronteras: http://borderzine.com/2011/05/segundo-barrio-a-living-history-lesson/

Darder, A. T. (1997). Introduction. In A. T. Darder (Ed.), *Latinos and Education* (pp. xi–xix). New York: Routledge.

Del Castillo, A. R. (1993). Covert gender norms and sex/gender meaning: A Mexico City case. *Urban Anthropology and Studies of Cultural Systems and World Economic Development, 22*(3/4), 237–258.

Gonzalez, G. G. (1997). Culture, Language, and the Americanization of Mexican Children. In A. T. Darder (Ed.), *Latinos and Education: A Critical Reader* (pp. 158–173). New York: Routledge.

Gonzalez, J. (2011). *Harvest of Empire*. New York: Penguin Books.

Hartman, G. (2003). The Roots Run Deep: An Overview of Texas Music History. In L. Clayton, & J. W. Specht (Eds.), *The Roots of Texas Music* (pp. 3–36). College Station: Texas A&M University Press.

Klor de Alva, J. E. (1998). Our Next Race Question: The Uneasiness between Blacks and Latinos. In A. a. Darder (Ed.), *The Latino Studies Reader: Culture, Economy & Society* (pp. 180–189). Malden: Blackwell Publishing.

McDougall, C. (2009). *Born to Run: A Hidden Tribe, Superathletes, and the Greatest Race the World Has Never Known*. New York: Alfred A. Knopf.

Moises Simons Rodriguez. (2020, June 8). Retrieved from es.wikipedia.org: https://es.wikipedia.org/wiki/Moisés_Simons

Nájera-Ramírez, O. (2012). Américo Paredes as a Guiding Force in Transcending Borders. *Journal of American Folklore, 125*(495, Winter), 86–90.

Peña, M. (1985). *The Texas-Mexican Conjunto: A History of a Working-Class Music*. Austin: University of Texas Press.

Sánchez, G. I. (1997). History, Culture, and Education. In A. T. Darder, & A. T. Darder (Eds.), *Latinos and Education: A Critical Reader* (pp. 117–134). New York: Routledge.

Songfacts. (2020, n/a n/a). *Begin the Beguin-Cole Porter-Songfacts*. Retrieved from YouTube: https://www.songfacts.com/facts/cole-porter/begin-the-beguine

Treviño, R. R. (2003). Facing Jim Crow: Catholic Sisters and the "Mexican Problem" in Texas. *Western Historical Quarterly, 34*(No. 2, Summer), 139–164.

Updike, William A., Borderlands. National Parks, 02768186, January/February 2001, *75*(1–2), 46.

Vélez-Ibáñez, C. G. (1996). *Border Visions: Mexican Cultures of the Southwest United States*. Tucson: University of Arizona Press.

CHAPTER THREE

Llorarás, Llorarás: Life and Music in Juárez

It was supposed to be just another errand on that day in 1943. Since her childhood, Aurora had accompanied her grandmother to do the grocery shopping there, in Ciudad Juárez. The border separating Texas from Mexico was just a short walk from home and the monetary exchange valued the dollar higher than Mexico's own peso, so they would go there, to get more food for their money. Sometimes they would also visit friends and relatives living there. When she became an adolescent, she was assigned this chore. So, on that day, she would go to Juárez to shop for groceries. She would think about visiting her sister. She would not know that on that day, she would encounter the nightmare that would catapult the life of an innocent child into one of a woman fighting to survive.

¡No Me Quiero Casar! / I Don't Want to Get Married!

Aurora was only a child when he accosted her as she was approaching *el Puente*, the physical bridge that was the international border, to return home. She had been visiting her older sister, Berta, who had moved out of the house to live with a friend in Ciudad Juárez. *Abuelita Juanita* had condemned Berta's rebellion and would have forbidden Aurora from visiting her, had Juanita known. Berta's girlfriend had two brothers: José, who had become Berta's suitor, and Martín, who unbeknownst to anyone then, had set his eye from afar on the unaware and unsuspecting little sister. On that fateful day as she walked alone, he seemed to appear out of nowhere, blocking her step, and ominously told her she would be his. He terrified her. She was equally scared of the consequences awaiting her at home for arriving late. Shaking with fear, she begged him to leave her alone. Hoping to dissuade him, she said that her family would come looking for her. He warned her not to tell anyone about that encounter. To prove his point, he uncovered the gun he carried hidden under his jacket. When the tears poured out of her eyes, he stepped aside.

On one of her next shopping trips, he kidnapped her. She was only fifteen years old. Lying by telling her that they would get her to the border faster so that she could get home sooner, he and an accomplice put her in a car. Instead, they drove her to the city's outskirts. For two days he locked her in an isolated, windowless building in the outskirts of the city, in what seemed like the desert, possibly the then-colonia[1] San Lorenzo. He violated her while the other man served as the lookout. The next day, Martín called her father to tell him Aurora was with him. Her father left work and he and Juanita went to Juárez, to find out what had happened. Martin told them that he wanted to marry Aurora, making it seem that it was a planned elopement. She cried that it was not true, *"¡no es cierto!"* and pleaded to go home. While relating that story again, at age 93, her eyes revealed the pain of that experience:

> *Yo iba a cumplir quince años. Él y el chofer se pusieron de acuerdo. Yo no sabía a donde me llevaban. Yo creía que me llevaban al puente. Y resulta de que le dieron para otro lado. Y le dije a Martin, 'para acá no queda el puente' y me dijo, si, pero para acá hay otro puente. Fíjate! ¡Como estaría yo de inocente! Me llevaron a un hotel y allí me encerraron. ¡Y el chofer, andavete! Quien sabe donde se metería. Era como un hotel, pero en un rancho, en un desierto. Yo creo que era como, San Lorenzo. San Lorenzo apenas empezaba. Quien sabe. Ahora esta muy diferente, ahora es una ciudad. Yo le suplicaba a Martin que me llevara al puente, que me llevara con mi abuelita porque ya era muy tarde. Yo le tenia mucho miedo a mi abuelita. Desde las tres de la tarde hasta las ocho de la noche, ¡ya estaba oscuro! ¡Y Martin no me llevaba! Otro día, le mandó hablar a mi papá y mi papá dejó de trabajar por ir con mi abuelita y la familia, a ver de que se trataba lo de Juárez. Pos qué? Que se quería casar conmigo. Y les decía yo a las muchachas, a Berta y a Carolina, '¡Yo no me quiero casar!, ¡Yo no me quiero casar!' Y nomás estaban una y otra al lado, no me decían nada. Y yo decía, 'yo no me quiero casar, yo no me quiero casar.' Es todo lo que me acuerdo. Y Martin estaba al otro lado allá, muy retirado y nomás me estaba viendo, me estaba viendo. [Sighs] ¡Que vida! Y ya de allí no sé que pasó. Yo no me quería casar. Yo no quería a Martin, no quería a nadie. Yo estaba muy chiquilla. Yo lo que quería era irme a mi casa. Y ya no me llevaron. El papá de Martin y sus dos hermanas estaban allí con él. Un montón de gente estaban allá, separados de nosotros, había muchos, y todos estaban apoyándolo a él. A mí nomás mi papá y mi abuelita, y Berta y Carolina. Yo diciendo, 'Yo no me quiero casar, yo no me quiero casar' y el juez estaba recitando*

todo, 'el casorio' y no se qué. Y ellas no decían nada, ellas nomás calladas. Y de lo demás, ya no supe nada. Ni como me metieron a la casa de ellos. Ya no supe nada, no me acuerdo de nada.[2]

[I begged my sisters who were there, Berta and Carolina, 'I don't want to get married.' They didn't say anything, they just stood there. And I would beg, 'I don't want to get married.' That's all I remember saying. Martin was on the far side of the room, he was just looking at me, looking at me. [Sighs] God, what a life! And from there I don't know what came next. I didn't want to get married. I didn't want Martin. I wasn't in love with him or with anyone, I was a just a kid! I wanted to go to my home. But they didn't take me home anymore. Martin's father and sisters were there, with a lot of people on the far side of the room with Martin, supporting him. I only had my father and grandmother and two of my sisters there, and I was saying, 'I don't want to get married, I don't want to get married' and the judge was just going on, reciting the marriage ceremony and I don't know what, anyway. After that, I didn't know anything that was happening. Everything went blank. I don't know when they took me to their house, I blanked out on everything.]

She wanted to return home. She wanted to go to school. She was barely in the eighth grade. Shame, modesty, fear, and inexperience with relevant language prevented her from describing the true events of her ordeal with Martín. She could only beg, through her sobs, not to be forced to marry. *¡Yo no me quiero casar!* In spite of her denials and protestations, and considering her as damaged goods, her father and grandmother forced her to marry Martín: *Me forzaron a casarme. Yo no quería. Yo quería ir a la escuela* [They forced me to marry. I didn't want to. I wanted to go to school.] Accustomed to showing obedience, cast out of her home, forced into the hands, home and country of her attacker, and still a minor with no one to protect her rights and interests, Aurora had no choice but to submit to the immediate marriage.

Nine years older than her and savvy to the ways of the world, Martín turned to courting Aurora. In celebration of their civil wedding ceremony, he bought her the biggest steak she had ever seen and the first she had ever eaten. She focused on those things she had never enjoyed at home:

> *Muy temprano en la mañana, llevaban los frascos para la leche. ¡Ay, y como me gustaba la leche de Juárez! ¡Y el pan dulce! Como lo hacían en la panadería que estaba allí en la esquina, se llamaba 'La Antigua.'*
>
> [Very early in the morning, they took the glass bottles for milk. How I loved the milk from Juárez! And the sweet bread! They made it at the bakery that was just around the corner, it was called 'La Antigua.']

Martin would take her out to eat, to the movies, or to listen to music. Learning of her love for music, he bought her an old piano, salvaged from the belongings of a recently deceased old neighbor. Humble as it was, it symbolized for Aurora the beginnings of a home of her own. He also showered her with sweet words:

> *Él me decía que me quería mucho, que era la reina de sus camelias yo comprendía que me queria y poco a poco a poquito lo empezé a querer. Él ya tenia veintycuatro años, aún no me sentía enamorada de él.*

[He would tell me that he loved me very much, that I was the queen of his camelias, and I understood that he loved me and little by little, very little, I began to love him. He was already 24 years old; I still did not feel in love with him.[3]]

Unaccustomed to receiving attention, Aurora began to respond to Martín's gestures with a strange affection, eventually believing that she was in love with him, but the marriage soon turned into a series of abuse and literal confinement. When he left for work, Martín would lock Aurora in their 2-room house, located in an isolated and then-sparsely populated Arroyo Colorado, a *colonia* far from the city center. Her sister Berta, by then married to José, shared a similar abuse by her own husband. The couples shared adjacent housing units, so the women were each other's sole support and companion. Martín had gotten rid of the piano, jealous of how it had captured Aurora's attention. He disapproved of women playing musical instruments, ridiculing it as what he considered to be unacceptable, masculinized behavior, ¡*eso es para hombres*! Aurora discovered a trap door in the roof of the small house, through which she sometimes escaped. Her escapades were limited to getting walnuts from the only nearby neighbor, a sympathetic street vendor who shared with her the treats he used to sell. Her defiance grew bolder when Berta's husband acquired a guitar. While the husbands were at work, the sisters enjoyed walnuts while Aurora began to explore the musical wonders of the guitar.

Mistress and Motherhood

By the time she was twenty-three years old it became evident that Aurora was unable to bare children. In a socio-cultural system that idealized motherhood and equated it with a woman's adult status, with respectability, and generally with a woman's social value, Aurora's infertility was emotionally devastating to her. The social and emotional scars left from her motherless childhood made her yearn to experience the joy of the mother and child bond that she had almost no memory of having known as a child. For years she suffered and cried over her infertility, and no doctor was able to offer a remedy. She proposed adoption to Martin, who rebuffed the idea. At first, in her ingenuous inexperience, my mother interpreted my father's increasing inattentions toward her and his thinly covered transgressions as due to her incompleteness as a woman. Not long after learning that her inability to have children was permanent, she also learned of his long-time mistress, and of their several offspring. Aurora resolved to confront the mistress, something that would prove to be eye-opening for my mother in life-changing ways.

The woman was not the image of the rival Aurora had envisioned:

> *Era una mujer panzona, vieja, casi jorobada, los senos le colgaban hasta acá. Caminaba así ... Ella era una mujer de mucha experiencia, con una boca de cantinera, lo que le gustaba a él.*
>
> [She was a big-bellied woman, old, had sagging breasts, nearly hunched posture and bowed legs that caused her to walk like this .... She was a woman with a lot of experience, with a saloon-woman's mouth, something that was to his liking.]

That woman was street-smart and well-learned in the art of ruthless offense, as Aurora found out when she confronted her and Martin. Taking his gun from its drawer, my mother went to the mistress's house, uncertain of her own plan other than to have it out with Martin and his lover:

> *Yo no sé, realmente, qué intenciones llevaba yo, o cuál era mi propósito. Cuando llegué a esa casa lo alcanzé a ver por la ventana que estaba sentado. Y allí se quedó mientras que ella salió para afuera a enfrentarme.*
>
> [I really don't know what intention or reason took me there. When I got to that house, I could see through the window where he was sitting. He stayed there while she went out to face me.]

The mistress went out to face Aurora while Martin stayed inside. In the verbal showdown that ensued, Aurora was no match for the other woman's bar room wisdom. Aurora's gun brandishing turned into a humiliating display of weakness and defeat. When she speaks of it, her eyes still reveal the indignity that enveloped her at that moment: *Me dijo que yo no tenía dignidad. Me sentí tan humillada. ¿Cómo iba yo, una mocosa, a compararme con esa mujer, una mujer de la calle?* [She told me that I had no dignity. I felt so humiliated. How could I, a snot-nosed kid, compare myself with that woman, a street woman?]

In the other woman's words Aurora heard a hard reality about herself: She was indeed a child, who publicly lay her dignity at the feet of a man who did not value her, thus demonstrating how unprepared she was for the battles of life.

That humiliating event was pivotal in my mother's life. It awakened in her a new perspective on matters of marriage, love, and self. She resolved then to leave her unhappy marriage and the man she no longer wanted, and she vowed never again to acquiesce her personal worth. She convinced her father to help her leave her violent and unfaithful husband. My grandfather purchased her ticket and arranged for her to go live with family friends, an older couple residing in Chicago. Determined never to return, she boarded the train in El Paso and embarked on a journey to remake her life.

Cuando lejos me encuentre de ti
cuando quieras que esté yo contigo
no hallarás un recuerdo de mí
ni tendrás más amores conmigo/
Yo te juro que no volveré
aunque me haga pedazos la vida
si una vez con locura te amé
ya de mi alma estarás despedida(o)/
No volveré
te lo juro por Dios que me mira
te lo digo llorando de rabia
no volveré/
No pararé
hasta ver que mi llanto a formado
un arroyo de olvido anegado
donde yo tu recuerdo ahogaré/
Fuimos nubes qu'el viento apartó
fuimos piedras que siempre chocamos
gotas de agua qu'el sol resecó
borrachera que no terminamos/
En el tren de la ausencia me voy
mi boleto no tiene regreso
lo que tengas de mí te le doy
pero yo te devuelvo tus besos/
No volveré
te lo juro por Dios que me mira
te lo digo llorando de rabia
no volveré/
No pararé
hasta ver que mi llanto a formado
un arroyo de olvido anegado
donde yo tu recuerdo ahogaré.[4]
[When you find that I am far from you
and you yearn to have me with you
you'll find nothing that is part of me
and you'll have no more lovemaking with me/
I swear to you that I will not return

even if life tears me to pieces
if one day I was crazy in love with you
from now on you are ousted from my soul/
I won't return
I swear to you as God is my witness
I tell you this crying with rage
I won't return/
I will not stop
until I see that my tears have formed
a river of flooded oblivion
where your memory I will drown/
We were clouds that the wind drew apart
we were rocks that always collided
drops of water dried by the sun
drinking binge that never subsided/
On the train of absentia, I leave
my ticket has no return
what you have of mine I give you to keep
but I give you back all of your kisses/
I won't return
I swear to you as God is my witness
I tell you this crying with rage
I won't return/
I will not stop
until I see that my tears have formed
a river of flooded oblivion
where your memory I will drown.] (Translation my own)

The Marriage *Bond*

For the first time in her life, my mother was about to take control of her own life. In Chicago she began working in a lampshade factory, an industry still largely associated with female Mexican labor in the 1950s. She was determined to keep her independence, and in order to do so, had sworn her father to secrecy as to her whereabouts. A few months later, acting remorseful, Martin convinced him to reveal her hiding place and got her family to help bring her back. The piano was gone, and he could offer her no other reason to return.

  I was to be the remedy for a failed marriage. While I was still in the womb and my birth was imminent, my biological parents agreed with Martín that what he and Aurora needed for reconciliation was a child to bond their marriage. Twelve days after my home birth, I was presented to Aurora, with the condition that if she accepted me, she would have to return to her husband. She returned to re-enter into the bonds of marriage, this time as the mother of a newborn daughter.

I was no more than five years old that day that I followed the sound of sobbing coming from the living room. At the doorway I paused at the sight of her crying, handkerchief in hand, sitting on the couch; my teenaged cousin, Chalía, seated on the floor, her head on my mother's knee, trying to console her while answering her questions. The meaning of their words was unmistakable. Chalía and her brother, Rafael, who lived with us at the time, were relating to my mother that my father brought "the other woman" and their children to our home, spending a day there, in full view of the neighbors, all while my mother and I were away visiting family in California. Even at my tender age I understood intuitively the reasons for my mother's crying that day. Her tears and anguish were not of passion, love or heartbreak; they were of frustration from feeling herself unable to escape abuse and humiliation. She was in an unenviable trap.

The whispered, fragmented and encoded conversations of the women in our neighborhood speaking with my mother of the known or suspected wanderings of husbands always produced the same response in her: *¿Todavía está con ella?* The women would ask, was her husband still involved with his mistress, and she would lie, *No, ya no*. Of course, Martín's infidelity was not unknown to Aurora, nor likely to anyone else who knew him. Martín and Aurora lived in an unstated understanding that kept her from questioning his activities. She knew well where he spent most days and nights of the week. But confronting him risked receiving his physical and emotional abuse. Police protection for women against domestic violence was a concept more than a practice. Aurora had no assistance from relatives and returning home was not an option. Her grandmother Juanita had died before I was born and her father, re-married, was unwilling to help. Employment was scarce, especially for women, who were caught between the need to escape and the need for support with few prospects for making a living on their own for themselves and their children. Moreover, divorced women or those living on their own faced the stigma of being a *Mujer Sola*,[5] the social casting of a lone woman as vixen, available, masculine, or otherwise deviant to the socially expected roles of wife and mother, and so, socially shunned. The lack of police protection, plus the public stigma of being a woman with a wandering husband, or worse, a lone woman, involved facing real physical risks. Outward denial was my mother's way of saving face, of staving off more indignities in her life, and of stalling a situation that she could not immediately resolve. It was in practice, the pretense that Del Castillo described about Mexican women who cover up the cultural failings of men to maintain their own respectability.

It happened one night, when I was about seven or eight years old. I do not know how many other times it had occurred. This time, he came home angry at my mother who, taking me along, had gone to his workplace asking for him. She had disobeyed his orders to stay housebound except for activities he approved, specifically Mass, grocery shopping, and occasionally a movie. Martín defined any other social interaction she could potentially have as *andar en la calle y hablando con gente*, derelict behavior with useless conversations. In reality, he had seen her when she spotted him flaunting his new conquest at his workplace. His anger doubtless masked his fear of losing her, as she had left him before, when she fled to Chicago, even having been so young and naïve at the time. If she confirmed his new infidelities, she might leave him again, perhaps for good, lest he subdue her courage to do so. He came into the room, with an unblinking stare. He spoke slowly, in an ominous, even tone. Though his face was partially averted from my vantage point, I saw it turn cold, losing all expression as his gaze fixed on her. She began to speak but her words faded hopelessly away. I stood frozen at the doorway of their small bedroom, unable to move while watching my mother retreat from him, seeking safety against the bed, as he launched toward her, arms swinging and hands slamming against her face. Horror and disgust took over as I heard my mother plead for him to stop. Then again. And again.

Our house was inhabited by the ghost of my parents' marriage. My father's presence, sporadic and infrequent, still loomed there like a mine field. No way to know when he might show up. He tended to check at random on my mother, driving by our house day or night, facilitated by his occupation as a taxi driver. My mother cried quietly and alone many nights; many times, overheard by the child lying nearby. Less often she cried outwardly, muffling her sobs only by their depth within her body. The emotional void my father dug in my mother's heart cast a sad and somber loneliness over her that shadowed me throughout those years of my own childhood. I listened to her pain-filled cries; they seemed to keep tempo, like the ticking of our clock.

> *Lloras, lloras porque estás abandonada*
> *Sufres, sufres porque estás desesperada*
> *Cuanta amargura te dejó la vida*
> *Toda la dicha para ti, perdida*
> *Sufres, sufres al pensar que la amargura*
> *Mata, mata tu hermosura bien amada*
> *Ya no llores tanto que el destino te ha de dar*
> *Un buen camino no estarás abandonada*[6]
> [You cry, you cry because you are abandoned
> You suffer, you suffer because you are desperate

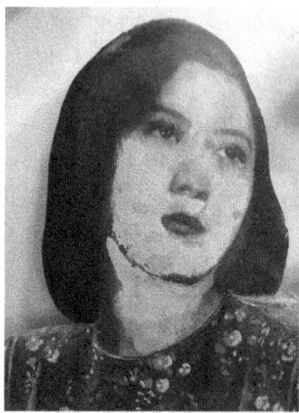

Photo 3.1: Aurora Prado, 1950s. From the author's private collection.

> So much bitterness life gave you
> All happiness to you, lost
> You suffer, you suffer thinking that the bitterness
> Kills, kills your well-loved beauty
> Do not cry so much, for destiny shall give you
> A good path and you will no longer be abandoned] (translation my own)

Emotional Survival

In one of my adult moments of reflection, I asked myself how my mother survived the emotional traumas of her marriage. The images that quickly filled my mind reminded me that Martin's dominant role as head of our household was in truth, a vulnerable position that was hard to sustain. His physical dominance was tangible, and the lack of social support or police protection made my mother fear him. But in the Foucauldian reality of human power relations, my father's dominance always provoked my mother's resistance.

Music was my mother's greatest resistance to my father. In our life in Mexico, music was ubiquitous: live on the streets, markets, church, and school; in films of Mexico's Golden Era, made so by the music they featured and introduced; on the record player or the radio, broadcasting artists' recordings or the *aficionados*, the hopefuls seeking a break to stardom on the radio's amateur hour. The sounds of *rancheras, corridos, boleros, huapangos, sones, danzones, valses, chachachás*, and more, always coming from one or another neighbor's house. Hearing it daily helped my mother and me sharpen our musical ears and enriched our aural knowledge of our

Photo 3.2: Aurora Prado, c1955. From the author's private photo collection.

Mexican music. Like her, my musical learning came from watching, listening to, and following what we heard. My music appreciation also came from watching some of my mother's self-taught instruction and her efforts to collect knowledge from anyone willing to share it.

Don Pascual was an old street musician, a man who was blind and well-known for his immense repertoire and his occupational longevity as a local musician in Ciudad Juárez. He worked on the busy *Avenida Juárez*, the street that welcomed border-crossers from the United States. The street was lined with curio shops, clubs, restaurants and cabarets, from which live music and young women's singing voices could be heard day and night. Like many other individual and group musicians who strolled along the avenue playing and singing for the tourists' dollars, Don Pascual played guitar and sang for passersby. He knew Martín and of Martín's shenanigans and was sympathetic to my mother. He would secretly lend her a guitar to take home, on which she would repeat the steps she learned from him, like different styles of strumming the chords and plucking the strings, and other specialized techniques that he would show her.

On the many days and nights of my father's absence, music washed the sadness from my mother's eyes. She and I would sit on the edge of her bed, me with my child's short legs dangling, she with one leg crossed, sometimes holding the guitar that she borrowed from Don Pascual and which we would hide from my father. Usually, our only instrument was the sound of two sticks we beat together, pretending they were *la clave*, or we just sang accompanied by each other's voices. She would follow my voice while she sang harmony: *Haz primera, yo te hago segunda*, when we sang together songs like the one titled, *Marta*, for example.

My mother was robbed of her childhood. She never had toys or playtime like other children, and Martin viciously and inhumanely ended her innocence. Her forced marriage erased any opportunity to partake in the extra-curricular activities that her schoolmates and agemates were able to enjoy, like playing baseball and running track, both of which she loved and excelled at, but in which she was never allowed to participate because her father and grandmother forbade it. They considered it useless and an excuse to get out of doing housework. She had managed to sneak in some playtime and attend both track and softball practices, until her father caught her in the ball field one day and ordered her to go home, where she would later receive a beating. With her forced marriage to Martin, his violent jealousy and her social isolation made her married life similarly brutal. By the time I reached school age, my mother was still very young, and her innocent hunger for fun and adventure was as alive as when she was fourteen.

The women and all the children of our neighborhood knew and liked my mother. I do not know how she managed to befriend them, given my father's restrictions on her socializing. Late in the days and on evenings, mothers would sit outside their front doors to watch over their kids at play on our street and converse with each other, sharing in their *chismes* each other's observations of the comings and goings and behaviors and relationships of other households. These *viejas chismosas* or *chirinoleras*, as my father referred to the neighbors, denoting "gossipy women" in his lexicon of derogatory terms, proved to be priceless for my mother's ways of reclaiming her childhood while emasculating her controlling husband. I have a vivid recollection of playing jacks (a child's game played with pick-up pieces and a mini rubber ball) sitting on the sidewalk at my front door while my mother played baseball on our street with the young and teenaged kids from our neighborhood. Everyone knew to watch out for my father's car, recognizable as it was as a taxicab. Lookouts were posted at every corner, and upon spotting his car as it turned toward our street, they would yell the code word, ¡*Aguas!* Some of the kids would form a roadblock by pretending to be playing on the street, while others helped hide my mother as she ran a full block at the speed of her Tarahumaran ancestors and she and I scrambled into our house. By the time he walked through the door, everything seemed as he expected. His arrogance did him no favors with the neighbors, and it may have been too late for him to act out his anger by the time he learned, if ever, about the good laugh they all would have at his expense.

In my early childhood we had a beautiful, long haired dog named *La Pinta*, which had a special bond with my mother. My father was fond of the dog, but not as much as he was of a prize rooster he planned to train for the cockfights. Every day since the cock arrived at our house, it would taunt and attack *La Pinta*. My mother pleaded with my father to get rid of the rooster, pointing out the physical damage and pain it inflicted on our dog, but my father refused. One day, while my father slept, as he worked nights at the time, the rooster turned especially brutal on our dog, causing it serious injury. My mother walked into our yard to address the problem. When my father awoke that evening and sat down to eat dinner, he had the best *mole* dish my mother had ever prepared. After finishing a second helping, he remembered he had not heard the crow of the cock, and asked about it, *¿Donde está mi gallo?* My mother calmly replied, *en el mole.*

While my mother's forms of resistance to my father's dominance seemed clever and calculated, I had not known my mother to confront hostility directly, until an event with a neighbor occurred. Virginia lived next door, in a housing tenement where she and her husband and their eight children shared a two-room apartment. In contrast, ours was a single-family dwelling, and humble as it was, it represented a comparatively higher socioeconomic status. A resentful Virginia often brought attention to that difference by flinging insults at my mother whenever she was within earshot. When my mother ignored them, Virginia began to throw the garbage she collected daily from her kitchen, on our sidewalk. Neighborhood residents took pride in maintaining the sidewalk spanning their homes. Sweeping and watering the public face of one's residence every morning and evening, especially in summer, was a common practice. Virginia's efforts to instigate a fight with my mother, therefore, were definitely noted by all the neighbors. They also knew her temper outbursts. In public, she would mercilessly beat her oldest child, fourteen-year old Carmela, with clenched fists, for meaningless reasons such as failing to bring a sibling indoors. The situation grew to unbearable lengths when Virginia's insults and threats began to prevent me, then about eight years old, from stepping outside our house.

It was a summer evening. The neighbors, mostly women, had been sitting on the kitchen chairs they placed outside their front doors, talking with each other and watching their children play on the street. I do not know how it began, but before I realized what was happening, I saw and heard a crowd gather at our sidewalk. Somewhere in the center of the cacophony I could hear Virginia's typical insults, and thought I heard my mother say something like, *¡A ver ahora, ándale pues!* [Well, let's see now, let's go!] With the light cast by the street lamp at the corner, I saw my mother tangling with Virginia. I was stupefied. Perhaps I was afraid that my mother would be hurt. Then a sense of awe and pride swept over me when I realized that the crowd was emboldening my mother to beat the other woman. They used their endearment name for her to tell her: *¡dele, Licha, dele!* When Virginia soon retreated, running back inside her home, the crowd laughed and cheered. She never bothered us again, and after that event even sought my mother's friendship with friendly greetings and salutations. I never knew my mother to be physical again, nor to advocate for violence, yet I gained a healthy respect for her conviction to set limits and ability to stand by them.

Models of Women's Independence

Entrepreneurship was one of few means of survival for lone women, *mujeres solas*. The tortilla cottage industry was a prime example. Some women would convert their (usually) two-room apartments into *tortillerías*, tortilla factories. Production equipment consisted of large-sized *comales*, smooth-top metal griddles, placed over large stones heated by charcoal over the dirt or cement floors. The women businessowners contracted neighbor women to work: one group on the large *metates*, footed milling stones on which women, squatting on the floor, grounded the lime-treated *nixtamal*, turning it into *masa*, or refined the already milled *masa*. Another set of women divided the *masa* into *testales*, small pieces, then worked each *testal* between their two hands, turning it into a tortilla. The fastest production was done with the tortilla press, but handmade tortillas were favored by the clientele and hence, were higher priced. The well-organized *tortillería* was as much a work of art as it was a demonstration of women's business acumen and agency in financial independence. This local economic system based on the tortilla commodity, included besides the *tortillería* owners and workers, the local *carbonera (charcoal seller)*, *molino* (mill) owner, and the corn and lime vendors. Though this system involved men, the top tier was woman-owned and controlled. That fact was not lost on anybody. *Tortillería* owners were assertive women and demanding bosses. Equally so was the *carbonera*, a mean-mouthed woman whose natural looks were always covered by the soot of her product. The *tortilleras* and the *carboneras* were known for their fast tempers, sharp tongues, and piercing wit.

Other women applied their business skills in more-or-less effective ways. For example, neighborhood street vendors commonly sold fruit, sweets, or cooked delicacies, or sold birds they caught and caged, herbal remedies, or native arts. Late at night, a single light bulb lit a lone woman seated at a table placed outside her front door, with a charcoal grill on which she cooked menudo or champurrado she would sell to late-night passersby. Some women offered cleaning services door-to-door. Doña Pepa, who lived alone in a two-room apartment across the street from our house, was a known *bruja* to some people, a *curandera* (shaman) to others, an occupation from which she derived her livelihood. Some people believed in and sought her healing skills; others mocked or feared her; still others made fun of her yet sought her services when they exhausted other options. Most of her clients were adult men seeking relief from a curse or illness believed to be caused by the men's errant ways against women. Two or three young and beautiful women neighbors sold their affections as kept women, with varying degrees of commitments to their relationships and hence, varying material benefits. Young Tarahumara women who populated the city typically sold items from gum to textiles, from which they derived means to feed the young children they carried on their backs, swaddled in native-made shawls or slings that hung across the mother's neck or forehead.

While gaining respect for their business savvy and management, businesswomen often paid a price as social outcasts. The *tortillería* owners and the *carbonera* were stereotyped as brash and dirty, respectively. Street vendors were associated with negative financial mobility and the low social status of its consequential continuous poverty. Respect for native healers like Doña Pepa hinged on their status within a family system in which their specialized cultural knowledge could be validated. Indian women like the Rarámuri living in the urban environment occupied the lowest rungs of a society that dislocated their families, disrupted their social organization and encouraged their men to find solace in liquor. For them, social life was different than for those practicing their traditions and ways of life in the copper canyons of the Sierra Madre. Rather than being respected for their entrepreneurship, the Indian women were often taunted for enabling their husbands' alcoholism. For the other women, whose company affluent men rewarded with comforts coveted by neighbors, their occupational branding tended to become permanent and usually with deteriorating compensation over time, reducing both financial rewards and social acceptance. Although no doubt with some exceptions, women at that time in general faced difficult barriers to their financial independence; the relatively few who dared to confront them did so to survive, or also to live life on their own terms.

When I was about nine years old, my mother obtained seasonal employment at the Hicks jeans factory across the border, in El Paso. Like Farrah and other factories located in that city and the border region at the time, Hicks used largely Mexican immigrant and migrant female labor. The work was arduous and exploitive, paying minimum compensation for the quota-based piecework done by the women workers like my mother. She would walk northbound across the border every day and spend 8–10 hours daily hunched over an industrial sewing machine. Her job was unsteady, but it provided some much-needed financial assistance to our household in Juárez. Although my father controlled even the money that she earned, she would keep some of it for her work-related needs. Perhaps it was in that way that she managed to pay the entry for the two of us to attend the live performance of a rising star in the record charts, Javier Solís, who would follow Jorge Negrete's and Pedro Infante's fame. He was on tour and the crowd was abuzz with excitement. The show was held in an outdoor patio with a tile floor and beautifully landscaped trees that lent a typical Mexican atmosphere to the approaching evening. We sat on wooden folding chairs, almost front and center from where he stood performing, with the accompanying mariachis behind him. He was a handsome man, dressed in his light brown *traje de charro* and matching sombrero. His voice was melodious and strong, and it seemed even more beautiful to me than those of the many gifted singers whom I heard so often. I believe that among the songs he performed that evening was *Llorarás, Llorarás*, one of his *bolero-rancheras*, for which he became immortalized after his career ended with his untimely death in 1966 at the age of 34, shortly after that Juárez performance. We returned home after dark, but my mother made no mention of my father's possible outburst if he should learn that we had been out that night. Everything about her that evening seemed different, confident, resolute. That song kept playing in my head, and I wonder now if it did so in hers as well.

> Llorarás, llorarás, mi partida
> Aunque quieras arrancarme de tu ser
> Cuando sientas el calor de otras caricias
> Mi recuerdo ha de brillar donde tu estés
> Has de ver que mi amor fue sincero
> Y que nunca comprendiste mi penar
> Cuando sientas la nostalgia de mis besos
> Llorarás, llorarás, llorarás ... [7]
> [You will cry, you will cry, my departure
> Even if you try to tear me from your being
> When you feel the warmth of other caresses
> My memory shall shine wherever you may be
> You must see that my love was sincere
> And that you never understood my grieving pain
> When you feel the nostalgia of my kisses
> You will cry, you will cry, you will cry] (translation my own)

The entrepreneur women in our neighborhood were good role models for my mother. When I was almost eleven, she began selling Stanley Home Products, akin to the "Avon Lady." She was a good salesperson and soon convinced my father that she needed her own car if she were to earn her full potential. They purchased a used Plymouth for her use, which, typical of the model, had a corroded floor that gave us a good view of the road underneath but proved to be a reliable enough form of transportation. It turned out to be a means for my mother to ultimately gain her independence. She and I would journey throughout Ciudad Juárez and its outskirts, as well as El Paso, selling the products and meeting many people. Then my mother got the idea of augmenting her income by selling tacos, burritos, and *elotes*, to factory workers in El Paso during their lunch break. She would cook *chile verde con carne, arroz, frijoles*, and tortillas early in the morning, and we would be set up at the factory's back door, pots of food in the trunk of our car, before the 11:30 lunch shift. At the sound of the lunch whistle blowing, workers would surround the trunk of our car with food orders. My mother, my cousin and I would form a service line: a waxed paper sheet, tortilla, and the fillings. Our clientele grew so much and kept us so busy that on one occasion we forgot the most necessary ingredient, when a woman lamented that she had gotten the food served only on the waxed paper: ¿*Y mi tortilla?*

Tia Eduvijes

My tía (aunt) Eduvijes was the widow of my father's eldest brother. She had spent most of her life in the *rancho* of her birth and had lived through the many injustices of the *Porfiriato*, one of which was her unregistered birth, which left her, like other enslaved peasants, uncounted in the record of human existence and unable to know or to prove her exact age; another was her illiteracy, causing her inability to know even the spelling of her own name. Both effectively disenfranchised her from the powers of society. She was of *abuelita* vintage by the time she came to live with us, as suggested by her missing front teeth, silver hair, the lines on her face, and her rounded figure. Like most elderly poor women in Mexico at the time, her only source of support was the assistance that relatives would or could provide, so I moved to the sofa and she occupied my room, located above the kitchen. She wore her waist-length hair in a bun, and in public covered her head with her *rebozo*, the ends swung over each shoulder. She owned one pair of shoes and one dress, plus the *huaraches* (Indian-made sandals), grey peasant shirt and black skirt she wore daily, covered by her muslin apron. Her daily enjoyment was smoking a stub from the box of the cheapest cigarettes sold, *Farolitos*. I would read the newspaper to her as she would sit barefooted on the patio floor, her back against the wall, to take in the afternoon sun and enjoy her smoke. In my child-like curiosity, I would ask her about my deceased uncle, who I never met, and about her youth, and I learned that her parents, serfs to the rich agrarian landowner, had taught her to be obedient to men, power and authority in order to survive. I was always treated to her talent for telling an adage from her enormous repertoire and told in her rural speech style, among them, *Te casates te fregates*, [You got married, you got screwed]. Her sky-blue eyes, evidence of a landowner's imposed sexual will upon a female peasant ancestor, hinted at a bittersweet journey back in time, to the memory of her parents, her two children, and the love of her life, her husband. She described him as a kind man who expressed his love for her intimately in a song that brought tears to her eyes:

> *Una noche, serena y oscura,*
> *Cuando juramos amarnos los dos*
> *Cuando en silencio nos dimos un beso*
> *Y de testigo pusimos a Dios*[8]
> [One night, dark and serene
> When we vowed to love one another
> When in silence, we gave each other a kiss
> And as a witness we called upon God.] (translation mine)

Tia Eduvijes seemed decades older than my father and as such, though deferential to him, he treated her with a distinct measure of respect. That was why, when one day in an outrage, he slapped my aunt, everything turned momentarily silent as each member of our house stood still in horror, fear and disbelief. With her bun slackened from the impact and some loosened hair framing her face, her eyes pierced him as she mumbled words that immediately transformed Martin's facial expression into one of terror. She ran upstairs preparing to leave our house, while my mother raised her voice to my father for the first time in her life: *¡¿Pero como se pone a hacerle eso a ella, una anciana?! ¡Dios quiera que no le mande una maldición!* [How dare you do such a thing to her, an elder woman? God help you from her curse of damnation!]

For the first time in my life, I saw my father afraid, repentant, and tormented by his own actions. He tried uselessly and foolishly to explain and justify his deeds to my unsympathetic and unyielding mother, who looked back bold-facedly at him saying: *No, ni hubo motivo ni hay excusa para lo que usted acaba de hacer. Pídale a la Virgen que lo ayude porque solo Dios sabe si tenga perdón.* [No, there was no cause or excuse for what you've just done. Pray to the Virgin (of Guadalupe) to help you because only God knows if you will be forgiven.]

My father turned into a very small figure at that moment, figuratively and literally. He begged my mother to help him make amends, to talk with my aunt and broker her forgiveness. My mother went upstairs to talk to and check on my aunt, but my aunt refused his apology. Then my mother reminded my father that Eduvijes had nowhere to go, and that he could try begging her forgiveness while reminding her that, for now, this was her only home. He succeeded in obtaining what we all knew signified only a reprieve from the punishment due his abhorrent behavior.

The episode with my *tía* Eduvijes was steeped in our spiritual beliefs and practices, that part of the cultural means of defense available to women in a paternalistic society. My father had never been a religious man. Due to his fear of God though, he occasionally would visit a church only to cross himself. But he had deeply ingrained beliefs about the power vested in Our Lady of Guadalupe to oversee God's men. Within that belief system, mothers and elderly women were the human vessels of sacred power. Although mothers and old women were often the butt of men's jokes or referenced in street obscenities e.g., *chinga a tu madre, hijo de puta* [fuck your mother, son-of-a-whore], this had its limits, for to disobey, disrespect, or lay hand on one's mother or an elderly woman could provoke her *maldición*, a curse that could result in the transgressor's lifelong misery or immediate death and eternal damnation, as the moral theme in many *corrido* songs often reminded us. In addition, my father's native beliefs also involved the sacredness of our spirit ancestors and our obligation to fulfill our promises and honor their earthly wishes. As was customary for younger siblings, my father had revered his eldest brother in life, and in death was obliged to respect his spirit and his legacy. To mistreat his wife was to dishonor him as well as his memory, itself cause for grave consequences.

Origins and Religious Legacies

According to my Catholic training, in the year 1531, the Indian Juan Diego, walking in the pre-dawn hours to get help for his dying old uncle, suddenly was met by a radiant brown-faced heavenly figure appearing to him, elevated above the ground, upon the hill known as El Tepeyac, near what is now Mexico City. She instructed Juan Diego to take her message to the archbishop, that on that site was to be built her shrine, so that all her people would know of their Holy Mother and of her protection over her oppressed children. Because he was an Indian, Juan Diego was disbelieved and dismissed by the archbishop. Juan Diego returned to the same spot, where the Holy Lady reappeared and told him to try again. When he did so the next day, the archbishop asked for proof. Juan Diego walked up the hill again, whereupon he saw the third apparition. She told him to return to her the next day and she would provide him the needed proof. On what is believed to have been December 12, Juan Diego beheld the Holy apparition for the fourth time. She instructed him to hold his *tilma*, his Indian tunic, folded into his arms, and to deliver the contents she placed therein to the archbishop. When Juan Diego did so, a cluster of Castilian red roses spilled out of his *tilma*, and on it was imprinted the image of the brown-faced heavenly Lady. The presence of the roses defied explanation because it was winter, when flowers would not grow, and the flowers were foreign to that arid region. Equally baffling was the imprinted image, which the archbishop and the clergy interpreted as being a brown-faced Virgin Mary.⁹

As an anthropologist, I gained a post-colonial understanding of Christianity in Mexico's history, including Juan Diego's encounter with Our Lady of Guadalupe. The apparition supposedly took place on the same sacred spot on which the shrine of the deity *Tonantzín,* also known as *Coatlícue,* the Holy Earth Mother of the Nahua people, had existed before its destruction by the Spaniards. Chicanx scholars have posited that the origin and application of the name "Guadalupe" is the transliteration into Spanish of the Nahuatl name Coatlícue or *Tecuatlanopeuh,*¹⁰ or transphoneticized from Coatlashuape.¹¹ When she spoke to Juan Diego in his native tongue, he believed her to be his native Holy Mother, evidencing what some have viewed as a syncretism, or others see as an indigenous resistance to imposed Christian doctrine. In any case, native Indians continued worshipping at the Holy site, demonstrating a resistance to Christian beliefs that caused the Spanish Christian colonizers to construct a shrine at the site and later expanded it into a small church to Our Lady of Guadalupe to honor the apparitions. The imprinted *tilma* is displayed at the altar of the Basilica of Our Lady of Guadalupe in Mexico City, which remains both a Catholic pilgrimage site visited by millions yearly and among the most visited sacred sites in the world.

During my mother's upbringing in Texas, as in part of my own in Mexico, Catholic Mass was celebrated in Latin. This functioned to elevate the symbolism of its rites, words, and readings, reinforce the Mystery of Faith, and maintain the perception of the priest's spiritual superiority over the congregants. My mother's family did not own nor read a bible, nor did our own family. As I recall during my own childhood, the Catholic church in Mexico forbade lay people to read it, because only priests were entrusted to interpret it correctly.

My mother's Catholic upbringing was based on practice more than theology. I believe it constituted the façade of Catholicism that her grandmother intended as a way to shield her family from the dangers of being identified as Indians, true as much in the period of the Revolution, when Juanita fled Mexico, as in any other time in the institutionalized anti-Indian racism that is historical and still exists on both sides of the border. From attending Catechism in preparation for my First Holy Communion, I learned that as the holiest act, receiving Communion required confession and overnight fasting to help cleanse the body and prepare one's soul to receive the Host. This relieved us of our sins and kept us from going to hell unless we sinned again. From my mother, I learned that we went to church every Sunday for about an hour, we sat and stood up a lot when we watched the other people around us doing so, we were quiet and didn't play, eat, chew gum, or stick out our tongue at people while in church because it might be a sin, and we kissed the priest's hand whenever we saw him outside of Mass.

My mother grew up respecting authority and power, the reason why she feared God, but our Catholic devotion in Mexico was to Our Lady of Guadalupe, who we saw as the Holy Mother. Our house was decorated with her image, lighted in a frame about 36 by 24 inches in size and built into our outdoor patio wall, above the kitchen door. Throughout the year, my father would stand in front of the image and cross himself to pay his respects and receive her blessing before leaving our house. When I was old enough to follow along, I began praying the yearly novena with my mother, beginning on the 4rd of December. We would be joined by our neighbors, mostly women and children, as we all knelt on our patio floor for the rosary and prayers for nine evenings. On December 11, our house was enlivened with the sounds of my father's hammering as he installed the trellises for the decorations around the framed image, while my mother, Tia Eduvijes, and some of the neighbor women cooked *tamales, champurrado, buñuelos*, and other delicacies in our kitchen in preparation for our celebratory feast of the day of Our Lady of Guadalupe, December 12. Our celebration would begin that night with the novena. We would then attend one of the Masses continuously offered throughout the night of December 11–12 at Our Lady of Guadalupe Cathedral, where *mariachis* played *Las Mañanitas*, the traditional Mexican birthday song. The number in attendance was so great that the Mass was heard over loud speakers by seemingly thousands of people overflowing the church and filling the plaza, where the sacred celebratory dancing by the *matachines* would take place throughout the night and the next morning.

The *matachines*, referring to the dance and the dancers, have particular religious significance. The dance performance, with its colorful plumage, the stomping huaraches, and sound of the drum and rattles, is not entertainment; it is a form of ritualized prayer with a fervor that surpasses ordinary religious worship. The different troupes usually name themselves according to the deity or regional saint to which they are dedicated.[12] For major religious events such as the celebration of Our Lady of Guadalupe, several troupes convene to create a continuous *danza*,[13] a testament to Guadalupe's heightened importance in Mexican Catholicism.[14]

Notes

1. "Colonias" in Mexico are early sub-urban settlements that develop into more permanent neighborhoods. They also are: "a residential area along the Texas-Mexico border that may lack some of the most basic living necessities, such as potable water and sewer systems, electricity, paved roads, and safe and sanitary housing" (Texas Secretary State of, 2016).
2. Conversation, December 8, 2020.
3. From interview, January 16, 1993.

4. Song title: No Volveré, by Manuel M. Esperón and Ernesto E. Cortazar (Strachwitz, 2020).
5. Del Castillo, 1993.
6. Song title: Abandonada, Pedro Zagarra, composer (Strachwitz, 2020).
7. The song title: Llorarás, Llorarás, is credited by most sources, including Strachwitz La Frontera, to Rafael Ramírez, composer, in most of its recordings; however, in one recording, by artist Goyo Flores, this same source credits its composition to Pablo Flores (Collection, 2021).
8. Song title: Una Noche Serena y Obscura. Available information on this song varies on its origin and first recordings, and dates are unknown. Its recording artists include Lupe Martinez and Pedro Rocha Duo con Guitarra; Gómez, Fierro and Domínguez; and Dueto América.
9. Many other, more detailed accounts exist, including with interpretive analyses of the socio-political and other significance of Guadalupe.
10. Anderson & Chavez, 2009, p. 205.
11. Broyles-González, 2002, p. 124.
12. In the binational borderland region that includes Ciudad Juárez, San Judas Tadeo and San Lorenzo are two of the saints celebrated with *matachines* at yearly festivals in their respective sub-regions (e.g., Colonia San Lorenzo, now a suburb of Ciudad Juárez). According to one source, the oldest *matachin* troupe in Ciudad Juárez is *La Danza Real Apache de San Juan Bautista*, brought from the city of Torreón by its founder, Prudencio Villalobos, in 1932 (Vianney, 2018).
13. Some debate surrounds the origin of the Matachines. One theory is that when the Spanish colonizers witnessed the dance rituals of the Chichimecas, the native nomadic people of the region that is now northwestern Mexico and the United States Southwest, the Spaniards called them *matachin*, a word derived from the Arabic, *mutawajjihin* and meaning buffoon. Another theory is that the origin of the word is from the Nahuatl *malacotzin* meaning to gyrate, and therefore suggests that this was a native tradition.
14. Regional variations in forms of worship and specific saints characterize Mexico's Catholicism. More than mere adaptations to colonialism, they are both ancient and ongoing survivals of our Indianness, veiled in the religion of the Spanish colonizers as necessary to avoid physical and cultural genocide but simultaneously, as Broyles-Gonzalez shows, marginalizing true Catholicism (2002, p. 124).

References

Anderson, C., & Chavez, E. (2009). *Our Lady of Guadalupe: Mother of the Civilization of Love.* New York: Doubleday.

Broyles-González, Y. (2002). Indianizing Catholicism: Chicana/India/Mexicana Indigenous Spiritual Practices in Our Image. In N. Cantu, & O. Najera-Ramirez (Eds.), *Chicana Traditions: Continuity and Change* (pp. 117–132). Urbana and Chicago: University of Illinois Press.

Del Castillo, A. A. R. (1993). Covert Cultural Norms and Sex/Gender Meaning: A Mexico City Case. *Urban Anthropology and Studies of Cultural Systems and World Economic Development, 22*(3/4), 237–258.

Marquez, R. R., & Romo, H. D. (Eds.). (2008). *Transformations of La Familia on the U.S.-Mexico Border*. Chicago: University of Notre Dame Press.

Stratchwitz Frontera Collection. (2020). https://frontera.library.ucla.edu/recordings/no-volvere-71

Stratchwitz Frontera Collection. (2021). https://frontera.library.ucla.edu/es/recordings/lloraras-lloraras-17

Texas Secretary of State. (2016). Las Colonias in the 21st Century. https://www.dallasfed.org/~/media/microsites/cd/colonias/background.html#:~:text=The%20Texas%20Office%20of%20the,Paved%20roads

Vianney, I. G. (2018). Los Matachines le oran a Dios por medio de su danza en Ciudad Juarez. Medium.com; https://medium.com/revista-arena/los-matachines-le-oran-a-dios-por-medio-de-su-danza-en-ciudad-juárez-aab19fba2dfc

CHAPTER FOUR

Mexican Education, the Golden Age of Cinema, and National Identity

My public elementary education in Mexico in the 1950s and 1960s was a legacy of the Revolution. It promoted a nationalist ideology that professed rejection of foreign domination, privilege and exploitation, and encouraged self-sufficiency and cultural pride. Schoolchildren like me were taught academic subjects rigorously, and were expected to show self-discipline, mutual respect, and self-reliance, and to learn about and appreciate our pre-colonial, revolutionary, and folk cultural history.

My mother's stunted educational attainment and the racist context of her Texan education had robbed her of the opportunity to learn about her cultural heritage. She was also tragically thirsty for the knowledge a formal education should provide, so she was interested in the lessons that I brought home from school. One of her favorite subjects was history. She would listen to me tell her about Mexican history and its leading figures such as Moctezuma, Cuauhtémoc, Miguel Hidalgo y Costilla, Morelos, and Benito Juárez, and about the heroic women whose lives and works were socially transformative, such as the prolific writer, poet, arch-feminist Sor Juana Inés de la Cruz, and the heroine facilitator of the insurgency against Spain, Doña Josefa Ortiz de Domínguez. Some of what I learned and shared with my mother could be summarized as follows:

After centuries of conquest and colonialism, Mexico's war of independence from Spain officially began on the night of September 15–16, 1810. A *Criollo* (Mexico-born person of pure Spanish descent) priest named Miguel Hidalgo y Costilla, carrying a Mexican flag and a flag with the imprint of Our Lady of Guadalupe, gave the *Grito de Dolores*, the famous yell that led the native fight against the Spanish colonialists. The native indigenous and Mixed-race (Mestizo) Mexicans wanted racial equality and a Reformation that would honor their land rights, independence from Spanish rule, and the end of the dominance of the Catholic church in national politics. When the Spaniards captured and executed Hidalgo for insurgency, José María Morelos succeeded him in leading the rebellion, along with Mariano Matamoros and Vicente Guerrero. A Mexican of Spanish blood, Agustín de Iturbide, negotiated the 1821 independence, but the Catholic church maintained its powerful position and those of pure Spanish blood remained in control as Mexico's elite.[1]

Benito Juárez, a Zapotec Indian native of the state of Oaxaca, became Mexico's first indigenous president in 1858. By 1861 the French intervention forced him temporarily out of power. In the ensuing war against the French, the historic *Batalla de Puebla*, the battle in the city of Puebla, took place on May 5. *Cinco de Mayo*, 1862, became historically important because, though Mexican forces were considered the underdogs, as many fought on foot and employed clubs as weapons, they forced a French retreat. The final expulsion of the French invaders took place in 1867, when President Juárez, restored to power, had the imposed French emperor, Maximiliano, executed. Although still a controversial figure in history and among factions at the time, Benito Juárez became known as the Reformation president, associated with principles like education, land rights for peasant and indigenous peoples, the nationalization of natural resources against foreign interests, and the separation of church and state, policies reflected in his slogan: *El Respeto Al Derecho Ajeno Es La Paz* (Respect for the Rights of Others is Peace), a principle that endeared him as an historic figure to my mother and me. After Juárez died in 1872, the former military general, Porfirio Díaz, who had contested Juárez's election in 1871, also challenged his successor. Díaz fraudulently gained the presidency in 1876, becoming Mexico's dictator for the next thirty-six years, eventually causing the uprising against his tyranny in the Mexican Revolution of 1910–1920.[2]

Porfirio Diaz had seized massive areas of Indian-owned land and turned it into lucrative agricultural enterprises run by the elites, dealing brutally with opposition and dissent, leasing resource-rich Mexican land to foreign investors,[3] and leaving the country's majority population, millions of Mestizo peasants and indigenous peoples, displaced from their subsistence lands and victims to the rich landowners (hacendados) who controlled the land and treated its people as serfs and slave labor. Some agrarian landowners opposed Díaz' government control and joined the Revolution. Among them was Francisco I. Madero, who challenged Díaz in an uprising in Ciudad Juárez, forcing him into exile. Madero became president in 1911 but special interest factions, including from the United States, soon weakened his power and he was assassinated in 1913.

The 1910 Revolution's rebel leadership was divided into a coordinated effort between the country's north, led by Francisco (Pancho) Villa, and the south, led by Emiliano Zapata. Villa and Zapata together fought the military power of Victoriano Huerta, who the rebels defeated and overthrew. Venustiano Carranza, a rich landowner-turned revolutionary ultimately betrayed Zapata and Villa to gain control of the country and eventually became president. He drafted the Constitution, adopted in 1917, but it failed to reflect the plan for reform that many viewed as Benito Juárez's legacy or as Pancho Villa's and Emiliano Zapata's goals for the rights of the people. Carranza defeated Pancho Villa and assassinated Emiliano Zapata in 1919, but in turn, allies of Villa and Zapata assassinated Carranza in 1920, ending the Revolutionary period.

The parts played by Villa and Zapata, as critical as they were to the Revolution and outcome of Mexico's history, were not taught during my own formal public education. At the time I was in school, national educational policy still interpreted the two insurgent leaders as outlaws, as my teachers explained. Students like me were curious about them, because we could discern an inconsistency that taught us about the importance of the Revolution in the fight for social equality and justice but denied us an explanation for not acknowledging its popular leaders. This flaw in policy would subsequently change, but not before I left my Mexican schooling.

My mother and I would have long conversations especially about Emiliano Zapata and Pancho Villa because we would watch movies that lionized them, their outlaw status fueling their portrayal as romantic heroes and thus their popularity. My school curricula included *canto*, during which we practiced the lyrics and melodies of traditional Mexican folk songs and *corridos* like *La Feria de las Flores, Gabino Barrera, Cuatro Milpas* and others that we also heard in the movies and that glorified revolutionary heroes and heroines and ideals such as familism, honor, justice, rebellion, patriotism, and love, and extolled the virtues of women, mothers, the poor and the oppressed.[4] My mother and I would practice singing the songs I learned in school, and many others that were also popular and that we would hear repeatedly on XEJ or XEW, the most popular radio station, or from the live musicians that played at *El 5%*, the club and cantina located down our street, or the many other ways in which music surrounded us.

Illiteracy was still widespread in Mexico in the 1960s, especially among rural people, Indians and Mestizos, many of whom had migrated to towns or *colonias*, creating rapid urbanization. Many peasants like my father's family of birth, left their ranchos for the development that followed in the decades after the Revolution. Many of those peasants, if not most, had an incomplete elementary education or no formal education at all. Martin only attended school through the second grade, but like most adults with at least a minimal education, he read the newspaper religiously every day. In that sense the newspaper functioned as a main source of public education and was one of the most effective media for public information, along with the radio and the cinema.

The nationalist ideology fomented a Cultural Renaissance following the Mexican Revolutionary period. This was evident in art, architecture, music, and cinema. Each of these forms of cultural production demonstrated the country's heightened interest in native creativity, and each demonstrated a push toward deconstructing classism and oppression in Mexico, but after centuries of conquest and colonialism, and a chaotic Revolution, Mexicans needed a unifying identity. Cinema effectively used cultural communication to foster, validate, and define the sense of *Mexicanismo* and to introduce Mexican culture to the world while giving Mexico international acclaim.

Films of the Golden Era portrayed Mexican society, culture, race, class, gender, sexuality, religion, foods, regionalism, indigenous peoples, geography, architecture, native manual arts, the Revolution, politics, dance, and especially music, so effectively as to become the single most influential media in defining Mexican society and identity to the Mexican masses. My mother lived in Mexico during the 1940s-1960s, and like much of the rest of the country, she absorbed that Mexican cultural identity presented through film, and it would thereafter underlie her stage persona and musicianship.

The Golden Age of Cinema

The Golden Age of Cinema spanned from the 1930s to the 1960s.[5] It was a period when Mexico became a globally recognized leader in filmmaking, and the center of the film industry in Latin America. Actors, songwriters, singers and other artists from all over Latin America, the Caribbean, Spain, Russia, the United States, and other countries, lured by Mexico's filmmaking stature, converged and many became famed artists of Mexican cinema and/or interpreters of Mexican song.[6] Films featured a multitude of Mexico's folk music and songs that represented our Mexican national history. Films also introduced many new musical compositions and songs that were made famous, some internationally, and became classics in the repertory of Mexican cultural music. Mexico produced various film genres, including comedy, romance, musical, folklore, and nationalism. Cinematic productions based on Mexico's revolutionary history abounded, as did themes of poverty, political and economic oppression, illiteracy, and more. Dominant cultural themes included gender norms and roles, familism, morality, and Catholicism, with references to God and Our Lady of Guadalupe in most storylines, from a visual component to being a main part of the theme of the film. Films also created iconic archetypes that typified and glorified, or challenged and questioned cultural norms, portraying strong-spirited and rebellious women and emotionally vulnerable men. Some juxtaposed the virtues with the iniquities of women effectively reinforcing the paternalistic ideology applied to women's roles, while others portrayed women as victims of society's infamy in its imbalanced assignment of power and privilege, a critical and sympathetic theme that applied to gender relations as much as it did to social class and racial distinctions.

Politics, Social Justice, Gender, and Indianness

The individual artist whose work had the greatest social significance, in my view, was the Mexican artist, Mario Moreno, known as Cantinflas. Beginning in the 1920s with his work in the traveling tent shows, known as *carpas*, he created the character that launched his career and which he used as the comical and quick-witted platform to expose Mexico's class oppression and to criticize the elite and defend the poor. His own humble beginnings included working as a circus acrobat, a toreador, a dancer, and a boxer and he deployed those experiences artistically in his humorous characterization of "the poor man,"[7] epitomized by his signature ill-fitting, droopy pants held up with a rope for a belt, and a small, squashed hat. His portrayals made him relatable to the masses and combined with his intellect and fearless way of exposing corruption, tyranny, and injustice, it also made him an ally of the underprivileged class.[8] His films used the unique quality of comedy and its power to provide his Mexican countryfolk with a formidable voice against social inequity.

It was films about Mexican folklore and the Mexican Revolution, that most reflected and simultaneously guided a sense of Mexican identity from the 1940s through the 1960s. A prolific filmmaker, director and actor of the genre, Emilio Fernandez (aka El Indio Fernandez), (who also directed a number of films of a genre known as rumberas), produced a string of films that strongly portrayed the social justice foundations of the Mexican Revolution as national ideals.[9] This genre typically involved portrayals of glorified revolutionary men and women, though it also defined a hierarchical gender structure. Fernandez also produced films of the Folklore genre, which showed the tragedy and sadness of Indianness in a socially unjust Mexican society. Typically, however, the films idealized a social, political, and spiritual innocence of Indians, yet seemed to suggest that the futility of their ambitions to overcome their social and economic status was either divinely ordained or a consequence of disturbing the social order, thus demonstrating the fundamental paternalism that was so ingrained in our socio-cultural and socio-economic systems.[10]

Movies romanticized the cause, heroes and heroines of the Mexican revolution of 1910–1917, defining gender roles within a hierarchical framework. A series of films starring the ruggedly handsome Pedro Armendáriz playing the iconic revolutionary hero, and Mexico's most popular bombshell, Maria Félix, playing roles of the legendary *La Adelita*, the strong-willed and beautiful female coronel, most represented the Revolution theme of that film era. Adelita epitomized *la soldadera*, the female revolutionary soldier, who was idolized as much for her loyalty to the revolution and agility in the battlefield, as for her supportive role as a camp follower, cook, munitions loader, and overall submissiveness to the dominant revolutionary hero.[11] Thus, the Mexican Revolution theme presented a model for female agency, rebellion and assertiveness, albeit framed within a consistently paternalistic, binary theme of male dominance and female subordination.

Films about the Revolution made effective use of the music closest to Mexican nationalist sentiment, *rancheras* and *corridos*. Female figures of the Revolution that were revered in folk lore for leading revolutionary battles against the oppressive *Porfiriato* became personified in films titled like the famous *corridos*, the ballads, that told the stories of those heroines, naming the protagonists in the movies like their namesake songs, such as *La Adelita* and *Juana Gallo*.[12] The films portrayed them as beautiful, subordinate, and submissive to their male lovers while also being strong-willed and rebellious women who flouted conventions and norms to follow their hearts and their political convictions.

Films that promoted nationalism pulled on the heartstrings of Mexicans with images and sounds of national idols such as Jorge Negrete, and many featured the nationally popular Mexican station, XEW. Negrete, who starred in over 50 films, became the icon of *Mexicanismo* while popularizing the song, *Mexico Lindo y Querido*, as Mexico's emblematic *ranchera*.[13] The station, which began broadcasting in 1930, continually brought entertainment along with educational programming to the public, thus forming and informing on, Mexican history, identity, and nationalism.[14] This station also was the first to present *los aficionados*, new artists, singers and composers hoping to break into showbusiness, to a sitting audience while live on the air. That program helped shape the music of Mexico while launching the careers of many famous artists.[15]

Blackness and Mexican Racial Contradictions

Our Indigenous, African and Spanish genetic *Mestizaje* produced a spectrum of skin tones, blurring color lines save for the binary extremes, facilitating for the estimated 90% national majority of brown-toned Mestizos, a high degree of social "passing" compared to the United States. Hence, open discrimination in Mexico was most often and most openly shown on the basis of socioeconomic status and social position. Nevertheless, whether overt or covert, racial discrimination has been an historical reality, and has operated in the tacit denial by the white elite that neither Blacks nor racial discrimination exist in Mexico, while simultaneously, whiteness is favored, blackness is denied, demeaned or rejected, and the country prides itself on its Mestizo identity. As Christina Sue writes, Mexicans deal with race and color "in an ideological terrain littered with contradictions."[16, 17]

The Golden Cinema promoted a nationalist narrative that idealized the country's Indians and Mestizos, while simultaneously excluding or marginalizing Afro-Mexicanos by exoticizing or downplaying the significance of blackness in our Mestizaje. In the musical film genre known as Rumberas especially, Afro-Latino artists were always presented as the musicians, singers or dancers, never as the hero or heroine protagonist. Movie plots sidelined black character roles and promoted exaggerated stereotypes played by black, mixed-raced, or white actors in black face, such as in the film, Angelitos Negros.[18] Rumbera films thus treated Blackness as a performative component of our national identity, repeating the country's official complacency toward blacks and people seeming to have black ancestry, often called *Mulatos*.[19]

Two films especially exemplified how the reference to God and heaven, which ran throughout the productions of the Golden Era, were applied in films dealing with blackness. *El Derecho de Nacer* used the intersectionality of race-color/gender/class to affirm the spiritual goodness of the poor and the black while laying out that women should maintain their own virtue or else either accept their resultant motherhood, or subject themselves to the strictest forms of penance in order to gain social and Christian redemption. Thus, for blacks, as for women, inclusion in heaven as in society became conditional upon a demonstrated self-sacrifice that helped expiate their own offenses (being black or being an unvirtuous woman) and those of others. In *Angelitos Negros*, the Christian reference is made as an assertion that black angels also go to heaven, countering the ideology that they do not; but the film's ending gave a melodramatic gloss to the paternalistic message again about the goodness of blacks and blackness, rather than dealing with society's accountability for the inequitable participation or exclusion of Afro-Mexicanos in our national identity.

Jarocho, Rumberas, and Bolero Music

Films of the folklore genre set in Veracruz, located on the Gulf coast of Mexico, were set in its *Jarocho* style, an Afro-Indigenous-Euro cultural mixture, in music, dances, and artists.[20] Among those was the *copla jarocha*. A *copla* is a four-verse poetic composition and a form of musical public duel taking place between two singers who improvise rhyming verses to get the better of each other.[21] Notable performers of other *jarocho* and *bolero* music in those films included the region's natives, Toña La Negra, who introduced the bolero, *Veracruz*, an homage to the city composed by Mexico's then-most famous composer, Agustín Lara, and Andres Huesca, a brown Mestizo and renowned harpist credited with defining the music known as *son jarocho* and introducing to the world the now famous *La Bamba*.[22]

Musicals and musical hybrids, including musical dramas, showcased Mexico's traditional music and introduced new musical styles and artists from Mexico and the Caribbean, especially Cuba, such as Mexican bolero interpreter Toña La Negra and the orchestra, Son Clave de Oro, both featured in the film, *Maria Eugenia*, introducing the *bolero* song, *Alma de Veracruz*.[23] The orchestra comprised Cuban and Mexican musicians, each a unique artist in their own right.[24] The orchestra, the radio station, and the song interpreter together influenced the popularization of the music and dance style associated with cabaret nightlife known as *danzón*, to Mexico and other parts of Latin America.

The unique film genre known as *Rumberas* emerged in Mexico from the 1940s through the 1950s. They were musicals and melodramas characterized by their use of Rumba, a music from Cuba and of African origin. Mexican folklore films had featured rumba dance acts as early as the 1930s, especially with the famous Afro-Cuban rumba dancers, Estela and Rene, but films of the Rumbera genre spotlighted the female dancer (also called "rumbera"). Mexico produced over one hundred of these films, creating a wave of Cuban-born artists who became stars of the Mexican film genre.[25] Although it grew out of the Afro-Cuban cultural production, the Mexican rumbera films appropriated the rumbera tradition in visibly significant ways: Its folk show dress was imitated with yards of ruffled organza-like fabric and brilliant adornments that re-defined its artists as vedettes: star performers of cabaret shows, and although the creative dance style developed by Estela and other Afro-Cuban artists were the prototypical influence, the new Mexican rumbera artists were all white. Thus, the rumbera film genre re-defined the rumbera (dancer) racially. It also broke with societal attitudes that constrained women's sexuality.

The Rumbera films had two principal veins: In one, the protagonist was portrayed as a naïve victim of poverty or circumstance falling prey to an evil man, usually a gangster, who forced her into prostitution, thus ruining her life and usually causing her tragic demise.[26] In the other version of the genre, the protagonist is a woman who uses her physical attractiveness to escape the limitations imposed by poverty and class. In contrast to the women of the Revolution, who rebuffed gender dictates to fight alongside male soldiers for a greater good, women in this version of Rumbera films defied moral and cultural codes for selfish reasons, usually for an illicit affair with a man who could provide them wealth and status.[27]

Both veins of the Rumbera films characteristically implied a two-sided morality of women, in whom good and evil seemingly reside simultaneously in constant opposition.[28] Whether as victim or fortune-hunter, the woman protagonist in this film genre typically ended up as the film title, matched to the *bolero* composed for it, which defined her, e.g.: A *Perdida* [Fallen Woman], *Pecadora* [Sinner], *Aventurera* [Adventuress], *Bien Pagada* [Well-Paid], *Perversa* [Perverse Woman], or *Pervertida* [Perverted Woman].

The Rumbera genre (aka cabaret films) made three major contributions to Mexico's cultural identity through cinema: It pivoted the plot's focus to women as protagonists, and affirmed women's sexuality, thereby challenging established conceptions of morality; and it introduced music and artists, especially of the *bolero*,[29] whose work defined a new musical era throughout Latin America.[30] As the music in the films evolved from the rumba to the new *danzón*, it also introduced other styles of music that soon were added to the film productions, including the tango, mambo, and cha-cha-chá. They ushered in music of composers and artists from Mexico, Cuba, Puerto Rico, Peru, Ecuador, and other parts of Latin America, some of whose music also would later be adopted into the music played by mariachi.

Notes

1. History.com, 2020.
2. The Revolution lasted from 1910 to 1917, although the continued unrest did not cease until at least 1920.
3. Including Hearst, Guggenheim, Rockefeller, and Texas Oil Company (Raat & Beezley, 1986).
4. I also learned other Latin American genres in school that related to the misfortunes of the poor, the suffering, and the vindicated, such as *Adios Muchachos*, a tango, which I also shared and sang at home with my mother.
5. Cinema, 2020.

6. Some of these artists included Argentinian singer/actress Libertad Lamarque, Spaniard singer/actress Sara Montiel, Honduran actor/songwriter/musician Juan José Laboriel, Spaniard singer/actress Elvira Quintana, Chilean singer Lucho Gatica, Cuban singer/pianist/actress Rita Montaner, Cuban reciter/actress Eusebia Cosme, Czech actress Miroslava, and many more.
7. Cantinflas's film titles and leading roles typified the working class, including a letter carrier (*Entrega Inmediata*), a schoolteacher (*El Profe*), a bank janitor-turned fugitive (*Soy Un Prófugo*), a boxer (*El Boxeador*) a gendarme (*El Patrullero Desconocido, El Patrullero 777*), a film extra (*El Extra*), a man who was illiterate (*El Analfabeto*), and many more.
8. With his uniquely clever, funny, and rapid-fire delivery of, likely his own improvised lines (though I cannot prove this) he made use of an overly accented street vernacular, in nonsensical ways, always confounding dialogues in which he got the better of others, particularly those in positions of authority or power.
9. Emilio "El Indio" Fernandez was the son of a Mexican revolutionary general and a Kickapoo Indian mother. His own participation in an attempt to subvert the Mexican president, Álvaro Obregón, caused Fernandez's temporary exile to the United States. While working as an extra in Hollywood he met the Russian film director Sergei Eisenstein, whose later film, ¡Viva Mexico! would further influence the ideology behind Fernandez's subsequent filmmaking career when he returned to Mexico. As an actor, Fernandez became famous for his role in the film, Janitzio (c. 1934), (an island in Mexico's Lake Pátzcuaro located in the Purépucha (Tarascan) Indian region of the state of Michoacán), to which his Indian features added to the film's story about a racialized Mexico. In the 1940s and 1950s his films about Mexican folklore and the Mexican Revolution became his signature genres. With the screenwriter Mauricio Magdaleno, cinematographer Gabriel Figueroa, and actors Dolores Del Rio and Pedro Armendáriz, he directed the classic, *Maria Candelaria*, the first Mexican film to become a Cannes Golden Palm prize winner, and in 1947, *La Perla* (The Pearl), starring Pedro Armendáriz and Maria Elena Marqués, in which John Steinbeck collaborated with Fernandez in the screenplay adaptation. It won multiple awards between 1947 and 1949 including at the Venice Film Festival, the Silver Ariel award for best picture, best male actor, and best cinematography; the Hollywood Press Award of 1949; and the Best Cinematography award at the Festival of Madrid (en.wikipedia.org, 2020).
10. For example, the story of *Maria Candelaria*, a classic film in which a young couple (Dolores del Rio and Pedro Armendáriz) suffers from the jealousy and envy of others to the point of a tragic ending. The movie became Mexico's all-time iconic film in the genre of Indianness, romance, and Mexican folklore. Its outstanding imagery of Mexico's romantic Lake Xochimilco, with its flowered floating gardens and traditional native rituals exemplified how Gabriel Figueroa's black and white photography captured and projected Mexico's most beautiful and dramatic landscapes in Fernandez's films. Such images gained this film and its photographer Figueroa, the prize for best photography, as they did for his similar films that featured Mexico's art and architecture, as well as his unique ability to capture human emotions in facial expressions (en.wikipedia.org, 2020). Another film classic of this genre was *Tizoc: Amor Indio* (Indian Love), a film by Ismael Rodriguez and starring María Félix and Pedro Infante, with Andres Soler, Carlos Orellana, Julio Aldama, and Alicia del Lago. The film's exceptional cinematography of Oaxaca's rural landscapes and pre-Columbian ruins assist this love story about a Mixteca Indian persecuted for his Indianness and caught in an ongoing family feud that keeps him from the Indian woman he loves, until a new love enters the picture, adding complexities of race and class to the plot.
11. Herrera-Sobek, 1992.

12. Maria Felix, Mexico's claim to having the most beautiful woman in the world, and also the most popular female actor, starred in Emilio Fernandez's production of *Enamorada*, about the daughter of a relatively wealthy man and supporter of the Federal government. When a rebel troop comes through the town, its general (Armendáriz) eventually meets the beautiful Beatriz (Félix), and falls in love with her, letting her know in several ways, including serenading her with a trio's rendition of Malagueña Salerosa (performed by Trio Calaveras). Rebuffing his attentions, she puts him through all manner of problems, including lighting firecrackers under his horse, startling the animal and causing it to send the colonel flying across the compound, knocking him out, much to his chagrin, in full view of his soldiers. In the end she renounces her privileged life to follow him as his lover and foot soldier, but not before the film makes clear its intended message about some of the foundations of the Revolution: to fight the creation of a serf peasantry by the oppressive colonialist elite, the historically complicitous role of the Catholic church, and the unfulfilled benevolence owed Mexico as portrayed by a painting by Nicolás Rodriguez Juárez in 1698 titled, *La Adoración de los Reyes* [The Adoration of the Kings].

    The 1959 classic, *La Cucaracha* (produced, directed and co-written by Ismael Rodriguez), titled after its Revolutionary *corrido* song, had an all-star cast led by Maria Felix and Dolores Del Rio, with Pedro Armendáriz, Antonio Aguilar, Flor Silvestre, Emilio Fernandez, and Ignacio Lopez Tarso. It also featured the famous singing and musical artists Cuco Sanchez, Los Dorados, and Dueto America. The film depicted a romantic triangle where the love for the same man, a revolutionary captain, pits two women against each other: one, a brash peasant who dons men's clothing and rebukes conventional dictates of what befits a lady; the other, a respectable and widowed señora. In the end, both women follow the captain as *soldaderas*, the goal of winning the Revolution taking precedence over individual rivalries.

    Juana Gallo, a film written and directed by Miguel Zacarías, also titled after its namesake *corrido*, presented the music and singing performances of José Alfredo Jiménez, Ernesto Juárez, and Trio Hermanos Michel. Maria Félix plays the courageous female colonel who leads soldiers into battle and in the process, after having previously lost her father and husband to the war, also loses the three men in her life: her lover, her friend, and her loyal sergeant, yet she continues to lead the fight.

13. From 1937 until his death in 1953, Jorge Negrete appeared mostly in c*omedias rancheras*. His natural charisma, striking good looks, and opera-trained voice made him Mexico's singing idol. In the film, *Siempre Tuya*, in 1952, his singing in the starring role would permanently associate his voice with, *Mexico Lindo y Querido*, a song composed by Chucho Monje in 1921, and turn that composition into the country's emblematic *ranchera* song. Negrete became internationally recognized as the original icon of Mexico's ranchero spirit. In this film of the nationalist genre, he affirms his *Mexicano ranchero* identity by rejecting a piano and asking instead for a mariachi group accompaniment. He played the role of a subsistence farmer forced by drought and poverty to move to the city, where employment is highly competitve and times are hard. He enters into and wins a radio amateur hour (on the famous station, XEW) singing contest, which transforms his life. When his eventual fame leads him to be seduced by an American woman (Joan Page), he leaves his Mexican life and marriage, but eventually returns after rediscovering his true feelings for his Mexican wife and country.

14. For example, the *Grito de Independencia*, the traditional Yell of Independence ritual reproduced every year by the sitting President in Mexico City, was initiated when it was broadcasted

nationally and internationally for the first time in history by this station on September 15, 1930, with then-President Pascual Ortíz Rubio.

15. Including: "Emilio Tuero, Juan Arvizu, Luis Arcaraz, Nicolás Urcelay, José Mojica, Alfonso Ortiz Tirado, Tito Guízar, Los Panchos, Maria Luisa Landín, Maria Victoria, Panzón Panseco, Los Cuates Castilla, Mario Moreno Cantinflas, Germán Valdés "Tin Tan", Agustín Lara, Toña la Negra, Angelines Fernández, Angel Garasa, Carmen Rey, Pedro Infante, Jorge Negrete, Pedro Vargas, Jose Alfredo Jiménez, Fernando Fernández "El Crooner de México", Gustavo Adolfo Palma de Guatemala, Luis Aguilar, Eulalio González "Piporro", Antonio Aguilar, Francisco Gabilondo Soler "Cri Cri", Viruta y Capulina, Javier Solís, Los Tres Ases, Los Tres Diamantes, Hugo Avendaño, Lucha Villa, Amparo Montes, Héctor Martínez Serrano, Juan "El Gallo" Calderón, Paco Stanley ..." (es.wikipedia.org, 2020) and many more.

16. Sue 2013, p. 18

17. Mexican history includes African Blacks who were brought by the Spanish conquerors in the Atlantic slave trade mostly to Veracruz, as well as descendants of Black immigrants from places such as Cuba, central America, and the United States. Black slaves intermarried with the native and mixed populations and in northern Mexico, including the Mexico-United States borderlands, Seminole Indians formed marital unions with slave runaways, from both Mexico and the United States, thus originating the communities of descendants existing today, one of which is in El Nacimiento, Coahuila. Other small concentrations of Afro-Mexicano and their descendants live in the geographic pockets where runaway Africans in the 17th century fought to resist enslavement and formed settlements, specifically in coastal Oaxaca and in the state of Guerrero, itself named for the mixed-race independence leader. The largest Afro-Mexicano population lives in the state of Veracruz, where the first community of self-freed blacks in the Americas formed in 1609, after fighting for their freedom from the Spanish in a forty-year struggle, led by Gaspar Yanga, a runaway slave.

    In spite of their significance to the formation of Mexico, Afro-Mexicanos have been kept largely as an invisible component of Mexico's official history. The national census, for example, did not include Black or Black-mixed racial categories until the 2015 count, which showed that about 1.38 million people claimed African descent, equivalent to only about 1.2% of the total Mexican population. The small number notwithstanding, some DNA evidence suggests that almost all Mexican Mestizos, Mexico's overwhelming majority, carry some African genetic heritage (en.wikipedia.org, Afro-Mexicans, 2020).

18. Two films, I believe most exemplified the oppressive paternalism of colonial elites toward blacks and Indians in Mexico's history. One was the 1948 production of *Angelitos Negros*, starring Pedro Infante, with Rita Montaner, Emilia Guiú, Chela Castro, and Titina Romay. The story decries the open racism with which the protagonist Ana Luisa (Guiú), a blonde, light-skinned woman, treats her black nanny Mercé (Rita Montaner), openly rejects her husband's black friends (Chela Castro in black face and Black actors uncredited in the film's listed cast), and hates and rejects her own daughter, Belén (Romay), when the child is born with black skin. Ana Luisa is unaware that she is herself the daughter of Mercé, who in self-deprecation, excuses Ana Luisa's abusiveness toward her for being black. When Ana Luisa gives birth to Belen, a priest convinces Luisa's husband, Jose Carlos (Infante), to assume the "blame" for the child's color by pretending to have a Black heritage himself, fearing that learning about her own blackness may send Ana Luisa into shock. The racism against dark skin and the racial and class privilege accorded to whiteness is operationalized in the "protection" of Ana Luisa and her White fragility. The film's plot centers

racial prejudice by treating racism as if existing only when demonstrated in blatant forms. The film's contradictory message pertaining to race includes the friendship between brown-skinned Jose Carlos and his Black and black-mixed friends as a supposed disclaimer, the appropriation of Black subjectivity by Jose Carlos' appearance in black face, and the rejection of black identity represented in Belén's attempt to use talcum powder to change her skin color in order to gain her mother's love.

The film was named like the song, which Pedro Infante introduced as a bolero style in the film, though it was adapted from a poem originally written in the 1940s by the mixed-race Venezuelan poet and activist, Andres Eloy Blanco, who titled it "Píntame Angelitos Negros." Manuel Alvarez "Maciste" Renteria composed the music for the song, which was launched in Mexico by the eminent bolero singer Toña La Negra in 1942. It was also recorded in 1953 by Eartha Kitt in her RCA Victor album, The Bad Eartha (en.wikipedia.org, 2019) and in 1969 by Roberta Flack in her album, First Take. Both of these American idols of R & B and soul recorded it in Spanish, in both cases with a discernable Afro-Latino pronunciation. It has had several adaptations and translations into other languages and has been sung and recorded by artists internationally. Delgadillo (2006) traces the international reproduction of the song to show how it effectively helped construct and disseminate the African American Diaspora Movement against racism throughout the hemisphere. As Delgadillo notes, the poem, the song, and the film, call forth our understanding of how, though acknowledging our different geographies, histories and contexts, our Mestizaje and the African American Diaspora share points of contact in our subjectivities.

The 1952 film, *El Derecho de Nacer* (The Right to be Born) was made in Mexico after it ran in Cuba as a popular radionovela. Like the first version, the 1966 remake of the film, starring Julio Alemán and Maricruz Oliver, depicts a rich, brown-skinned father of a young woman who gives birth out of wedlock. He secretly arranges to have the infant killed to protect the family's social standing, but the family's black servant, Mamá Dolores (Eusebia Cosme), enlists the cooperation of the black manservant, Bruno (Juan José Laboriel) to keep her secret when she rescues the child and runs away with it to raise it herself in the city. When the child grows to adulthood, he becomes a physician with strong pro-life convictions who intervenes in the decisions of his patients seeking abortions, convincing them to reconsider. The end of the film shows that the boy's mother renounced the love of a man and became a nun to atone for having a child out of wedlock and to deal with the sadness she felt over losing him; the boy's grandfather, remorseful of having attempted to kill his grandson, ends up grateful to Mamá Dolores for saving and raising the boy and purchases a house for her as recompense for her selfless love and for raising the child. The film is thus deeply grounded in Catholic and socially conservative anti-abortion values.

19. This word *Mulato* is part of the classification of races, particularly in Latin America, indicating a person who is a direct descendant of a White parent and a Black parent. According to some sources, its origin is from the Portuguese word for "mule," which is a mix between a horse and a donkey. I refer to it here to situate its social significance in the intended and unintended messages of the film, but also wish to bring attention to the term's offensiveness.
20. Veracruz's bio-diversity, cultural diversity, and gender, class and race stratification, were exemplified in the 1942 film, *Historia de un Gran Amor*, starring Jorge Negrete, Gloria Marín, and Sara Garcia: In the 19th century's post-independence period, in the highlands of Veracruz, a child becomes orphaned at age 12, after his father is swindled out of his home and property. The

child, impoverished and alone, is taken in to live with a priest and the old woman who raised the priest under similar circumstances. Due to his social status, the boy is treated by some people as a *recogido* (taken in) though others recognize the status of his privileged upbringing. As a man, he falls in love with the daughter of the man who robbed him of his home, but the young woman obeys her father and marries instead the rich owner of the town's biggest factory. Affirming that happiness is impossible against the power of a fate dictated by class structure, the story ends in tragedy. The film is rich in visual folklore, provided by Gabriel Figueroa's masterful cinematography, and features Negrete and others performing the improvisation characteristic of the *coplas* of Veracruz, and he and Marín dancing a *zapateado* to a *Jarocho* band performing *El Balajú* and other *sones Veracruzanos*.

Tierra Brava, a 1938 classic about the people and traditions of Veracruz, showed the people working in the region's production of tobacco, the folklore, including its community dances known as *fandangos*, its Easter celebrations that mimic the *posadas* of other parts of the country, and the regional *zapateado*, the staccato heel dance steps performed upon the traditional *tarima* (platform), particularly in the wedding dance, *La Bamba*, in which the couple ties a long cloth band into a knot using their feet while dancing to the music of the *jarocho* band. The film included *sones Veracruzanos* played by Escamilla as well as by Hermanos Huesca, and the singing of Trio Calaveras, Los Murcielagos, and Trio Asencio del Rio. The film was among the first to introduce the Cuban-origin rumbera music and dancing, here performed by the famous *rumbero* dancers, Estela and Rene, to the music of the bandleader Enrique Bion and his Cuban band, *Hatuey*.

21. The *copla* performers are either accompanied by musicians playing several instruments or they accompany themselves on guitars, depending on the music genre they represent. The 1936 production of *Allá en El Rancho Grande*, a *comedia ranchera* (comedy and folklore) starring Tito Guizar and Esther Fernandez, is credited as the first of the Golden Era and the first Mexican film to gain international recognition (agurza, 2016) (Grande, 2020). Along with its *ranchera* music and singing, it included the famous *coplas de huapango* performed by Guizar and Lorenzo Barcelata. In this case, the coplas are performed in the *huapango* genre. The film also introduced the *sones jarochos* music played by Andres Huesca y Sus Costeños, who used a harp associated with the music of Michoacán, a larger version of the traditional *jarocha* harp (es.wikipedia.org, 2020). The film was remade in 1948, starring Mexico's film and singing great, Jorge Negrete, who performed the dueling *copla* with Luis Perez Mesa, and co-starring the singer/actor, Lilia Del Valle. It featured the Trio Calaveras playing and singing *Lucha Maria*, and whose guitars also accompanied Jorge Negrete singing *El Gallero* (jkr1mc, 2013).
22. Andres Huesca was the first to record La Bamba, a song of African roots, in 1945. Ritchie Valens adapted it to the rock n' roll genre in his recording in 1958. Huesca also pioneered the use of the Michoacán harp, a larger version of the harp used in the older *Jarocho* musical tradition, to enhance its visibility in films. For example, the 1943 film, *Maria Eugenia*, featuring Andrés Huesca y Sus Costeños, also featured a *copla jarocha*, sung by Alfredo Varela and an uncredited artist.
23. *Alma de Veracruz*, by the famed composer, Manuel Esperón, is introduced in the film in a cabaret setting, showing the microphone of the popular radio station, XEW. The orchestra Son Clave de Oro was originally named Son Marabú. It was created by Agustin Lara in the early 1930s, specifically to accompany his famous bolero song muse Toña La Negra.
24. They included: "Absalón Pérez on the piano; Lalo (Eulalio) Ruiz de Mantilla, tresero of the original Son Cuba by Marianao; Domingo Vernier "Mango", flutist; Manuel Peregrino and Pablo Zamora Peregrino, percussionists; Manolo Güido, trumpeter; Mario Ruíz Armengol,

pianist; ... Juan García Esquivel, Ismael Díaz, Chucho Rodríguez, Homero Jiménez, Güicho Iturriaga, Mongo Santamaría and Armando Peraza. Its most important singers were José Vásquez "Chepilla", Pedro Domínguez "Muscovita" and Orlando Guerra "Cascarita", singer of the Orquesta Casino De La Playa" (discogs.com, 2020).

25. The best known included the Cubans Ninón Sevilla, Maria Antonieta Pons, Amalia Aguilar, Mary Esquivel, and Rosa Carmina, as well as Meche Barba, who was born in the United States and raised in Mexico.

26. A defining film of this version of the rumbera genre was the 1948, *Salon Mexico*. Its storyline, musical style and lyrics identified the nightlife, and its cinematic photography portrayed a context of poverty that evoked empathy. Starring Marga Lopez and Miguel Inclán, it ushered in the replacement of the rumba with *danzón* music, played by Son Clave de Oro, performing *Juárez no Debió de Morir, El Caballo y la Montura, Almendra, Nereidas, Sopa de Pichón*, and *Meneíto*. The plot includes a male character who is injured in his service in the United States military under General McArthur. The story thus helped raise public awareness about the participation of Mexico in World War II. The film was produced after Aaron Copeland's composition, El Salón Mexico, a symphonic piece meant to musically describe Mexico's complex nightlife and compiled from the different genres of music he heard played at a popular dance hall he visited in Mexico City, named El Salón Mexico (wikipedia, 2019).

27. An example is the 1954 film, *La Perversa*. Alicia is the self-centered, irreverent, over-ambitious, wicked woman (played by Elsa Aguirre), the opposite of her younger and equally beautiful sister, Gloria (played by Elsa's real-life sister, Alma Rosa Aguirre), who is virtuous, principled, and devoted to their loving, aging and sickly mother. Alicia discards her economically modest life with her mother and sister to live with Enrique, a wealthy but narcissistic man who showers her with luxuries on conditions that ultimately mean helping him gain sexual access to her sister. Reluctantly, Alicia agrees and tricks Gloria into the apartment where Enrique rapes the young woman. Filled with remorse and disgusted with Enrique, Alicia kills him, and although proven innocent, she pleads guilty and accepts imprisonment.

28. This coexisting duality was most obviously exemplified in the case of Maria and Magdalena, the two sides of the biblical sinner, Mary Magdalene, suggested in the characters of twins in the 1945 film, *La Otra* (The Other One). Dolores del Rio plays a double role of twin sisters: Maria, a hard-working lone woman on the edge of poverty, and Magdalena, whose unscrupulous ambitions made her a rich widow. In a reversal of character, the good sister kills the bad and assumes her identity and her wealth, only to find herself blackmailed by Magdalena's illicit lover and accomplice in the murder of her husband. In the end, Maria, who maintains Magdalena's identity, still gets a prison sentence for committing murder.

29. Agustín Lara, legendary bolero composer since the 1930s, was the best known for the songs that titled and described the cabaret films. Among them was the 1948 film production, *Humo en los Ojos*, [Smoke in the Eyes], with the title song interpreted by Lara's bolerista muse, Toña la Negra. The song has been recorded by various artists, but its most popular association is with Javier Solís; *Pervertida* (1950), starring Amalia Aguilar and sung by Pedro Vargas and Ana Maria Gonzalez, with the additional songs, *Contigo*, by Vargas, and *Adios*, by Gonzalez; *Pecadora* (1947), starring Ninón Sevilla and featuring performances by Miguel Aceves Mejia and Ana Maria Gonzalez, cabaret music played by the Brazilian group, Los Angeles del Infierno, and Agustin Lara singing more of his compositions, *Maria Bonita, Tus Pupilas*, and *Te Quiero*, as well as the film's namesake song, *Pecadora*.

Other examples included the 1952, *Yo Fui Una Callejera*, starring Meche Barba, with then-bolerista, Antonio Aguilar, which introduced Consuelo Velasquez's composition, *Qué Divino* and Mario Ruiz Armengol's *Soñaré Contigo*; Fernando Fernandez's interpretation of the Cuban Chucho Rodriguez's *No te Vayas*; the Trio Janitzio played and sang *Te Sigo Esperando*; and Trio Avileño, Trio Los Mexicanos, the *Jarocho* Trio Los Águilillas, and Luis Aguilar interpreted a Cuco Sánchez *ranchera* composition, *Yo Tambien Soy Mexicano* with Mariachi Pulido.

The 1950 film, *Amor de la Calle* [Street Walker], was themed and titled from the bolero song composed by Fernando Z. Maldonado (Wikipedia, 2020).

30. Rumberas also introduced new musical drama hybrids that introduced new boleros. For example, the 1948, *La Bien Pagada*, starring the Cuban Maria Antonieta Pons and Blanca Estela Pavón introduced the Puerto Rican composer Pedro Flores's bolero, *Amor Perdido*, sung by the bolerista Maria Luisa Landín, who became best known for this song; Cuban composer Bobby Collazo's *La Ultima Noche*; and the composers/duo (Carlos and Pablo) Hermanos Martinez Gil's, *Falsaria*; and the 1958, *Bolero Inmortal*, featuring compositions by some of the greats of *bolero* music and song, Trio Los Panchos, Pedro Vargas, Agustín Lara, Toña La Negra, Fernando Fernandez, Roberto G. Rivera, and Bobby Capó, and starring Elvira Quintana, who recorded these in her album, including: Cesar Portillo de la Luz's (Cuban), *Contigo en la Distancia*, Pedro Junco's (Cuban) *Nosotros*, Frank Dominguez (Cuban) *Tu Me Acostumbraste*; Consuelo Velasquez (Mexican) *Besame Mucho*, Alberto Dominguez (Mexican) *Perfidia*, Victor Huesca (Mexican) *Nochecita*, Gabriel Ruiz (music) and Ricardo Lopez Mendez's (lyrics) (Mexicans) *Amor, Amor, Amor,* and *Desesperadamente*; and Agustín Lara's *Por El Triste Camino,* and *Que te Quiero* (SecondHandSongs.com, 2003–2020) (en.wikipedia.org, 2020) (encuentrolatinoradio.com, 2020):

References

Cinema, G. A. (2020, July 7). *en.Wikipedia.org*. Retrieved from en.wikipedia.org: https://en.wikipedia.org/wiki/Golden_Age_of_Mexican_cinema

Delgadillo, T. (2006). Singing "Angelitos Negros": African Diaspora Meets Mestizaje in the Americas. *American Quarterly*, 68(2), 407–430.

Herrera-Sobek, M. (1992). *The Mexican Corrido: A Feminist Analysis*. Bloomington: Indiana University Press.

History.com. (2020, May 5). *This Day In History- August 24*. Retrieved from HISTORY: https://www.history.com/this-day-in-history/spain-accepts-mexican-independence

Jkr1mc (2013). Alla en el Rancho Grande.You Tube. May 11. https://www.youtube.com/watch?v=CT5U7BVJWr0&t=1145s

Raat, W. D., & Beezley, W. H. (1986). *Twentieth Century Mexico*. Lincoln: University of Nebraska Press.

Sue, C. (2013). *Land of the Cosmic Race: Race Mixture, Racism and Blackness in Mexico*. Oxford, UK: Oxford University Press.

Wikipedia: The Free Encyclopedia. (2019). The Bad Eartha. November 13. https://en.wikipedia.org/wiki/That_Bad_Eartha

Wikipedia-The Free Encylopedia (2019). El Salon Mexico. October 5. https://en.wikipedia.org/wiki/El_Sal%C3%B3n_M%C3%A9xico

Wikipedia-La enciclopedia libre (2020). XEW-AM. June. https://es.wikipedia.org/wiki/XEW-AM

CHAPTER FIVE

Naa, Na, Na, Na Naa: The Chicano Movement and the Birth of the East Side Sound

"As a people who have been stripped of our history, language, identity and pride, we attempt again and again to find what we have lost by imaginatively digging into our cultural roots and making art out of our findings."[1]

We traveled northbound on the Arizonan desert highway through the dark of night, as we did every other time that we went to California to visit our family. The car was fully occupied. It was a private transport service, one of the cheaper alternatives to the Greyhound that were advertised in the classified section of *El Fronterizo*, the popular newspaper in Ciudad Juárez. There was little conversation among the car's occupants. We all seemed consumed by our thoughts and apprehensions. For me, it was from knowing that I was leaving my childhood behind as my adolescent years were about to begin. My mother was always quiet and pensive on these trips, and I knew she was anticipating our living arrangements with our family in El Sereno and looking forward to stoking our close bonds, especially with her nieces and nephews, the godchildren she had helped raise as her own. I sensed that thoughts of my father figured most in her quietness, that this time was different than the others. Indeed, this would be more than a visit because unbeknownst to my father, he would be fading from the picture, and for my mother and me, this would be a one-way journey.

> *Estoy pensando en ti,*
> *mientras viva un amor*
> *que ya no siento/*
> *Los besos que te dí,*
> *me duelen*
> *Como duele, el pensamiento ...* [2]
> [I am thinking of you
> as I live a love
> I no longer feel/
> The kisses that I gave you,
> hurt me
> as the thought hurts ...] (Translation mine)

I attended Woodrow Wilson High in El Sereno, briefly. When I started high school in the United States, I was placed two years ahead due to the comparatively accelerated Mexican school curricula. My greatest challenge in my new schooling was the English language, and although I was in a largely Mexican American community, I was also experiencing culture shock. The Mexican cultural identity and sense of belonging that surrounded our life in Mexico was faint or absent among my new school peers who were of Mexican origin. I was not in a bilingual program, and, being more able to understand than to speak English, limited my ability to communicate and added to my sense of isolation. My Mexican-origin classmates spoke Spanish but usually not in school and most spoke a fractured version that could not sustain an entire conversation. I shied away from others, especially white kids, to avoid the language barrier. In our home the adults spoke only Spanish while the kids spoke a mixture of the two languages. We kept up with the news with a combination of the Spanish newspaper *La Opinión* and the daily English televised newscasts, which helped my understanding of English. For the first time in my life, a school official, a counselor, told me that I should choose an easier math class than I wanted because it would be too hard for me, contradicting the high expectations of my Mexican schooling and the reasons I was advanced two years in school in the U.S. The scenario resonated the culturally demeaning experiences that my mother had as a Mexican American student in Texas. The blow to my self-esteem from the tracking I was placed in and my counselor's advice provoked a setback in my academic achievement, but the cultural pride I was taught to feel during my Mexican education saved me from the kind of permanent damage that the same experience had caused my mother.

The music that filled the airwaves in the mid-sixties in East Los Angeles was an amalgamation of rock, rhythm and blues, soul, Mexican music, and Motown. Radio hosts Casey Kazem, Wink Martindale, Bob Eubanks, the Real

Photo 5.1: Promotional photo of Amalia Mendoza's performance at Teatro California, Los Angeles. From the private archives of Aurora Prado Pastrano, c1965.

Don Steele, Charlie Tuna, Charlie Van Dyke, Robert W. Morgan, "Emperor" Hudson, and "Huggy Boy," played top hits on "Boss Radio" KHJ, KRLA, and KFWB, and the "Mighty 1090" featured "Wolfman Jack," while *Radio KALI* competed by playing Mexican music. On Saturday mornings we cleaned house while listening to the record player blaring do-wop oldies but goodies and new sounds of Motown, mixed with Javier Solís accompanied by mariachi, and Eydie Gormé accompanied by the famed trio Los Panchos. Some evenings my mother would gather the children to practice singing. The older kids, Gloria and Pepe (Joe), would sing *boleros* while the younger kids watched and listened. Famous Mexican artists like Amalia Mendoza (Photo 5.1) and José Alfredo Jiménez, whose performance we once attended, would perform to a full house at venues like the Million Dollar Theater in downtown Los Angeles when they toured the United States. Like other Latinos, Joe and Gloria went dancing with their friends at The Hollywood Palladium whenever the famous Mexican orchestra, La Sonora Santanera, was playing. The song, Land of a Thousand Dances, with its catchy tune and the simple phrasing made famous by Cannibal, of Cannibal and the Headhunters, "naa, na, na, na naa ..." would be repeated seemingly by every kid at school throughout the day. Thee Midniters became famous with their cover of that song and with their mostly instrumental original, Whittier Boulevard, titled after the drag strip known to every Mexican American youth in East L. A. "Louie, Louie," by the Kingsmen, played repeatedly on transistor radios that students smuggled into school, along with Motown hits like Mary Wells's "My Guy," The Temptations' "The Way You Do The Things You Do," Martha and the Vandellas' "Dancing in the Street," and The Four Tops' "Baby I Need Your Lovin." That February, like millions of other viewers, my family witnessed the beginning of the "British Invasion," with The Beatles appearing on the Ed Sullivan Show on television. The camera panned over a live audience of young girls screaming and crying with delight at the band's performance of "I Want To Hold Your Hand." The adults in my house lamented such behavior, while the teenagers watched with excitement. I was mystified by the whole spectacle. In school I was introduced to the concept of extra-curricular social dances, and one was featuring a rising duo named The Righteous Brothers. I was curious and disappointed when my mother, saying I was too young to go to dances, would not allow me to attend. At my first after-school dance, I learned the local dance moves to the popular hit, "Shotgun," by Junior Walker and the Allstars, and had my first slow dance to Thee Midniters' 1965 cover of Jay Wiggins's 1963 original, "Sad Girl."[3]

My mother and I moved into a modestly furnished studio apartment located in Lincoln Heights. Though they were adjacent, Lincoln Heights was a less prosperous neighborhood than El Sereno, and demographically more Mexican immigrant/Mexican American. Lincoln High had few white students, and my schoolmates were less acculturated, that is, they were more Mexican in their family relationships, adherence to traditions, forms of expression, language, viewpoints, joking styles and the like; hence, it was easier for me to fit in and soon I made friends with a large group of Upward Bound students. Although I was in the heart of the Mexican American community, I began to bring home new ideas and viewpoints I learned from my peers, such as college attendance, and English increasingly was in our language use at home. As those things unfolded, the relationship between my mother and me began to strain.

Civil Rights Movements

My mother and I sat on the front steps of our apartment on an August evening in 1965, talking with our neighbor about the "Watts Riots," as they were called on television, happening less than twenty miles away. Watts was a section of the predominantly African American south-central area of Los Angeles. The scenes shown were frightening and the reports were scary and confusing. We did not really understand what was truly happening. People were being pulled out of their cars and beaten, stores were being looted, cars were set on fire and people were running through the smoke.

Around us the country was undergoing an historic period that would have monumental significance. The Black Civil Rights marches, along with the Freedom riders, had begun to take place in protest of the historical Jim Crow laws that institutionalized segregation in the south and denied Blacks their right to vote. On March 7, 1965, John Lewis[4] and Hosea Williams led the Selma to Montgomery march on what was to be remembered as "Bloody Sunday."[5] As we witnessed the events hours later on television, it was an awakening for my family and, I believe, for much of the country. We watched the nationally broadcasted images exposing racial violence that forced non-black people to confront the reality of injustice long suffered by African Americans. We watched the televised reports showing how other protests ensued as sympathy snowballed. These events introduced us to the Black Civil Rights Movement and to Dr. Martin Luther King Jr. Though my family and I did not fully understand the political process, we learned from these events that we were living an historically pivotal moment with significance to our own Mexican American community.

We witnessed the birth of the student Anti-War Movement on college campuses in United States history during that Civil Rights period. We watched the protesters shown on television, at the University of California-Berkeley, demanding the end of U.S. involvement in the war. The protesters were white, like the vast majority of students in higher education in the United States. My family presumed that they were also wealthy and privileged. My family, like almost all Latinos in the U.S., had known the destruction and devastation of war. We had a tradition of military service, in large part because of the racial and economic barriers that kept us from accessing higher education and good employment opportunities, which left military service the only viable option. It was also traditionally a matter of honor and distinction in our family and community for a young man to serve his country. But our Mexican American communities were suffering great losses from the disproportionate war casualties among our young servicemen. So, although it was strange to us, my family and those around me, to watch those white, rich students form a radical opposition to the war, we took serious notice. As those protests continued and gained momentum, they brought attention to how the Viet Nam war differed from others in which the United States had fought. The student voices, posters, and some news reports articulated the criticism that justified my family's and community's reluctance to send our young men to war in spite of our traditional patriotism: This was not just about privileged young white people refusing to go to war for their country; it was about how this country's leaders stoking a war because it was lucrative to U.S. investors, at the expense of human carnage, was immoral.

In my family, the Women's Movement that arose in the 1960s lacked the impact of the other Civil Rights Movements. From what we watched and read about the Feminist Movement's rhetoric as shown on television and the printed media, it did not inspire members of my family, friends or community. I was in early adolescence and did not yet understand the greater implications of our disinterest, but it seemed clear that that Movement was for and about white, relatively privileged women whose goal was personal fulfillment and whose objectives were liberation from male and sexual domination. The Feminist Movement protested gender inequality in educational, employment, salary, and other institutionalized ways that deprived women participation in society equal to that of men. Feminists also sought to overturn the patriarchy that denied women's freedoms, rights, and protection of their own autonomy and that underlay all of society's institutions, including religion and the family. In retrospect, the Women's Movement agenda of the 1960s–1970s (now called the second wave of the Feminist Movement) ignored the practical, everyday needs that women of color and poor women suffered as a result of discrimination, and the fact that our gendered oppression has always been compounded by our racialized and class-based experiences. The thrust of The Feminist Movement also hit at the heart of what we considered sacred: The family, religion, and cultural tradition. As Mexican American and Latina women, many of us did not relate to The Feminist Movement because it failed to understand the Mexican American family's function as a source of the material support as well as comfort, purpose, status, power, and control that society denied to us. It did not know the cultural value of women of color and poor women for their contribution to the cohesion of their families and communities through their relationships with children, parents, and other social ties. It also seemed to ignore how women like *Tia Eduvijes, Abuelita Juanita*, or our song artists deployed our cultural music, family sentiments, religious practices and other cultural means as tools of liberation, or the significance of Our Lady of Guadalupe as racial and gender counterpower to the Eurocentric patriarchy of the church. For many Chicana/Latina women, like those in my family, and for me, the Feminist Movement of the 1960s fell short of including our interests, history, and experiences.[6]

The Chicano Civil Rights Movement

In the spring of 1966, a retreat held at Camp Hess-Kramer in Malibu would be pivotal in Chicano history. Two-hundred youths from Los Angeles area high schools were invited to meet with members of the Los Angeles County Human Relations Council to discuss Mexican American youth issues, including gang membership, school dropout rates, and access to college opportunities. The faculty at Lincoln High were Anglo with few exceptions, like a Mexican American history teacher and student counselor named Sal Castro. He encouraged my then-boyfriend, Oswaldo (Ozzie) Reinoso to attend the meeting at Hess-Kramer. According to Ozzie, Mexican American students at the retreat gathered on their own in a separate lunchtime group to discuss a possible Movement against the discrimination with which they were treated by the schools. As an Ecuadorian immigrant, honor roll student, highest-ranked ROTC officer, and student body president-elect, Ozzie did not identify with the other, predominantly Mexican American students' experiences and sentiments:

> I met other students there. The Salas Brothers[7] were there. A colleague of Mr. Castro was there. They all told me about discrimination. They wanted me to influence [organize] other students, because I was a peer model. But I was the pet of the class, never had trouble with the law, I was picked to succeed. I felt anger. I was crying. I said 'No, I can't do that.' They went with other students.[8]

The retreat was repeated the next year, attended by some students from the previous year. According to a published account of these events,[9] among the students at that year's retreat were my former schoolmate, Moctezuma Esparza, and David Sánchez, from another school, both politically precocious. Sánchez met Richard Alatorre, the future second Mexican American U.S. congressman from the 30th Congressional District. With Alatorre's support, Sánchez sought and obtained funding the next year, to open a community teen hang-out called Piranya. He gathered some of the students he had met at the Hess-Kramer camp meeting and formed a community leader group called the Young Citizens for Community Action (YCCA). A passionate young activist of Cuban descent who related to Chicano life, Eleazar Rizo, began writing and distributing a paper titled, *La Raza*, which raised consciousness on educational issues, police brutality, and the overrepresentation of Chicano casualties in the Viet Nam War. The popularity of the publication and The Piranya served to foment a political consciousness and activism among Mexican American youth. The YCCA group evolved into the Chicano militant group that would come to represent the fight for Chicano liberation, called the Brown Berets.

On March 1, 1968, the student walkouts, called "blowouts," erupted. They started at Wilson High and continued the next week at Garfield, Roosevelt, Lincoln, and the other predominantly Mexican American high schools throughout East Los Angeles, with over 10,000 student protesters and over 15,000 students absent from their schoolrooms.[10] The Chicano college student organization, United Mexican American Students (UMAS), and members of other Chicano college student organizations, protested in solidarity with high school walkouts, which were happening throughout the country, especially all over the southwest. Students carried signs that said "Chicano" and "Chicano Power," announcing their political rebirth and their determination for change, respectively. The issues in East L.A. included the need for college preparatory courses and appropriate advisement, an end to the practice of tracking most Mexican American students into vocational classes for labor and service occupations, and the need of Mexican Americans to have an education that valued their cultural heritage, with available bilingual instruction, an end to corporal punishment, the hiring of more Mexican American faculty and counselors, and the integration of courses on Mexican American history and culture. Thus, the 1966 meeting at Camp Hess-Kramer, became what Rosales called the "genesis" of the events leading to the blowouts as a marker of the Chicano Civil Rights Movement.[11]

The students marching outside Lincoln High was a dramatic scene. I had graduated from that school the previous spring and was on the bus on my way to the trade-technical college I was enrolled in by then, instead of the University that I had dreamed of attending. I had become another casualty of the failed educational system; hence, I was intrigued by the protest and admired the students' revolutionary spirit. In the archival photographs of the events, one picture taken in front of the Lincoln High School's marquis, shows a sign carried by a student, depicting Miguel Hidalgo y Costilla, the Mexican independence leader and iconic symbol of justice and de-colonization.

Like all such revolutionary events, the young students' protesting would put them in the crosshairs of the authorities, including the FBI. The police reacted by clubbing and arresting the protesting high school students for walking, marching, or crossing the street. Administrators and school boards soon turned the blowouts into a persecution of Sal Castro, accusing him of inciting the students to revolt. He was dismissed from his teaching position and arrested, as were Moctezuma Esparza, David Sánchez, Eleazar Rizo, and some members of the Brown Berets, totaling thirteen people held on charges of "conspiring to create riots, disrupt the functioning of public schools, and disturb the peace."[12] In the next weeks, members of the community organized to support the "L A Thirteen," obtaining backing from governor Brown, Councilman Tom Bradley, and the Chicano Legal Defense Fund. Ultimately, a ruling found that a school demonstration did not constitute a felony. In spite of this landmark victory, the core issues continued and likewise the protests throughout the southwest.

A Philosophical and Political Divide

Not all members of the Mexican American community approved of the protests.[13] My mother was among those in the Mexican American community who disagreed and viewed the protesters as disruptive, disrespectful, and deviant. She reacted to the televised scenes of the protests with a head shaking in her most condemning way along with her disapproving, "¡*mira nomás!*" which meant, "just look at such behavior!" She interpreted the events the same way she had understood those of the Watts Rebellion, which, according to televised reports, turned into riots, with looting and rock-throwing that understandably produced public disapproval; but the reports did not cover the underlying social justice issues. The use of force by the police on the young Chicano students made my mother angry as much with the officers as with the marchers for exposing themselves to it with injudicious behavior, as she considered their overt act of protest. The protesters' proud self-reference as *Chicanos*, an historically ascribed socially demeaning term, and as *La Raza*, a cultural self-reference often used in our humorous self-deprecation, added to the shame she saw in their actions, missing in her assessment the new significance of the terms as cultural affirmation and political solidarity.

My mother was raised to obey and respect authority unquestioningly, under the threat of physical punishment. That was how *abuelita Juanita* survived political persecution for her Indianness in Mexico; that was how tia Eduvijez, as a peasant woman, survived the Porfiriato; and how Mexican Americans survived their poverty and subordinate social and political status. My mother's abusive marriage repeated the expectation of her obedience as requisite for her and her child to survive. Showing conformity and acceptance to authority and power thus meant survival, not just of oneself, but also of others; altruism was the foundation of good moral character. In my mother's view, in the young, such rebellion made us *malagradecidos*, ungrateful toward our parents, who we should honor by preventing social shame and other consequences of our rebellion to befall them. To my mother, such demonstrations of dissent thus fell within a framework not of a socially transformative deviance, as exemplified by Mexican revolutionary heroines like the iconic Adelitas, but as one of self-indulgence.

Her interpretations of the student blowouts did not originate in the context of her family upbringing; they were grounded in the colonization and cultural hegemony inherent in the racist and paternalistic educational system. It taught her as a school child in Texas and all brown children in the United States, to obey and conform; to be grateful for an education that shamed their native culture and language and colonized them with the idea that they should learn vocational skills because they could never be anything more. The damage caused by that message was tragically manifested in my mother's life. It would also produce a fundamental philosophical wedge that would permanently exist between us.

Identity, Sadness and Resistance

My mother has never been given to political activism. For most of her life in the United States she has been cynical about politics, perceiving power as only vested in the politicians, *"Para qué te preocupas tu tanto, hombre. ¿Que puedes hacer? ¡Déjaselo a los políticos!"* [Why do you worry so much? What can you do? Leave it to the politicians!] What could be considered her limited political involvement happened through her participation in musical performance. The first was in the spring of 1968, with Bobby Kennedy's campaign for the democratic presidential nomination. To support Bobby Kennedy's candidacy, *La Asociación de Artistas, Cantantes, y Compositores*, an association of artists and composers of which she was a member by then, held a fundraiser benefit show with guest artist performances. My mother and the rest of our family held great esteem for the Kennedys. She had admired JFK's decisiveness in the 1962 Cuban Missile Crisis, was empathetic to Jackie Kennedy over her miscarriages, and felt some religious closeness with the Kennedys' practiced Catholicism. She also was always happy to participate in musical events. It was not surprising, therefore, that Aurora Prado would be among the featured artists in the benefit. That event remains to my mother, among the most memorable in her music career. This is partly due to a mishap she had onstage with her dress and partly to her almost entire family's singular presence at her performance, but to whatever degree her performance contributed to the fundraiser, she speaks of it with notable pride when mentioning that it was to support Bobby Kennedy's campaign. In my experience, that event represents a highpoint of my mother's claim and affirmation of membership in a politically significant group, and that was as an American national. I use this term intentionally, because that is how I believe she feels about and describes her social, ethnic, and political identity.

Over the years, I have seen how my mother struggles to define her own ethnic identity. When conversations veered toward racial or political topics, she often contradicted herself in defining her own ethnicity or political views. Sometimes she followed with comments or clarifications that further complicated her explanations. For example, she would claim her Mexican identity and then *other* her own group by referring to them as invaders of her neighborhood, *Ya se está viniendo toda la Mexicanada para acá*. [All those Mexicans are coming over here.]

As the country spiraled into the depths of racism with the Trump administration, so grew her nationalism and attempt to show her belonging in this country by emphasizing that she is "American." In spite of her profound belief in equality and social justice, her understanding of the national protests over immigration and Black Lives Matter fell under the influence of Fox News and its delegitimization of the social motives behind the protests. Her vulnerability to such misguiding reports is a tragic remnant of the biases against Indianness and blacks that she internalized during her childhood and the societal attitudes towards blackness that she learned as a young adult, both in Mexico and the United States. As a result, she has always struggled with her perception of Mexican American status as either or, where being ethnically Mexican represents being inferior to and hence separate from, being an American citizen.

It has always been sad for me to witness my mother's fragile sense of belonging in her native country, and her struggle, yet obvious pride in, staking her claim in her rightful national citizenship. Though she expresses it differently than I do, it mirrors my own desire and that of other members of ethnic and other social groups, to be included, to belong. That struggle is rooted in our collective Mexican American experience as a people whose history includes being annexed, immigrants, and citizens, and our evolving attempts to survive as a group, from forced annexation to segregation, to assimilation, to a cultural renaissance that shows how throughout, we are a people with a cultural resistance and persistence.

The legacies of the Chicano, African American, Student, and Latina Women's Movements raised my political and cultural consciousness during my undergraduate and graduate education, and my career as a university professor of cultural anthropology and Latino/a studies in many ways strengthened me against the cultural hegemony that socially injured my mother. The price of my consciousness and my education, however, is a gulf that in her eyes, seems to divide us. Our social and political views have been in contention since my adolescence. For that, my mother has always resented and blamed my education, which she sees as making me uppity, *Tú con tus libros crees que sabes mucho.* [You with your books, you think you know so much.]

What I see in my mother is an unbendable inner resilience that is as personally defining as it is politically significant. When we are together, my mother and I spend our time singing old Mexican songs or watching old Mexican movies, and she can always name all the actors/singers as well as the songs played in every film. Our conversations are in Spanish, peppered with terms, names, or concepts that are easier to say in English. Unlike our more acculturated members of our extended family, we observe our Mexican Catholic tradition of setting up the altar, lighting candles, and praying the novena to Our Lady of Guadalupe, and all our prayers are in Spanish. We adhere closely to traditional Mexican cuisine and she is always quick to correct me if my dish is missing a key ingredient. We observe lent with its specialized food, *comida de vigilia,* crowned with its special pudding, *capirotada.* We both reach for *hierba buena, estafiate, manzanilla,* or *sávila,* indigenous Mexican botanical home remedies, instead of Pepto Bismol, aspirin, or other over-the-counter medications. She expects and receives the respect owed to the matriarch in a traditional Mexican family. These and many other basics in her life show the strength of her ties to her Mexican cultural roots, a testament to her own cultural resistance, while she simultaneously fights to defend her United States citizenship as her birthright. In spite of her lack of political consciousness, that is what the Chicano Movement was about.

The Chicano Renaissance

The most visible and lasting product of the Chicano Movement was the Chicano Renaissance, a nationalist rebirth in literature, visual and performing arts, and music. Chicano artists, writers, musicians, and performers infused our communities with cultural pride and Mexican nationalism, shaping and expressing our ethnic consciousness of resistance against white cultural hegemony. Murals and graffiti displayed in our communities' private and public spaces, produced by local artists, became valued visual memorials to our native history and our new era. Several streets and public places were renamed to honor our Chicano leaders or mark our Chicano history. These included the Plaza de la Raza (formerly Lincoln Park), and Cesar Chavez Av (formerly Brooklyn Avenue), both in East Los Angeles. Circumventing the racism of mainstream publishing outlets against Mexican American authors, Chicanas/os created new publishing houses, while the demands of Chicano student activists pushed colleges and universities to offer courses in Chicano studies, fund the creation of Chicano Student Centers, reform admission and hiring practices and hire Chicano/a faculty, and commit to the promise of equity and justice represented in Affirmative Action. Chicano/a scholars also turned their research attention to our own communities, rejecting and exposing the Eurocentric canon as fictitiously "objective" research, and actively chronicling our own story. Chicano/a literature in history, political science, fiction, sociology and other fields of research proliferated, along with filmmaking, theater, and Chicana/Latina/Latinx playwriters, filling the libraries of our new Chicano Centers in universities and communities with our own creativity, ideas, and testaments to our own known and lived reality.

The regeneration of our traditional Mexican cultural music was an integral part of the Chicano Renaissance. Our folk musical styles, especially *rancheras, corridos,* and *boleros* had long been part of our Mexican American history, geography and life as people of Mexican descent in the United States, but with the rise of the Chicano Movement, Mexican music came to represent not only the music of our *sentimiento*, but an affirmation of our cultural belonging.[14] It became vital in Chicano political consciousness, proof of our cultural resiliency, an historical document of the richness of our musical legacy and inherited culture, and therefore it became the essence of our new musical sound. Chicano music was political history in the making.

Chicano music is rooted in the work of the few pioneer Chicano artists who, facing segregation and exclusion, introduced Latin sounds to the musical mainstream, even before the era of the Chicano Movement. Tito Tosti recorded "Pachuco Boogie," bringing recognition to the non-conforming Mexican American youth Zoot Suit subculture of the 1940s and their adopted *caló* argot, in 1948. Lalo Guerrero, famous for his Spanish-language parodies of English-language ballads and other genres, about the Mexican American experience such as that of immigrants and farm workers, is recognized as The Father of Chicano Music. The first Mexican American rock and roll star was Ricardo Valenzuela, a seventeen-year old from Pacoima, California, in the San Fernando Valley. He was discovered by Bob Keene, who changed Valenzuela's name to Ritchie Valens, concealing his Mexican American identity to circumvent the prevailing racist barriers. In 1958, Valens put the Mexican traditional *huapango jarocho* song *La Bamba* to a rock 'n' roll beat, breaking into the national charts and becoming a top recording artist with it.[15] Other pioneer Chicano individual and group artists included the Jaguars, a racially mixed group (black, white and Chicano) from Fremont High in Los Angeles, whose hit, "The Way You Look Tonight" was recorded in 1956; and "Tequila", by the saxophonist Danny Flores, who was billed as Chuck Rio with a band called The Champs, and recorded in 1957.[16]

The East Side Sound

The Chicano musical brand known as the West Coast East Side Sound emerged in the 1960s in East Los Angeles. The East Side Sound diverged from assimilationist music of the 1950s with a unique fusion of sounds that developed "... based on borrowed, adapted genres such as rhythm and blues, soul, rock, funk, salsa, and Mexican traditional forms."[17] Some of the earliest and most popular Chicano bands and individual artists and their music included The Village Callers, who started about 1960–61 as a band called Marcy and the Imperials and were perhaps the first to introduce the use of Latin percussion in their R&B and Latin jazz-style.[18] The Premiers formed in 1962 and recorded their cover of "Farmer John," which became a national hit in 1963. Little Ray (nee Ramón Jimenez) recorded "Soul Stomp" with The Premiers in 1962, and then became lead singer briefly with Thee Midniters before being replaced by Willie Garcia, but Little Ray's own hit was "I Who Have Nothing" in 1965. The Blendells recorded "La La La La La", a Stevie Wonder cover, making it an East Side hit in 1964. These and other early Chicano bands and artists got recorded thanks to a record producer named Eddie Davis, known as "The Godfather of the Chicano East Side Sound." He and a friend named Billy Cardenas introduced and promoted many Chicano artists, among them, The Romancers, The Village Callers, The Premiers, Little Ray, The Salas Brothers, Cannibal and the Headhunters, The Blendells, and Thee Midniters.[19]

The most popular bands in the East Los Angeles community during my adolescent and young adult years, the 1960s–1970s, included: Thee Midniters, with their cover of Chris Kenner's "Land of a Thousand Dances" and their later original hit, "Whittier Boulevard," which spotlighted the Saturday night cruising strip of low-rider Chicano youths in East Los Angeles. They pioneered the combination of trombone, sax, congas, keyboards and electric guitars, baptizing it as the new Chicano Rock sound. With their talent and innovative musical sound they developed into a versatile band that could play Mexican music as well as compete with sounds like those of Chicago, Blood, Sweat and Tears, Paul Revere And The Raiders, and hard rock.[20] Cannibal and the Headhunters, whose leader, Frankie Garcia, introduced the "Naa, na, na, na naa" lyrics in "Land of a Thousand Dances," branded the song as the East Side Sound at the time. The Salas Brothers, Rudy and Steve, who began singing at ages 13 and 11 respectively and went on to form the band, Tierra, became one of the best-known Chicano East Side bands of the 1970s. Los Lobos first formed in 1973 and became perhaps the best known Chicano band nationally for their bilingual and multi-genre musical repertoire and movie soundtracks. The East Side sound also adopted the music of Chicano bands hailing from other areas, like Rosie and The Originals, from San Diego, who recorded their original, "Angel Baby," the lyrics composed by Rosie, a song that became an East L.A. Chicano music staple; from San Francisco, including Malo, who, among other great songs had the 1972 hit, "Suavecito"; El Chicano, whose original instrumental, "Viva Tirado" remained in the national top charts for over fifteen straight weeks; Santana, whose early Chicano Rock recordings included the hits "Suavecito" in 1969, "Black Magic Woman" in 1970, and "Oye Como Va" in 1971; and from Texas, Chicano artists like Sunny and the Sunglows's (aka Sunny and the Sunliners), "Talk to Me,"; the Sir Douglas Quintet's, "She's About a Mover"; Trini Lopez's, "Lemon Tree"; Sam the Sham and the Pharaohs', "Wooly Bully"; and Question Mark ("?") and the Mysterians', "96 Tears."[21] Cannibal and the Headhunters toured with, or performed on national shows alongside artists like Smokey Robinson And The Miracles, The Four Tops, Ben E. King, The

Temptations, Marvin Gaye, Wilson Pickett, Jerry And The Pacemakers, and Peter And Gordon, and they opened for The Beatles' second American tour.[22]

Hundreds of other local bands and individual artists performed live in the community, typically at high school dances, in the 1960s and 1970s and many also recorded. Many codeswitched or replaced entire verses with Spanish in the songs they covered, and/or used Spanish-language band names or their real individual names. They were the substance of the Chicano Sound because they were part of our communities, and they made otherwise abstract songs relatable to us, their Chicano audiences. They turned those songs into representations of our bilingual voices, claiming their Mexican and Latino cultural identity even though doing so risked facing barriers to national fame. To those of us growing up in the midst of their music, touched by it, the national recognition that most of those bands were denied did not matter; what mattered was that the music, though usually a cover, created a shared sentimental statement; the music they made was *our* music, for *us*, about *us*. For example, in his cover of the oldie, "Sincerely" by the Moonglows, which includes the lyrics:

> Oh Lord, won't you tell me why,
> I love that girl so
> she doesn't want me
> but I'll never, never, never, never let her go

Jesse "Chuy" Gonzalez alters and personalizes the message by directing it to a correspondent and replaces the original third verse English lyrics with colloquial Spanish:

> *Por Dios, dime tu si este amor,*
> *es irreal o es una illusion, si no me quieres,*
> *ya mas nunca, nunca, nunca, nunca, yo vuelvo a amar*[23]

Most of the hundreds of Chicano bands of the 1960s and early1970s also never got noted in the annals of Chicano music history. The reasons were varied. They broke up as members got drafted into the military and sent to Viet Nam, or the band changed members and eventually dissolved or got reconstituted into a different band. Mainly, they either did not record or their records did not make the national charts. Among those many East L.A. bands was one called The Big Beats.

Joe Chavira grew up hearing Mexican music in the East Los Angeles sections of Lincoln Heights, the Ramona Gardens housing projects, and El Sereno. He did not have the benefit of music lessons; he had something else: The influence and mentorship of his aunt/godmother, Aurora Prado. From the time he began to talk, she encouraged his musical ear, his gift for singing, and his love of Mexican music, like the *ranchera* song he liked to sing often when he was only four years old, *Tú Solo Tú*. From her he learned harmonic singing, practicing with her songs like *Perdón*, a song that is sung by a duo, one voice singing in half-notes and one in quarter-notes, then the voices re-join, harmonizing to the end of the song. At 15 years of age and pretending to be 21, Joe became the lead vocalist and drummer in a band called The Big Beats. The band started in Las Cruces, New Mexico and added Joe when its original members moved to Los Angeles. Like the many other Mexican American music groups in the cusp of the Chicano Movement, their band name did not claim their ethnicity, but their music did: doo wop, rock, ballads, salsa, and *boleros* popularized by artists like Javier Solís and Eydie Gorme. In 1962, The Big Beats appeared regularly at Millie's Lounge, a club located at the corner of Whittier and Atlantic Boulevards in East Los Angeles, where Joe Chavira and the rest of the group, which included the Nuñez brothers, Benny (bass guitar), Martin (lead guitar), and Juno (rhythm guitar), and Johnny Galvan (keyboard) (Photo 5.2), were among the many bands making history heralding the East Side Sound of Chicano music.

Photo 5.2: The Big Beats. Joe Chavira, second from the left. At Millie's Lounge in East Los Angeles, 1962. Provided to the author by Joe Chavira from his private collection.

La Estrella in the Chicano Renaissance

Aurora Prado was an unintentional part of the Chicano Cultural Renaissance in the late 1960s East Los Angeles night club circuit, as *La Estrella de la Canción Romántica*. She was a performer of *boleros*, mostly of yesteryear but also of contemporary Spanish and English love songs. Subjectively a racialized grassroots woman artist yet lacking a political consciousness, she nonetheless, through her musical performance, renewed and kept alive that part of our cultural music and helped imbue younger Chicanas/os and Latinas/os with cultural renewal. Her musical performance thus signified self-representation, a form of political activism similar to that of other Mexican music lovers and performers of *bolero* in other times and historical periods:

> ... disillusioned by the broken promises of politicians ..., these impoverished masses ... relished the bolero's inwardly directed expressivity. The bolero provided a release from the turmoil of displacement and poverty by providing a refuge within innermost emotional life ... the bolero helped give shape to new modes of gender/sex/class consciousness ...[24]

Notes

1. Anzaldúa 1998, p. 163.
2. From song titled: Tu Olvido, José Alfredo Jiménez, composer.
3. Wikipedia, 2019.
4. As I write this, we mourn the death of the great fighter for Civil Rights, John Lewis. With millions of others, my husband, son and I watched the services with pain in our hearts, especially in the very difficult socially and politically divided times of the Trump administration.
5. On that day, 600 peaceful marchers were attacked brutally as they were crossing the Edmund Pettus bridge, with clubs and tear gas, by heavily armed state troopers and the local sheriffs, sent by then-governor of Alabama, George Wallace.
6. For many Latinas of my generation, our own Latina Feminist Movement would directly address our own realities.
7. The Salas Brothers was a singing duo in what is known as the Chicano East Side music of the 1960s.
8. From personal interview, September 19, 2003.
9. Rosales, 1996, p. 187.
10. Rosales, 1996, p. 185.
11. Chicano Civil Rights Movement, 1996, p. 186.
12. Rosales, 1996, p. 192.
13. Some parents, who were not or not yet politically conscious, viewed the protests negatively, and some had strong reactions. Yet, for many of those parents, the blowouts and their aftermath

helped raise their consciousness, and they joined the struggle that their children had bravely begun. For example, Rosales (1996, p. 191) quotes Joe Razo, co-editor of *La Raza*, describing the following: "I saw a man in one of the East L.A. parks slapping his daughter around because she had walked out … she was crying but still arguing with him about the necessity for fighting for some of her rights and for changing the curriculum … I still remember this vividly … it was a family that at least a man had the interest enough to get involved with his kid … there were going to be a lot of long discussions in that family … as to why she walked out of school … it was not a matter of 'it's nice and sunny, I think I'll go to the park.' They were political. They really knew what they were fighting for."

14. Peña, 1985; Loza, 1993.
15. Valens's other hits included "Donna", "Come On, Let's Go", "That's My Little Susie", and "Little Girl."
16. Wikipedia, 2021.
17. Loza, 1993, p. 95; Hiesca, 2004.
18. Guerrero, 2019.
19. Guy, 2012; Guerrero, 2019; He began with his Faro label in 1958, his Linda label in 1960, Rampart label in 1961, Boomerang label in 1962, Prospect and Valhalla Records label in 1966, and Gordo Records label in 1968.
20. Reyes & Waldman, 1982; Loza, 1993; Wikipedia, 2020.
21. Quiñones, 2005.
22. Guerrero, n.d.; Wikipedia, 2020; Similarly other bands, like The Premiers, who toured with The Crystals and Gene Pitney and opened for The Rolling Stones and the Dave Clarke Five; The Blendells who shared a stage with The Dave Clarke Five, Roy Orbison, The Ventures, The Shirelles, The Drifters, and Chuck Berry; and among others, The Village Callers, who often appeared with one of the best horn section show bands, known as The Watts One Hundred Third Street Rhythm Band ("Express Yourself," "Loveland,") from South Central Los Angeles.
23. As recorded in the album, Chicano Oldies, Vol. 1, Los Soul Records label.
24. Broyles-González, 2012, p. 149.

References

Anzaldúa, G. (1998). Chicana Artists: Exploring Nepantla, el Lugar de la Frontera. In: Darder, A. & R.D. Torres, (Eds.), The Latino Studies Reader: Culture, Economy & Society (pp. 163-169. Malden: Blackwell Publishing.

Broyles-González, Y. (2012). Re-Membering Chelo Silva: The Bolero in Chicana Perspective (Women's Bodies and Voices in Postrevolutionary Urbanization: The Bohemian, urban, and Transnational). In A. J. Aldama, C. Sandoval, & P. J. Garcia (Eds.), *Performing the US Latina and Latino Borderlands* (pp. 146–164). Bloomington: University of Indiana Press.

Guerrero, M. (2019). *Mark Guerrero Singer/Songwriter*. Retrieved from The Village Callers: East L.A. Latin Rock Innovators: https://markguerrero.net/32.php

Guerrero, M. (n.d.). *Cannibal and the Headhunters*. Retrieved from Mark Guerrero Singer/Songwriter: https://markguerrero.net/10.php

Guy, E. L. (2012, April 12). *You Found That East Side Sound*. Retrieved from You Found That East Side Sound: East Side Producers – Eddie Davis: http://wwwyoufoundthateastsidesoundcom. blogspot.com/2012/04/eastside-producers-eddie-davis.html

Hiesca, V. H. (2004, 09). The Battle of L.A.: The Cultural Politics of Chicano/a Music in the Greater Eastside. *American Quarterly, 56*(3), 719–739.

Loza, S. (1993). *Barrio Rhythm: Mexican American Music in Los Angeles*. Urbana and Chicago: University of Illinois.

Peña, M. (1985). *The Texas-Mexican Conjunto: A History of a Working-Class Music*. Austin: University of Texas Press.

Quiñones, B. (2005, December 29). Naa Na Na Na Naa: How the West Coast East Side Sound changed rock & roll. *LA Weekly*, p. n/a.

Reyes, D., & Waldman, T. (1982, February 28). Thee Midniters. *Goldmine*, p. n/a.

Rosales, F. A. (1996). *Chicano! The History of the Mexican American Civil Rights Movement*. Houston: Arte Publico Press.

Wikipedia. (2019, November 2019). *Sad Girl*. Retrieved from Wikipedia The free encylopedia: https://en.wikipedia.org/wiki/Sad_Girl

Wikipedia. (2020, 10 23). *Cannibal and the Headhunters*. Retrieved from Wikipedia-The free encyclopedia: https://en.wikipedia.org/wiki/Cannibal_%26_the_Headhunters

Wikipedia. (2020, December 27). *Thee Midniters*. Retrieved from Wikipedia-: https://en.wikipedia.org/wiki/Thee_Midniters

Wikipedia. (2021, March 21). *Chicano Rock*. Retrieved from Wikipedia-The free encyclopedia: https://en.wikipedia.org/wiki/Chicano_rock

CHAPTER SIX

La Estrella de la Canción Romántica

In the 1940s and 1950s, Mexican female composers Maria Elena Valdelamar, Consuelo Velázquez, Maria Grever, and Maria Alma, led a unique and lasting musical era that centered women in a new bolero mystique. It was essentially a musical revolution, because the songs defied the norms of conservative Mexican society. Social dictates denied women their sexual feelings and relegated women's sexuality to the satisfaction of their husbands' desires. Women were to show modesty lest they be labeled "sinners." The songs of the new era's female composers broke women out of sexual and sexist confinement with unforgettable music and lyrics that expressed a passion and eroticism previously claimed only by male song composers and interpreters, as Estrada says in her review of Grever and Valdelamar:

> *En sus canciones, Grever se aventuró a expresar sus más íntimos deseos, situación mal vista por la sociedad conservadora de esa época ....*[1]

> [In her songs, Grever dared to express her most intimate desires, something frowned upon by the conservative society of the era ....]

> *Como las trovadoras de la Edad Media, Valdelamar expresaba sus pasiones por sus enamorados. Al tomar la palabra no sólo asumían la voz activa, configurándose a sí mismas como amantes, en lugar de amadas, sino que, además, situaban a los hombres como objeto de deseo ... .Estas trovadoras conocidas como las 'trobairitz' componían versos y luego los cantaban o recitaban, exactamente igual que sus colegas masculinos. Le cantaban al amor*

cortés, a ese amor imposible que las tenía en un estado de sufrimiento gozoso, un amor adúltero bajo apariencia de amor platónico.[2]

[Like the minstrels of the Middle Ages, Valdelamar expressed her passion for her lovers. In their words they not only took on the active voice, they also assumed the role of the lover instead of the loved subject, simultaneously situating men as objects of desire … . These female troubadours, known as *trobairitz*, would compose verses and then sing or recite them, exactly the same as their male colleagues. They sang to the well-mannered love, that impossible love that had them in a state of joyful suffering, an adulterous love hidden under the guise of a platonic one.]

The era of the female bolero composers created artists like Maria Victoria, icon of the female bolerista aesthetic, and many other famed Mexican and international boleristas. Over a decade later in the United States, Aurora Prado also rose to the stage, deploying those boleros to express or redefine her own reality (Photo 6.1).

The Bolerista Stage: East Los Angeles, 1960s

Aurora Prado entered as a contestant in *La Hora de los Aficionados*, an amateur radio show, in 1967. It was a live weekly singing competition aired on a local Spanish-speaking station on Thursday evenings and was partly sponsored by a

Photo 6.1: Aurora Prado, 1968. From her private collection.

local night spot, Club Flamingo. In the tradition of XEW, Mexico's famous radio station, the Los Angeles station introduced new talent to a live audience while on the air. The show's judge would sit beside the stage, fully robed and hooded so as to remain anonymous. If a performing contestant went off-key, forgot the lyrics, or sang the lyrics incorrectly, the judge would ring a loud cowbell disqualifying them from the week's contest. In her third round, Aurora was disqualified. For the first time in her life, she froze part-way into the song and forgot the lyrics while singing *Amor Perdido*. She related this story to me many years later. Even then, she found the experience disconcerting. Ironically, that short-lived failure would be the starting point of her professional life as a bolero musical solo artist.

La Asociación de Artistas, Cantantes, y Compositores, an organization in East Los Angeles for musicians, singers and composers, hosted the Thursday night amateur hour as a way to identify new talent. It also sponsored variety shows to recruit new artists into the organization. It promoted members of demonstrated artistic ability, and functioned as a central registry and talent agency in East L. A. That was how Aurora entered into the professional world of music.

In a conversation, I ask my mother how she learned about *La Asociación*. She tells me it was through Irene, her best friend, and I remember that we met Irene when we moved into a small apartment in El Sereno. She was a recent widow, still dressed *de luto* (in mourning) at the time. Her husband had been a musician very much involved in the East Los Angeles music scene. She was a music lover herself, so she knew many clubs and musicians there, with whom she acquainted my mother. The two women frequented clubs and restaurants that featured live Mexican music on Thursday and Friday evenings and soon Aurora made important connections:

> Aurora: *Empecé cuando me metí a la Asociación de Artistas, Cantantes y Compositores. Así se llamaba. Tenían programas los jueves, en el (sic) radio. Me acuerdo del que anunciaba. Era joven y payaseaba mucho cuando se subía al stage. Era chistoso. Agarraba el micrófono y decía, ¡'regístrese, regístrese!' Así invitaban a artistas a La Asociación.*
>
> [I started when I joined the Association of Artists and Singers. That's what it was called. They had programs on Thursdays that aired on the radio. I remember the MC. He was young and he would clown around when he got on the stage. He was funny. He would take the microphone and say, 'Get registered, get registered!' That was how they would recruit artists to join the Association.][3]

Alicia: How did you begin singing professionally? Where did you start singing?

Aurora: I started *en el* Flamingo, *allí en* East L.A., *así se* llamaba. It was in the 1960s. *Iba mucha gente, todos mexicanos. Era barrio mexicano. En el Flamingo eran los aficionados. Era todos los jueves, de las 9 a las 11 de la noche. Los Aficionados eran por la Asociación. Todavía no me oían cantar.*

[Lots of people would go there, everyone was Mexican. It was a Mexican neighborhood. The amateur show was held at El Flamingo club. It was on Thursdays, from 9 to 11 at night. The Association sponsored the amateur hour. At the time, they had not yet heard me sing.]

La Estrella de la Canción Romántica was born when *Promociones Serrano* featured an article and photograph of her and donned that label on her, lauding her also as the lovely, elegantly fashionable, and "well-mannered" Lady Star Interpreter of the Romantic Song (Photos 6.2 and 6.3a, b). She became popular as well among her peers: *Todos eran muy amables conmigo. No me llamaban Aurora, me llamaban Aurorita.* [They were all very nice to me. They didn't call me 'Aurora,' they called me 'Little Aurora' (a diminutive form indicating endearment).]

Photo 6.2: Promotion of *La Estrella*, 1968. From the private archives of Aurora Prado Pastrano.

Alicia: Where did you sing?

Aurora: *La Asociación promovía a los artistas. Yo no escogía el lugar. Ellos me llamaban y me decían a qué lugar iba a ir a cantar. Pero todos los lugares eran allí en East L.A. También algunos eran restaurantes adentro del Mercado Central en el centro, en downtown de Los Ángeles, o alrededor o pegados al Million Dollar. Yo cantaba con diferentes grupos, los que estuvieran tocando en el lugar. Uno de ellos era el grupo Papaloápan. Yo no era parte de su grupo, solo cantaba con ellos a veces cuando me mandaban a cantar a donde ellos se presentaban.*

[The Association promoted artists. I didn't choose the venue. They would call me and tell me where I was to go sing. All the venues were there, in East L.A. Some were also restaurants in downtown L.A. Some were inside the Central Market, or around or adjacent to the Million Dollar Theatre. I would sing with different groups; whichever group would be playing at the time. One of them was the group Papaloápan. I was not part of their group. I only sang with them on those times when I was sent to sing where they were appearing.[4]]

Alicia: *¿Como era la Asociación?* [What was the Association like?]

Aurora: *Cuando me metí apenas se estaba formando. A los integrantes nos cobraban una mensualidad, me parece que doce dólares al mes. Íbamos a las juntas. Nos dijeron que nos saldrían trabajos. Yo no quería eso. Yo quería nomas divagar mi música. Yo no quería negociar con mi música. Yo nomás quería, pos … desahogarme, yo creo. Me gustaba cantar, me gustaba participar en los eventos. Pero yo no pensaba ser número uno en ninguna forma. Y de eso se trataba La Asociación. Escoger a los mejores y tenerlos listos para cuando hubiera un evento grande. Cuando venían artistas que se presentaban allá en el Million Dollar Theater, la Asociación llenaba el background. No participábamos con el cantante que viniera de allá, sino que llenábamos el coro nada más, el background. Así nos iban distinguiendo. Así era como escogían ellos los artistas. Pero yo nunca di oportunidad para eso, porque yo no viajaba hasta donde ellos querían. Además, yo estaba sola, no tenía que decirle a nadie nada, pero estaba trabajando en la Broadway, y tú estabas en la escuela, yo no podía participar a las horas que ellos querían. Nomás los viernes. Me iba al Papaloapan, mejor. El Conjunto Papaloapan, a donde estuvieran ellos.*

[When I joined the Association, it was just forming. We paid a monthly membership fee; I think twelve dollars. We went to meetings. They told us we would get paid gigs. I didn't want that. I just wanted to propagate my music. I didn't want to commercialize my music. I only wanted, well, to vent, I guess. I liked to sing, I liked to participate in the events. But I didn't think about being number one in any way. And that's what the Association was about, choose the best ones and have them ready for when there were big events. When big celebrities came [from Mexico] to perform at the Million Dollar Theater, the Association filled the background. We didn't participate with the visiting celebrity, we just filled the chorus, the background. That was how new artists would stand out; how they would get chosen. I was alone, I didn't have to ask anyone, but I was working at The Broadway and you were in school. I couldn't travel or participate at whatever hours they wanted. Only on Fridays. I would go instead with the Papaloápan, wherever they were performing.]

Alicia: *¿Que canciones cantaba cuando andaba cantando sola?* [What songs did you sing when you were singing as a solo artist?]

Aurora: *Pues, muchas canciones, puras viejas, como Desvelo de Amor.* As she starts singing a song, *Perjura*, she says: *Esa canción la canté en uno de los lugares allí, en el downtown.* ["Well, many songs, old ones, such as *Desvelo de Amor.* I began singing that song in one of those places there in downtown."]

Alicia: *¿y le pagaban?* [Did you get paid?]

Aurora: *Si, por La Asociación. Cuando te inscribes, es para toda la vida. Iba la gente a la Asociación y preguntaban que a quien les recomendaban, y me recomendaban a mí. Entonces yo tenia que encontrar quien me acompañara, ya fuera trio, ya fuera guitarra, o ya fuera mariachi.*

[Yes, by the Association. When you join, your membership is for life. People would go to the Association and ask for a recommendation (for a performer) and they would recommend me. Then I had to find the accompaniment, whether a trio, a guitarist, or a mariachi group.]

Photos 6.3 a and b: From the private archives of Aurora Prado Pastrano. 1968.

Alicia: *¿No se acompañaba usted misma con la guitarra?* [Didn't you accompany yourself, with the guitar?]

Aurora: *Cuando empecé con los aficionados, yo cantaba sola. No sabía todavía suficiente para tocar la guitarra. Pero en una ocasión, ya cuando tocaba yo más la guitarra, entonces fui con Berta, a una estación de radio, no sé cual era, era por allá creo que en Hollywood. Una estación americana. ¡Era como los aficionados, y ella me animó 'vaya!' Y fue conmigo. Era estación americana y me dieron un cuartito y me dijeron, 'only three minutes, okay?' para que cantara Sabor a Mí. Pero me pasé de los 3 minutos, así que no me eligieron. Es que tocaba yo muy despacio. Era una sola vez. Esa si no se me olvida porque Berta se rio tanto de mi.*

[When I sang for the Amateur Hour, I didn't yet know enough of the guitar, so I used to just sing alone. But one day, by then I had picked up more on the guitar, I went with Berta, to a radio station, I don't know which one, it was over in Hollywood, I think. An English-speaking station. It was like the Amateur Show. She told me about it and encouraged me to go. She went with me. They gave me a little room and told me 'only three minutes, okay?' to sing *Sabor a Mi*, but I went over the three minutes, so they didn't choose me. It was only once. I don't forget that time because Berta laughed so hard.]

Alicia: *¿Cuales artistas la inspiraron a Usted?* [What artists inspired you most?]

Aurora: *Amalia Mendoza, número uno. Yo quería imitarla, pero no podía, no tenía la misma voz. La fuimos a ver cuando se presentó en el Million Dollar Theater, allí en Los Ángeles, en los 60s, pero no me preguntes cuándo porque no me acuerdo. ¿Sabes quien sabe mas? David, el requintista, porque él acompañaba a Amalia Mendoza. Eso me dijeron, que el acompañaba a muchos artistas de allá, inclusive a Amalia Mendoza.*

[Amalia Mendoza, number one. I wanted to imitate her, but I couldn't, I didn't have the same voice. We went to see her when she appeared at the Million Dollar Theatre, in Los Angeles, in the 60s, but don't ask me when because I don't remember. You know who knows more? David [Chanes], the requinto player, because he used to accompany Amalia Mendoza. That's what they told me, that he accompanied many artists who came from over there, including Amalia Mendoza.][5]

La Asociación de Artistas, Cantantes y Compositores held a Bobby Kennedy fundraiser event on April 27, 1968, at the State Ballroom in Los Angeles, the same hall where Association meetings usually were held. It featured some of its most established local artists, among them, Aurora Prado. She was accompanied by a mariachi group and performed to a full house. It was the only event that I recall our extended family members attending. I designed and made her dress for the show and styled her hair in "dancing curls," the popular hair style at the time

(Photos 6.4a, b). My mother usually mentions that occasion when we talk about that part of her life, as in the following:

> *Tengo el retrato. En el salón estaba el retrato de Robert Kennedy. Allí estaba sentada toda la familia, estabas tú con Ozzie. Es donde traigo el vestido que tu me hiciste. Los mariachis estaban tocando, parados atrás de mi. Yo estaba cantando, así que estaba parada en frente de ellos. Cuando sentí que se me desabrochó el ganchito del vestido, atrás, y se me abrió el zipper. No me podía concentrar y se me quiso olvidar la letra. Cuando acabé la canción, ellos luego luego se hicieron a un lado y me taparon para que me fuera a arreglar el vestido sin que se diera cuenta la gente.*[6]

[The whole family was sitting there; you were there with Ozzie. It was where I was wearing the dress you made me. The mariachis were playing standing right behind me. I was singing, so I was standing in front of them [facing the audience]. When suddenly I felt the hook closure on the back of my dress come undone, and the zipper opened up. I couldn't concentrate and almost forgot the lyrics. When I finished the song, they right away moved aside and covered me so I could get away and fix my dress without members of the audience noticing.]

Among the most lasting relationships that my mother established in those early years of her solo singing career was her friendship and musical relationship with the *jarocho* music group, Papaloápan, especially with one of its members, known as *Negro*. They were among the best-known groups in East Los Angeles for music of *Veracruz*, and among the few who became recording artists. Their album

Photos 6.4 a and b: Aurora Prado, performing at a fundraising event for Bobby Kennedy's candidacy. At the State Ballroom, Los Angeles, April 27, 1968.

was titled *Cantándole a Veracruz*, on the *Discos Corona* label. (see Photo 6.5). My mother recalls how she met them:

> *Al grupo Papaloápan los conocí cuando iba con Irene a oírlos. Ellos tocaban en un salón, pero ya no me acuerdo de los nombres de los lugares. Una de esas veces le pedí a Negro que, si me podían tocar una canción, ahorita no me acuerdo cual era, pero me dijo, 'sí, como no, con todo gusto.' Cuando la empezó a cantar él, yo la empecé a cantar también, y me dijo, 'Oh, ¿Usted la sabe? ¡Véngase, cántela!' y me invitó a que subiera al stage a cantarla con ellos. Me dijo después que yo tenía muy bonita voz, y me invitó a que cantara con ellos cuando volviera.*

[The group Papaloápan I met when I used to go with Irene to listen to them. They used to play in a club. One of those times, I asked *Negro* if they could play a song for me, I can't remember which one, and he said, 'of course, with pleasure.' When he began singing it, I also began to sing, and he said, 'Oh. You know it? Come on, sing it!' and he invited me unto the stage to sing it with them. Later he told me I had a very pretty voice and he invited me to sing with them again whenever I came back.]

The musically collegial connection that began that night between my mother and *Negro* would last years and would be followed by more memorable musical encounters.

Photo 6.5: Conjunto Papaloápan album cover. From the private record collection of Aurora Prado Pastrano.

On one occasion in 2010, *Negro* happened to be filling in for a member of the Trio Sol y Luna, at Del Mar Restaurant in Yucaipa, California. They performed their last song for the night at our booth, and my mother stood up and joined in the song, as she often did. A woman who had been dining in the back of the restaurant walked toward our booth and began to talk loudly with a man sitting in the next booth. I struggled to hear the song through the loudness of her talking. A few days later, I brought up the incident with my mother; she seemed unfazed by it, though it triggered a memory, and she told me the following story:

> *Una vez, estaba yo cantando en un salón, no me acuerdo cual era allí en East L.A., una canción con el mariachi que estaba allí esa noche, y había gente sentada en los dos lados del salón. En medio estaba vacío, era para que la gente bailara. Yo no sabía que, al fondo del salón, en la mesa en frente de nosotros, había estado sentado Anthony Quinn, oyéndonos. Cuando acabé de cantar la canción, se paró y me gritó, '¡Cánteme Camino de Guanajuato!' El mariachi la empezó a tocar para que yo la cantara y la empecé a cantar, pero una gente que estaba sentada en la mesa cerca de él empezó a platicar, haciendo mucho ruido. De pronto se levantó él y alzando los brazos, dijo en una voz alta, '¡Momento, momento por favor!' Luego los volteó a ver y les dijo, '¡Por favor! ¡Déjenme oír mi canción!'*

[One time, I was singing in a lounge hall, I don't remember which one, but it was there in East L.A. I was singing a song with a mariachi group that was playing there that night, and there were people seated on both sides of the hall. The middle of the lounge was a dance floor. I didn't know that at the far back of the room, at a table facing us, was seated Anthony Quinn, and he was listening to us. When I finished singing the song, he stood up and yelled to me, 'Sing *Camino de Guanajuato* for me!' The Mariachi began to play so I could sing it and I began to sing, but some people who were sitting at the table near him began to converse loudly, making a lot of noise. Suddenly he stood, and raising his arms he said in loud voice, 'One moment, one moment, please!' He turned and looked at them and said, 'Please! Allow me to hear my song!']

> *Eso fue antes de que yo me hubiera metido al mariachi. Yo había estado cantando con el Trio Papaloápan esa noche. Yo estaba allí con ellos, pero había cantado una canción con el mariachi que estaba tocando después que ellos esa vez, y fue cuando me oyó Anthony Quinn. Era una fiesta grande y creo que resultó que él había sido el guest of honor.*

[This was before I was part of the mariachi group. I was singing with the Trio Papaloápan that night, but I had stood up to sing a song with the mariachi group that followed after them that night, and that was when Anthony Quinn heard me. It was a big party and I think it turned out that he had been the guest of honor.]

The Association would send her to perform with different groups to help popularize her as *La Estrella de la Canción Romántica*. Occasionally, this meant that she would take the hard-earned spotlight from an established artist, which produced artistic jealousy and tension:

> ... (name) nomás me oía cantar uno de los boleros que yo sabía y me decía, déjemela a mí. Así lo hizo con la canción que yo siempre había cantado, Mucho Corazón. Todo el tiempo me hacía eso, hasta que un día vino una pareja a oírnos cantar. Él iba a empezar a cantar, cuando ellos le pidieron que me dejara cantar Mucho Corazón a mí porque me querían oír. Creo que querían grabarme porque llevaban una grabadora.

> [... (name) was very jealous. As soon as he heard me sing a *bolero* that I knew, he would say, 'leave it to me'. That's what he did with the song that I had always sung, *Mucho Corazón*. He always did that to me, until one day, a couple came to hear us sing. He was about to start singing, when they asked him to let me sing alone, because they wanted to hear me sing *Mucho Corazón*. I think they wanted to record me because they had a tape recorder with them.]

Aurora Prado was a *mujer sola*, an unattached woman, and the bolero has always had social implications for women: "Women bolero singers were necessarily public women, and their domain was the nightclub."[7] Aurora's acquaintances in the music circuit sometimes misread her association with the nightlife as a potential conquest:

> Muchos me hacían la lucha cuando yo andaba cantando. Hasta el director de La Asociación, ni me acuerdo cómo se llamaba. Una vez me dijo que me iba a llevar a la casa de una artista para que la conociera. Me llevó a donde estaba una en construcción. Creo que la de la artista estaba pegada, al lado. Yo no sabía. ¡Era tan inocente, tan pendeja! Me empezó a dar miedo, y le pregunté que dónde andábamos, y luego se me acercó. Le dije, ¡¿Qué está haciendo?! Me dijo, 'Kissing you.' '¡Oh no! ¡Usted se va de aquí y yo me voy!' Lo empujé y me fui. Yo siempre iba a todos los lugares sola o acompañada de Irene, o con Irene y Bobby. Así como yo iba, así regresaba a mi casa, sola. Yo no me metía con nadie. Yo sólo andaba en eso por la música. No me interesaba nada más.

> [Many men tried to get me interested in them when I was singing back then. Even the director of the Association, whose name I even forget. One time he told me that he was going to take me to the house of a famous celebrity so I could meet her. He took me to a house that was under construction. I think the celebrity's house was adjacent. I didn't know. I was so innocent, so stupid! I began to get scared, and I asked him where we were, and then he got close to me. I said, 'What are you doing?' He said, 'Kissing you' 'Oh no, you get out of here!' I pushed him away and I left. I always went everywhere alone or accompanied by Irene or with Irene and Bobby. The way I went is the way I returned home, alone. I never went with anyone. I was in it for the music. Nothing else interested me.][8]

A Dissonant Diva

Being artistically branded as *La Estrella de la Canción Romántica*, referencing the bolero with its descriptive name, cast Aurora Prado as what Vargas calls a *dissonant diva*.[9] She performed those songs of the 1930s–1960s era, songs whose characteristic lyrics of passion and sensuality, and their implications of sexual and emotional vulnerability, necessarily drew public attention to its female interpreter, while simultaneously, she was lauded for her elegance. Her gender defined the artist in the music circuit: Not just a singer, but an interpreter, that artistic measure of a bolerista's ability to dramatize through voice and mediate in body, the love, the loss, the heartache conveyed in the lyrics and melody. As Vargas explains in her review of the internationally famous *bolerista Tejana*, Chelo Silva, interpreting a *bolero* involves a special relationship between the song's lyrics and its vocalist:

> ... it is the connection between personal experience and musical narrative that marks performers like Silva not just as singers, but also as interpreters of song. Particularly within the *bolerista* tradition, there is a key musical distinction between the Spanish terms *intérprete* (performer) and *cantante* (singer) ... Herein lies a key distinction that is significant particularly as it pertains to gender, sexuality, and power in bolero performance. *Intérpretes* of boleros are more than mere conveyers of lyrics, more than simply *cantantes* or singers ... *Interpretando el bolero*—performing one's own interpretation of a song's significance and meaning—is not just a matter of the singer's voice and the lyrics. Vocal inflections, pauses, and bodily gestures during live performances, together with lyrics, constitute a singer's mark on a musical text.[10]

Aurora Prado's chosen lyrics in her public musical performances, though it was during the 1960s and 1970s, were the songs of the 1940s–1950s era of the bolero musical revolution. Those songs beckoned, provoked, questioned, challenged, condemned, or forgave and vowed unending love. Cushioned in the softness of a beautiful melody, her message was captivating. Her voice in song emanated both innocence and worldliness, with its tone of certainty, words of unwavering poignancy. Through her own stage aesthetic, she communicated a deep sentiment to those who allowed themselves to experience her performances visually and audibly, evoking an empathy that brought her audience into the depths of her life and her soul, accepting what she gave them: *Mucho Corazón*, all her heart.

The songs she interpreted represented her Mexican cultural belonging, yet she was never entirely defined by that cultural membership. The songs enabled and empowered her to define herself, often in contradiction to or defiance of gendered cultural dictates or socially dominant evaluative criteria. Thus, her cultural music was also very personal. She, as the performer, always evaluated the music as to whether it was significant, appropriate, relevant, and performable, and did so in tandem with her audience's culture-sensitive conception of what constituted beautiful music. She never appreciated classical religious music, for example, and I never heard her sing or play a hymn or psalm.[11] Recently I asked her why. Shrugging it off, she described them in one word that means corny, uninteresting, or dull: *Quien sabe. Nunca me han interesado. Siempre se me han hecho muy furris.* Her choice of *"furris"* for an adjective in her answer sounds funny, a blunt put-down in the vernacular, but I believe that at a gut level, she rejected the psalm and hymnal genre because of their Eurocentric indifference to her gendered, racialized experience. Through her selected music, intuitively or to some level of consciousness, she claimed her intersectional identities as a woman, Mexican American, Tejana, *mujer sola*, Mexicana, and American.

La Estrella became known for her vast song repertoire of the romantic bolero. She also interpreted light classics, *ranchera-boleros*, *rancheras*, tangos, English-language love songs, and other styles. None were ever just songs, and not every song was equal. Often the audience requested songs, or the musicians played out their playlist for the night. She typically met requests, but onstage or off, she would not sing songs that were what she calls *muy plebes*, by which she means crude, crass, sexually explicit, or otherwise what she considered unsuitable to her stage persona. *Tampoco cantaba bravías*, [I also wouldn't sing *bravías*] she tells me, the bravado vocalization some artists use to emphasize the *ranchera's* country style. This was true even in her vibrant rendition of especially animated *ranchera* songs, such as *Juan Colorado* and *La Feria de San Marcos*, which she sang with mariachi accompaniment. All this seems contrary to what Anzaldúa would call "*Haciendo Caras*/Making Face," the gesturing of subversion in defiance of the limits of gender norms; but Aurora's avoidance of *plebe* songs and *bravía* styles, both of which command attention by contradicting the gendered rules of normative behavior for women, were not her attempts to please or ensure favor with an audience, to align herself with a set of socially dominant social standards, or to avoid confrontation with "sexual, racial, or gender normativity."[12] Rather, they were part of her own criteria for self-representation and self-affirmation; perhaps she followed the model of Maria Grever, the first Mexican woman composer who broke through gender barriers to enter the musical world allowed only to men in the 1930s, and who was known for her romantic and elegant style.[13]

The songs Aurora chose to interpret were specific, meaningful, and relevant to her life. They were eloquent, not referring here to their level of sophistication, but to the artistic expressivity of their lyrics in describing her own emotion and capturing her own sentiment. The same applied to melody and vocalization style, both of which had to support, not compete with or overshadow the message conveyed in the words in the song. Some of the songs she performed seemed only distantly if at all pertinent to her own life, but on closer listening, they related to her life in the pain, joy, humor, suffering, or beauty they expressed. Any song's lyrics and melody had a subjective tie to her life, her story, her world view, if it was part of her chosen repertory. Through song and performance, she expressed what she would not or could not easily or otherwise articulate through normal speech communication. Music was her refuge because through song, she complained, cried, and received solace. Songs with lyrics that spoke of pain evidenced that someone else also had experienced and understood what she felt. She sometimes formulated her alternate reality, re-writing her life through song, as one in which she found the fulfillment that she had not actually known. Thus, through her stage performance, *La Estrella de la Canción Romántica* controlled her own narrative, she defined her Self.

Family Attitudes

Family members frowned upon my mother's involvement in the musical nightlife. They admired and enjoyed her musical talent within the family circle. Our family gatherings always involved music, and my mother never attended one without bringing along her guitar. She would accompany herself and other family members singing songs like, *Compréndeme*, *Eternamente*, *Para Morir Iguales*, and other songs that she sang in her singing engagements. While the songs were favorites of family members, they were also reminders of why some of our family considered her life as a public music performer socially provocative. Even her daytime engagements were cause for the family's tacit disapproval. Our family deemed her performing life as frivolous, on the fringe of respectability, and as irresponsible behavior for a woman with an adolescent daughter. Their attitudes showed a gender and age bias not applied to her nephew/godson Pepe (Joe), who at 15, was already playing with a band in a nightclub on Saturday nights.

In retrospect, I felt a weight of loss and loneliness throughout my teen years when my mother was involved in the music world. My mother cooked daily, stocked our refrigerator, washed laundry, worked a day job as a shipping clerk, and cleaned our house diligently. We attended Mass on Sundays and observed religious holidays and other forms of celebrations with our family. Neither drugs nor liquor were ever part of my homelife, nor among our chosen friends, though alcoholism left a sad mark on people close to us. Yet, it was not hard to understand why the family considered her music-related activities as neglecting her parental duties. Her lack of involvement in my high school life and apparent disinterest in my educational and career plans caused distancing between us. Conversations on those topics for us were rare and superficial, and for my mother, chore-free times usually belonged to her music activities: *Asociación* meetings or performance engagements. Conversely, I was unaware at that time of the challenges that she confronted in her artistic pursuits, or how she navigated them. Her support sources were my cousin Bobby, with whom my mother grew up and enjoyed a good friendship, and her friend Irene. The communication gap between us grew throughout my teens. Many of the questions, fears, doubts, and dreams I had in my adolescent years went silent. The closeness we had shared in Mexico through music was gone. Instead, music became the very cause of the distance between us in Los Angeles. The interest my mother had shown in my schooling in Mexico also was absent in L.A. Getting good grades, making the drill team or cheerleading were accomplishments about which I felt especially proud, but which she never asked about, and I never discussed with her.

My early pregnancy and marriage at age 17 solidified the family's condemnation of my mother's musical activities. By then I was in my second year of a 2-year degree in fashion design at Los Angeles Trade Technical College. I felt disappointed with that choice, because it was a vocation for which I did not feel I had the talent, and because it did not align with my academic interests and aspirations, so I felt discouraged by the life path I could foresee. Ten years later I had changed all that and was starting graduate school towards my Ph.D. in anthropology, but my academic journey was always independent of my mother.

My mother sang *Ave Maria!* at my first wedding, celebrated at Sacred Heart church in Lincoln Heights, from the balcony and accompanied by an organist. My father traveled from Juárez to attend the wedding, with hopes of reconciliation with my mother, but their marriage had been long over, and he was not welcomed in her house. Several musical groups who were friends of my mother played at the reception, held in my cousin's backyard. That was the first of many times that my mother insisted on putting me in the musical spotlight with her, to sing a duet. I now wonder if it was her last jab at my father, performing a song in public, which he had once forbidden, and doing so with their daughter, to boot. To obey and please her, avoid embarrassment by refusing, and at the encouragement of our guests, I agreed to sing with her. I was too nervous and scared of going off key, losing my voice halfway through the song, or otherwise making a fool of myself, to notice what kind of musical group accompanied us; I just wanted it over with. We sang a *ranchera* that my mother still likes for our combined voices, *Grítenme Piedras del Campo*, a Cuco Sánchez original.

Whether my adolescence would have been different had I been raised by my father instead of my mother, or with his presence and involvement during those years, I cannot know. What is certain is that because of her gender, my mother's musical profession was key to how others, including her daughter, would judge her parenting. In a recent conversation over the family attitudes she dealt with at the time, she told me:

> Mi familia me despreciaba porque yo andaba en mi música, pero no me importaba. A mí me encantaba la música, eso era lo que me importaba.

[My family spurned me because I was into my music, but I didn't care. I loved music, that's what I cared about.]

Becoming Aurora Pastrano

She was performing a bolero onstage in a piano bar in East Los Angeles, when he first saw her. She was beautiful, her song sensual, her voice enigmatic, but her attitude clear: she was unattainable. This was magnetic to him, a man unaccustomed to subtleties. Encountering someone like her here, in a cabaret in East L.A., his old neighborhood, was poetic. This was the start of a relationship that would have inspired a 1940s *Rumbera* cabaret movie of the Golden Era of Mexican Film.

> Yo estaba cantando en el stage, con el conjunto Papaloápan, allí en Marty's[14] en East L.A. It was a piano bar. Y se sentó él. Él acababa de salir de la cárcel. Y luego me habló, y no le hice caso. Y luego fue a donde yo estaba con Irene sentada y me dijo, ¿'Porqué eres tan orgullosa?' Así. Y le dije, 'Yo no te conozco. Ni tú me conoces. ¿Porqué voy a platicar contigo?' Y me levanté y me fui. Irene se quedó platicando con él. Y así fue como nos conocimos.[15] La siguiente semana volvió, y así, seguían yendo él y Larry, el amigo, y allí se sentaban. Yo no le hacía caso. Hasta que un día, Larry me dijo: 'You should pay attention to him. He's a good man. And he's in love with you.' Después, un domingo en la mañana estaba yo muy dormida cuando sonó el teléfono. Era él. Le dije, ¿'quien te dio el número de mi teléfono?' 'Tu amiga.' Irene le dio el número. Después, un día, yo no sé cómo supo donde vivía o quien le ha de haber dado mi dirección,[16] fue hasta donde vivía. Yo tenia una station wagon y se me había descompuesto el mofle. Yo estaba abajo del carro tratando de arreglarlo, y él llegó, andando. Y me dijo, 'what are you doing?' 'I'm trying to tie up this muffler. It's dragging.' Y desde entonces, Nick me llamaba, iba y me ayudaba con el carro. Él no andaba en carro. No podía manejar porque le habían dado un DUI.

[I was singing onstage, with the group Papaloapan, there at Marty's, in East L.A. It was a piano bar. And he sat down. He had just gotten out of prison. And then he talked to me and I didn't pay any attention to him. And then he went over to where I was sitting with Irene and he said, 'Why are you so conceited?' Just like that. And I told him, 'I don't know you. You don't know me. Why should I talk with you?' and I got up and left. Irene stayed there talking with him. And that's how we met. The next week he returned, and like that, they kept coming by, he and his friend, Larry, and they would sit there. I didn't pay attention to him. Until one day, Larry said to me, 'You should pay attention to him. He's a good man. And he's in love with you.' Later, one Sunday morning I was sound asleep when the telephone rang. It was him. I said to him, 'who gave you my telephone number?' 'Your girlfriend.' Irene gave him my number. Then, one day, I don't know how he found out where I lived or who gave him my address, but he went there. I had a station wagon, and something was wrong with the muffler. I was under the car, trying to fix it, when he arrived, on foot. And he asked me, 'what are you doing?' 'I'm trying to tie up this muffler. It's dragging.' And since then, Nick would call me, he would go over and help me with the car. He couldn't drive because he had gotten a D.U.I.]

The Association of Artists was holding an event that was to take place on Catalina Island, and Aurora was an artist on the program. That occasion gave a jump-start to their relationship:

> *Cuando le dije del evento, y supo que yo iba a ser una de las artistas, compro el boleto y fue. También fueron Irene y Bobby, y así fue como resultamos siendo dos parejas esa vez, y desde entonces.*

Photo 6.6: promotional poster of Mother's Day event sponsored by Thrift Furniture Co. Aurora Prado was among the performers on the program.

Photo 6.7: Promotional poster of performance program on Catalina Island, 1968. Aurora Prado, among the featured artists. From the private archives of Aurora Prado Pastrano.

[When I told him about the event, and that I was going to be one of the featured artists, he bought a ticket and went. Bobby and Irene also went, and that was how we ended up being two couples that time, and since then.] (see Photos 6.6 and 6.7)

Nick Pastrano had lived a hard life. He was adopted in infancy by a loving mother of Mexican origin and an abusive father of Italian heritage. Though he was too young, Nick joined the military by lying about his age, to escape his father's abuse. He was intelligent, articulate, and street-smart. Before meeting my mother, he had been imprisoned for attacking the man who had been his best friend, after catching that man having an affair with Nick's wife. In a fit of passion, Nick threw him against a wall, causing him major injury and a permanent limp. I never knew Nick to be violent, but neither did I know him to have a charming side.

Although I had already married and left home when their relationship began, Nick was a silent barrier between my mother and me for almost three decades. According to her, he resented sharing her attention and affections with anyone, and as the closest to her, that meant especially with me. He and I never said harsh words to each other, and we never told each other how we felt about one another, but we were never friends. Most of our family disliked and disapproved of Nick and we all reluctantly accepted him as my mother's husband, but generally her relationship with him distanced her from most of her family until his death.

To me, Nick was what my mother saw as a man she felt she could trust. She had never been in a relationship with a loving, protective, supportive partner, and Nick was her version of that partner. In their early relationship, he told her about the underworld he had once been part of, one she had only seen in movies. She thought of him as worldly, wise, exciting, and experienced, as someone who kept her from that evil underworld, mentored her, guided her, protected her. He was like the gangster with the bad façade and the good heart who turns out to unselfishly show his undying love for the protagonist in the movie:

> *Era muy sincero. No era ventajoso en ninguna forma. ¡Y que era un hombre de la calle! Sabía mucho. Cuando yo quería cantar en algunas partes en East L.A. él me decía, 'nuh huh, don't' y yo le decía, 'what's wrong?' y me decía, 'just mind me, just believe me, don't sing there.' Después me di cuenta porqué. Era de puras prostitutas, y yo no sabía. Cuando lo conocí me llevó a Chinatown, y me dijo, 'This is where I used to work.' Allí underneath, tienen basements los chinos, de puro gambling, contra la ley, escondidos. Él me llevó y me enseñó, y me dijo, 'never come in here.' Porque te engañan y te meten para abajo, porque al mismo tiempo que era casa de juego, también tenían prostitutas. Andaban con los hombres y los llevaban para abajo. Era un escondite. Él había trabajado de dealer. Por eso era que Nick era tan vulgar. Conocía las lenguas, pero nunca las usaba en mi casa; no hablaba cochino.*

[He was very honest. He wasn't one to take advantage of anyone in any way. And he was a street man! He knew a lot. When I wanted to sing in certain places in East L.A., he would tell me, 'nu uh, don't' and I would say, 'what's wrong?' and he would say, 'just mind me, just believe me, don't sing there.' Later I found out why. It was a place of prostitution, and I didn't know. When I met him, he took me to Chinatown, and he told me, 'This is where I used to work.' There, underneath, they have basements that are just for gambling, against the law, hideaways. He took me and showed me, and he said to me, 'never come in here.' Because they trick you and they take you down below, because at the same time that they are gambling houses, they also have prostitutes. They are with the men and then they take them downstairs. They're hideouts. He knew, because he had worked there as a gambling dealer. That's why Nick was so vulgar, he knew that kind of language, but he never used it in my house; he never used obscene language.]

Nick shared with Aurora's family a dislike of her involvement in the music business, but like everything else, this would not stop her from performing music. Although it caused arguments and discord that strained their relationship, he accepted her public life as a musical artist. In her view, his objections had merit, unlike those of her ex-husband, Martin:

> *Y así fue como empecé aquí, en East L.A. En Juárez, pues, ya sabes, donde quiera que había música yo me metía, pero no era nada profesional. Ni siquiera lo pensaba por Martin. Pero aquí, pues, me tocó la misma mala suerte con Nick, que tampoco le gustaba que yo anduviera en la música. Pero Nick tenia razón, porque yo a veces andaba afuera muy noche. Llegaba a la casa a la una, a los dos de la mañana. Eso era cuando yo andaba cantando en East L.A.*

[So that's how I started here, in East L.A. In Juárez, well, you know, wherever there was music I would go in, but nothing professional. I didn't even think about that because of Martin. But here, well, I had the same bad luck with Nick, who also didn't like for me to be in the music business. But Nick had good reason, because I would be out late at night. I would get home at one, two o'clock in the morning. That's when I was singing in East L.A.]

She became Aurora Pastrano when she married him almost twelve years after they started living together. Regardless of his shortcomings, some that she acknowledges, some that she attributes to his being "misunderstood" or "unappreciated": *La familia lo despreciaba porque no lo conocían* [the family disliked him because they didn't really know him]. She speaks of him as the only man who ever loved her, the one who never lied to her, the two reasons why she loved him, in spite of what anyone else thought about her feelings for him.

> *He encontrado en tu amor*
> *la fe perdida,*
> *ahora tiene mi vida una razón/*
> *No se si fue el embrujo de tus ojos*
> *que les dijo a tus labios,*
> *róbale el corazón/*
> *Yo sé que en los mil besos*
> *que te he dado en la boca*
> *se me fue el corazón/*
> *Y dicen que es pecado*
> *querer como te quiero*
> *quizás tengan razón/*
> *Pero que ha de importarme*
> *todo lo que me digan*
> *si no te he de olvidar/*
> *Que si es pecado amarte*
> *yo he de seguir pecando*
> *¿Porqué lo he de ocultar? /*
> *Te he de seguir amando*

*te he de seguir besando
aunque me vuelva loca/
Hasta que me devuelvas
el corazón que en besos
yo te dejé en la boca.*[17]

[I have found in your love
the faith I'd lost
and now, my life has a reason to be/
I don't know if
it was the bewitchment
of your eyes/
that told your lips
steal her heart/
I know that in the thousand kisses
that I left on your mouth
I left you my heart/
And they say that it's a sin
to love the way I love you
perhaps they are right/
But why should I care
about what they say
if I cannot forget you/
For, if it's a sin to love you
I shall continue sinning
why should I hide it? /
I will continue loving you
I will continue kissing you
even if I go insane/
Until you return to me
the heart that in kisses,
I left on your mouth.] (Translation my own)

Their relationship lasted until his death. After being his widow for more than ten years, she entered into a new relationship, one she claims was of mutual convenience.[18] Nothing would ever replace the way she felt about Nick, as she tells in the song that she wrote to him years after his death.

El único que me quizo muy sinceramente fue Nick. Nick fue el único que me quiso. Este no. Este por pura conveniencia, eso es todo. Creo que últimamente si me ha agarrado un poquito de cariño ... Pero, pues, no le tengo cariño como de hombre. Lo quiero, porque me ayuda mucho, pero no le tengo cariño como a Nick. A Nick sí lo quise mucho. Era MUY sincero. Nunca me engañó, nunca me contó mentiras. Eso era para mí una cosa muy principal.[19]

Duramos Nick y yo juntos doce años antes de casarnos. En 1979 me casé con él, pero antes de eso vivíamos nomás juntos, y pues, casi los treinta años.[20] *Fue el único que yo quise. Y todavía lo recuerdo mucho.*

[The only man who truly loved me was Nick. He was the only one. Not this one. This one for convenience, only. I believe that lately he's grown to have affection for me, but, well, I don't love him like a man. I love him, because he helps me a lot, but not like the love I had for Nick. I loved Nick very much. He was VERY sincere. He never deceived me, never lied to me. That was a major issue for me. Nick and I were together 12 years before we were married. In 1979 I married him, but before that we were only together and, well, a total of almost 30 yeas. He was the only one I ever loved. And I still remember him very much.]

Notes

1. Estrada, 2017a.
2. Estrada, 2017b.
3. From interview, October 18, 2020.
4. Ibid.
5. March 4, 2016.
6. March 4, 2016 and October 20, 2020.
7. Broyles-González, 2012, p. 157.
8. From interview, November 2, 2020.
9. Vargas, 2012.
10. Vargas, 2012, pp. 88–89; Italics in original.
11. The exceptions are Ave Maria!, which she sang at my first wedding, and years later showed interest in Amazing Grace.
12. Vargas, 2012, p. 185.
13. Estrada, 2017a.
14. From interview, October 24, 2020.
15. From interview, March 7, 2016.
16. From interview, October 24, 2020.
17. Song: Los Mil Besos, Ema Elena Valdelamar, composer. As interpreted by Maria Victoria.
18. Ironically, Frank would be the man I came to love dearly, as a father.
19. From interview March 7, 2016.
20. From interview, March 4, 2016.

References

Broyles-González, Y. (2012). Re-membering Chelo Silva: The Bolero in Chicana Perspective (Women's Bodies and Voices in Postrevolutionary Urbanization: The Bohemian, urban, and Transnational). In A. J. Aldama, C. Sandoval, & P. J. Garcia (Eds.), *Performing the US Latina and Latino Borderlands* (pp. 146–164). Bloomington: University of Indiana Press.

Estrada, T. (2017a, May). *Correo del Maestro*. Retrieved February 2021, from Creadoras del Bolero: Maria Grever: Una Mujer Juglar mexicana en Nueva York: https://www.correodelmaestro.com/publico/html5052017/capitulo5/creadoras_del_bolero.html

Estrada, T. (2017b, April 1). *Creadoras del bolero: La Senora de "Mil Besos" Ema Elena Valdelamar*. Retrieved February 2021, from correodelmaestro.com: https://www.correodelmaestro.com/publico/html5042017/capitulo6/creadoras_del_bolero.html

Vargas, D. R. (2012). *Dissonant Divas in Chicana Music: The Limits of La Onda*. Minneapolis: University of Minnesota Press.

CHAPTER SEVEN

Volver, Volver:[1] Mariachi Music and Performance

Mariachi is an original product of Mexico. Its music is not a genre but a compilation of genres and stylistics representing the history, cultures, geographies, and human condition of Mexico, as well as the folk music, songs, beliefs and practices of Mexico's indigenous, African, and Mestizo rural people. Its first instruments were adaptations of earlier versions introduced to Mexico from Spain. By the mid-20th century, the instruments identified with mariachi included the trumpet, the *vihuela*, the violin, the guitar, and an optional harp.[2] The *guitarrón*, essential in a true mariachi ensemble, is believed by some to be Mexico's unique adaptation to the Spanish large-bodied bass, *bajo de uña*.[3] Thus, in my view, Mariachi represents both a form of cultural persistance and an adaptation to centuries of Spanish colonialism.

The term "Mariachi" can refer to the band, the music, or the performer(s). When the first Mariachi group organized is unknown but is believed to have been sometime in the late 1800s and is credited to the state of Jalisco, home of the oldest and most famous group, Mariachi Vargas de Tecalitlán. Today, although Mariachi music and musicianship appears all over the world and includes music and songs made famous by *trios, orquestas, bandas, grupos, conjuntos*, and the artistic innovations of innumerable artists, Mariachi remains identified by the music and styles of its Mexican roots. The symbolic performance *traje*, worn uniformly by every member of the group (though colors vary according to the group's choice), honors the horseman, rural, and folk idealized heritage of this tradition. Mariachi musicianship requires both singing and playing an instrument in the group. The exception is the solo guest singing artist accompanied by the mariachi group. In that case, the guest artist may also wear the mariachi *traje*, if the guest artist is male, or a skirted version if the guest is female.[4] To represent the regional sounds of its traditional cultural music faithfully, a respectable mariachi ensemble should include at least between eight and twelve musicians, although many groups have more or fewer members, depending on the scope of their repertoire, abilities, or whether they are a permanent group, such as the show group, or have ad hoc membership, such as groups that stroll on the street or from restaurant to restaurant, playing song requests (called *al talón*). The minimum number of musicians in the group necessary to create the sound expected by most audiences, is eight. In any case, a mariachi group must have a repertoire that includes the many songs most often identified with mariachi, including its signature group of songs, *Son de la Negra, Jarabe Tapatío, Las Mañanitas, Malagueña Salerosa, Cielito Lindo*, and others representing history and life from Mexico's pre-revolutionary times to the present.

Mariachi became emblematic of Mexican national identity by the 1920s.[5] The development of the radio helped broadcast the sounds of Mariachi throughout Mexico as well as the border areas of the southwestern United States. With the birth of cinema came the production of films that featured Mariachi groups, spreading the popularity of the music and introducing and helping to immortalize artists such as the iconic Jorge Negrete and Pedro Infante, and other artists of the mariachi song. By the 1940s and 1950s, mariachi music and performers had become internationally recognized, yet mariachi music and folk musicians were snubbed by Mexico's musical elite, because it was identified with Mexico's poor, rural, Mestizo population, and it was learned informally among the people. It was also played in public places such as cantinas, and not in theaters like the symphonies or philharmonic, in which mariachi groups also play today. In his comprehensive review of Mexico's music from Aztec through the early 1950s, for example, the early ethnomusicologist Robert Stevenson included the Euro-inspired musical styles and composers influencing, and identified with, Mexican music, yet omitted mariachi music and its prominence as the music of the Mexican Revolution, cultural identity, and nationalism.[6]

Genres in Mariachi Music

Mariachi music[7] has always been identified with *rancheras* and *corridos*.[8] The *corrido* (ballad) traditionally glorifies a male hero protagonist in the context of adversity, conflict, rebellion, or violence, themes that continue in the growing appearance of female protagonists in Mexican American *corridos*.[9] The *ranchera* encompasses various themes related to Mexican life and its human contexts and relationships but love and passion permeate the genre, especially in its *romantica ranchera* hybrid style.[10] *Ranchera* music dates back to the 19th century and is more complex than what some might call "country" music.[11] Gustavo Arellano best describes the *ranchera* genre:

> Ranchera isn't so much a genre as it is a *sentido*-a way of life, of viewing the world in all its melancholy, grandiose beauty. It's no surprise then, that ranchera is the quintessential Mexican music in a land with a dizzying variety of music. Ranchera embodies everything that Mexicans think of themselves when they're at their best-macho, romantic, dressed in splendid outfits, and stubbornly stuck in a myth of a bucolic Mexico that never truly existed. There's no corollary for it in American song-it ain't country music, it ain't Tin Pan Alley, it ain't even Western swing. It's ranchera, dammit ....[12]

The other music genres of the Mariachi repertory include *boleros*, *sones*, *huapangos*, *jarabes*, *danzones*, *polcas*, *pasodobles*, *cumbias*, *valses*,[13] and a variety of hybrid musical styles.[14] Among the most famous songs played by mariachi is *Son de la Negra*, which often opens the performance or musical set, and the internationally known mariachi staple, *Malagueña Salerosa*. The best known *jarabe* played by Mariachi is probably *Jarabe Tapatío*, often renamed by non-Spanish speakers as "The Mexican Hat Dance."[15]

Gender and Age

Traditional Mariachi has been defined by heterosexuality, masculinity, and presumed youth. In its assumed binary gender definition of romance, traditional mariachi performance privileges and emphasizes a maleness that infers a virility personified in the performer, while also not rebuking an older or less-than physically perfect male performer. Dressed in the black (or brown) fitted *traje de charro* (cowboy suit) adorned with rows of *botonadura* (silver button adornment) down the sides, and matching large sombrero, the traditional Mariachi image idealizes the hacienda life and the *charro* (Mexican cowboy) in his *campesino* (country) life as he portrays the imagined physically strong and handsome horseman riding confidently through the countryside doing or overseeing the work of the hacienda.[16] This hyper-masculinized image is further supported by the romantic song, whether a *corrido*, *ranchera*, *son*, *huapango*, or *bolero-ranchera*, in which male sexual desire and prowess are underscored, yet thinly veiled in the lyrics. The narrative often employs humor as a measure of decorum, as in the popular *ranchera* song, *La Feria de Las Flores*. The song's lyrics exemplify both the macho image through the male's active role as the sexual aggressor, armed and prepared to take the "flower" from her male protector. As is typical of the *ranchera* genre, the traditional male-centered standpoint of the lyrics serves to shroud the male performer in a youthful masculinity, real or imagined. In contrast, the female is the correspondent in the song and is portrayed as a blushing, virginal, and passive object of his desire. Implied in this portrayal of binary male and female sexuality, is a youthfulness that drives sexual passion.

Throughout most of its history, composers of the *ranchera* have been men, so that *ranchera* lyrics consistently portray a male protagonist and the narrative is developed from a male standpoint. As the reigning and historically longest genre tied to Mexican nationalism, it has traditionally involved a cultural accommodation for its interpretation by female artists, while also supporting its fundamental machismo. Some *ranchera* songs refer to events, places, or topics other than love, facilitating the female artist to assume the protagonist standpoint. In the male-centered *ranchera* narrative however, women artists either change the gendered nouns in performing or recording the song, if the composition allows, or they sing the song as composed, from the male perspective. In the latter case, the female's strong, often throaty voice with a tone of bravado becomes the complement to machismo; her voice assists the image of femininity that is simultaneously tough of character, while her *traje de charra* or regional dress helps personify and maintain the feminine image. For women artists, the typical ranchera song can signify a gendered barrier that the singer often negotiates with her voice, thus helping to make it gender-accessible through performance.

Whether written in the usual third person or in its occasional first person, the *corrido* has been paternalistic in character and youth is either directly referenced or implied. References to women generally fall into thematic archetypes: lover (good or evil), mother (good or bad), goddess, or soldier.[17] In the non-romantic song or songs with non-romantic portrayals of women, lyrics typically reference the woman as either the beloved mother or the iconic Holy Virgin. Yet even in such songs, the male protagonist sings from a youthful standpoint, in this case, that of a son, and the female in this case, is aged, wise, suffered, lovingly protective of her son or her children, or empowered by her maternal status to exact moral punishment through a *maldición*, (curse) to an errant son or daughter. The female here is extolled for her maternal altruism or appealed-to for forgiveness, guidance, or protection, in any case distinct from physical appeal, romance, or emotions related to human sexuality and its vulnerability, in contrast to the tough, strong masculinity of the *charro*.

In its characteristically romantic lyrics and musical style, the *bolero* often assumes an unspecified gender, which makes this musical style more gender-inclusive than the *ranchera*. The sensuality in the bolero narrative is dramatized vocally through performance and particularly so in the female performer.[18] Its poetic lyrical style, along with its use of innuendo and double-entendre, is ambiguous to the extent that, depending on the song, it can be heterosexually binary or gender-neutral, as in the highly sexualized lyrics in the bolero song, *Quizás, Quizás, Quizás*, where gender is unspecified. The sensuality in the lyrics of the *bolero* tends to imply a youth corresponding to the burning urge of desire, or the pain of suffering over an uncommitted, unrequited, lost, or betrayed love, unless it specifically refers to a love of the protagonist's past youth that is recalled in the present, such as in the song, *Aquellos Ojos Verdes*.

Mariachi in the United States

Mariachi music has been popular among Mexicans in the U.S. since before the 1930s,[19] but in the 1960s, at the rise of the Chicano Movement's Cultural Renaissance, Mariachi reigned as an expression of Chicano cultural identity, particularly in the Southwest.[20] Other genres of Mexican music were also popular among Mexican Americans, including *boleros* by trios and new styles developed by young Mexican American performing artists. The Renaissance was most vibrant in Los Angeles,[21] the city with the largest Mexican population outside of Mexico, particularly East Los Angeles, the heart of that community, and home of *Las Generalas*.

Mariachi is similar to jazz in what Gardner calls a "street-level" musical tradition.[22] That is, as the music of the people and rooted in history and folklore, it has not been traditionally associated with or restricted to formal instruction, the affluent, or the elite. Its learning is often lyrical, that is, self-taught, by apprenticeship from other self-taught or learned musical people such as street musicians, family members, and others. Traditionally, mariachi musicians with profound musical inclinations who had the opportunity and resources, pursued formal academic and long-term instruction to reach stardom or public acclaim. Since the period of the Chicano Renaissance in the United States southwest especially, formal instruction in mariachi music and musicianship has become much more available and that form of learning is now more common among new generations of mariachis.

The Mariachi tradition transcends national borders, but U.S. Mariachi performance assumes the additional dimensions associated with the Mexican diaspora. Mariachi's distinctive music, instrumentation, style, songs, and *traje* (performance wear) remain integral to traditional performance and public expectations (in both Mexico and the U.S., the traditional women performers' *traje* includes a long skirt, decorated similarly to the traditional *traje* of the male mariachis). Its musical repertory also continues to be distinguished by its representation of Mexico's colonial, revolutionary and rural past; however, in their musical repertoire, the Mexican American mariachi groups must be able to please transnational audiences with the most culturally recognizable songs, popular on both sides of the border. For Mexican American audiences, the mariachi must also provide a particularly nationalist repertoire through which the music enjoins the listeners to a feeling of belonging to their Mexican roots. In this case, the *ranchera* song, *Mexico Lindo y Querido*, is particularly emblematic of Mexican identity, especially in the following stanza:

> *México lindo y querido,*
> *si muero lejos de ti*
> *que digan que estoy dormido*
> *y que me traigan aquí/*
> [Mexico beautiful and beloved,
> if I should die far from you,
> may they say that I am asleep
> and return me to you.] (Translation my own)

Mariachi groups in the United States also expertly adapt to the ethnically diverse context of the country and to the political climate affecting Mexican Americans and Mexicans in the U.S. Mariachi groups in the U.S. borderlands have led in such adaptations, for example, by singing in English.[23] Some groups also pepper their performances with *corridos* about the border crossing and immigrant experiences and other relevant narratives, or with the occasional crowd- or client-pleasing adaptations of Anglo songs, some of which are intentionally comical and often requested by audiences, as for example, Happy Birthday, which becomes phonetically translated by mariachis as *Apio Verde* (Green Celery).

In Los Angeles, a variety of mariachi groups abounds. They include groups that are showcased in theater concerts and/or accompany famous celebrity vocalists; groups that are salaried by establishments (*plantas*) such as restaurants in which the clientele's entertainment is supplied by *la casa*; groups that play by *chambas* (gigs) at community venues such as parks, centers or marketplaces, community events, or private events such as weddings and *quinceañeras* (the age fifteen version of "sweet sixteen"). In both the United States and Mexico, a *chamba* is a way to earn a living in a tough economy and job market, as it is for many street mariachis and

Photo 7.1: Poster purchased by the author, of the International Mariachi Conference in Tucson, 2006. From the author's private archives.

other *músicos*, street musicians or semi-professional mariachi groups that play *al talón*, moving bar-to-bar, playing requests.

Venues associated with mariachi artists and mariachi social life in the United States also have their own Mexican American history. For example, Mariachi Los Camperos, founded by the late Natividad (Nati) Cano, though famous in both countries, is the U.S.'s answer to Mexico's oldest, Mariachi Vargas de Tecalitlán. Cano's Los Angeles-based Los Camperos broke tradition by originating the stage-show mariachi in the U.S., which they instituted at La Fonda, the restaurant they own and in which they perform for dinner audiences. Cano also included the first female mariachi musician, Rebeca Gonzales, in his Camperos show mariachi, an otherwise all-male group. Cano also instituted the annual International Mariachi Conference in Tucson, Arizona (Photo 7.1).[24] *Plaza Garibaldi*, the "Mariachi Central" of Mexico City, *La Plaza de los Mariachis* and *Teatro Degollado*, both in Guadalajara, in the state of Jalisco, Mexico, have had their counterpoints in the "Hotel Mariachi," *Plaza del Mariachi* of Boyle Heights, *Plaza de la Raza* (formerly

Photo 7.2: Program from the Mariachi Festival X (10th) Anniversary, June 19 & 20, 1999, at the Hollywood Bowl. From the author's private archive collection.

named Lincoln Park) in Lincoln Heights, Mission San Gabriel church, and *El Mercadito*, all in or bordering East Los Angeles, among others, the Million Dollar Theatre in downtown Los Angeles, and *La Placita* on Olvera Street, located in the historically oldest Mexican-occupied section of downtown Los Angeles. Other venues abound in which mariachi groups are or have been showcased, including Carnegie Hall, Colleges and Universities, the White House, and the famous Hollywood Bowl (Photo 7.2), as well as international venues and events.

A great part of mariachi's uniqueness is its relationship with its audience. In etiquette as in showmanship, mariachi professionalism, in the United States as in Mexico, demands the connectedness of mariachi with its public. For those playing *al talón, de planta*, or as a *chamba*, the performance is preceded by a brief friendly conversational or salutatory exchange. Often, the performance stimulates the small audience to get up and dance, or audience members to let out the "*Ay, ay, ay, ay!!*" yell of approval and camaraderie with the performers. The nature of the professional show mariachi restricts the same kind of interaction as the bar-to-bar or table-to-table version, but the stage performers' engagement with their audience is in how they evoke whistles and yells, culturally recognized as signs of enjoyment that gauge the public's rating of the performance's artistic merit. The repertoire itself also produces interaction, along with the musicians' sensitive responsiveness to the audience. For example, every mariachi group knows how to play the songs *El Rey* or *Volver, Volver, Volver*, perhaps the most recognized for evoking the interconnectedness of performers and audience. In the latter song, the lead vocalist introduces the first verses and the excited audience completes the song with the chorus, assisted by the rest of the mariachis (rather than the other way around), so that the audience not only joins but becomes the performer. What underlies the audience-performers connection in this case is not so much the song's narrative, but rather how its verbal simplicity facilitates the unstated but understood expression of a shared nationalism implied in the interaction. This nationalist spirit of mariachi performance is heightened in the United States, among audiences of the Mexican diaspora, who lament their physical dislocation from their homeland and self-identify with a Mexican heritage, a sense of shared cultural roots and belonging. Even the *pocho*, the Anglo-acculturated and limited or non-Spanish speaker yet culturally attuned fan, attempts to communicate his request for "that song, you know, the one that goes, 'Come Back, Come Back, Come Back!'"

Interactions and relationships among mariachi group members also are sensitive to inter-group differences in the United States in ways not likely to occur in the same ways in Mexico. Examples include variations among the mariachi group members in levels of Spanish language and acculturation to the dominant Anglo culture. Since the 1970s, mariachi groups increasingly have included members whose backgrounds are not Mexican, particularly Anglos. This can present tensions that limit the potential for camaraderie or strain the social cohesion of a group whose members are by necessity in almost daily contact as required by long and frequent rehearsals and the needed communication for collaborating to successfully synchronize a performance.

Mariachi continues to grow in popularity among new generations of musicians. This is especially noteworthy given the history of racial discrimination in the United States against Mexicans and their music, the popularity of contemporary music among younger people, the attraction of electronics especially among the young, the dominant English language, evolving gender and sexual socially claimed and recognized identities and politics, urbanization, globalization, industrialization, individualism, changing attitudes toward religious practices and religiosity that are often part of the songs in the mariachi repertoire, changing family structures, and the Euro-centered cultural hegemony that legitimizes musical production and performing arts only when they are products of academic training, all factors implicated in the music and performance of Mariachi. The school-sponsored mariachi music curricula now offered in many public schools, colleges and universities, community centers, and private schools, especially throughout the southwest, and the rise of mariachi conservatories, conferences, concerts and sales in recordings, attest to the status of mariachi as among the prominent music styles of the Americas, and in other parts of the world. While this signifies its cooptation by the Euro-centered system of formalized instruction, it also evidences Mariachi's importance in Mexican American cultural persistence.

Notes

1. Song title, Fernando Z. Maldonado, composer; made popular by Vicente Fernandez.
2. Sheehy, 2006.
3. Museum, 2021; Wikipedia, 2021.
4. Although, the performance dress worn by mariachis may reflect their claimed gender identity.
5. Sheehy, 2006.
6. Stevenson, 1952.
7. Mariachi music and songs that I refer to here are just some of the most popular and recognizable ones, because the mariachi repertoire would be too extensive to list here. I also mention only a few of the artists who have reached stardom singing with mariachi.
8. Both genres allude to the life, love, sorrows and other conditions of the common people, but as ballads, *corridos* specifically provide a folk history because they refer to events, places, or folk heroes, popular leaders such as Pancho Villa, or outlaws of crimes of passion. *Corridos* typically glorify revolutionary soldiers, heroes and heroines, victories or defeats of revolutionary battles, or relate stories of tragedies or love affairs, and some are even about the animals of heroes or protagonists.
9. Herrera-Sobek, 1992; Tatar, 2015; Some *corridos* also relate stories, sometimes humorous, about experiences of Mexicans on both sides of the United States-Mexico border. The oldest *corridos*, still integral to mariachi music, include songs about the Mexican Revolution of 1910–1917, and may have several versions or additions over time. For example, the great Mexican American folklorist, Américo Paredes, documented seven versions of the corrido, *Benjamín Argumedo*, composed over a period of fifty-four years since it was initially performed (Paredes, 1993). Even the best known old corridos are too numerous to list, but a minute sample includes: *Gabino Barrera, Rosita Alvirez, La Carcel de Cananea, La Toma de Zacatecas, Carabina 30–30, Corrido de Pancho Villa, La Cucaracha, La Valentina, La Adelita, Juana Gallo, Siete Leguas, El Caballo Blanco*, and many, many more.
10. Many artists of this sub-form have been popular over the years but even before the 1950s, the composer/singer Cuco Sánchez was perhaps best identified with this style. His songs became classics internationally because of his uniquely soulful, melancholic guitar arrangements accompanying the sorrowful lyrics referring to a broken heart, his typical theme. Some of his many songs include *Fallaste Corazón, La Cama de Piedra, Siempre Hace Frio, Guitarras Lloren Guitarras, Anillo de Compromiso, Qué Manera de Perder* and *Gritenme Piedras del Campo*.
11. The *ranchera* artist/composer most known and associated with a mariachi sound since the early1950s has been the legendary José Alfredo Jimenez. He wrote over 1,000 songs and his name, like his songs and his voice, are still the most recognizable of the *ranchera* and *corrido* styles. He also composed and sang many songs in styles known as *huapangos, sones*. and variants of the genres, such as *boleros* and *ranchero-boleros*. such as *Serenata Huasteca, Cuando Sale La Luna (aka Deja Que Salga La Luna), El Jinete*, many others considered his signature classics. A robust

repertory of his compositions, especially the transnationally popular *El Rey*, remains a must among Mariachi musicians. His songs have been interpreted since the 1950s by renowned and countless local male and female artists. A very small sample of his songs includes: *Qué Bonito Amor, Camino de Guanajuato, Corazón Corazón, Cuatro Caminos, El Cielo de Chihuahua, Ella, Guitarras de Medianoche, La Enorme Distancia, La Media Vuelta, Llegó Borracho El Borracho, La Retirada, Me Equivoqué Contigo, No Me Amenaces, Pa' Todo El Año, Paloma Querida, Para Morir Iguales, Llegando a Ti* (aka "*Poco a Poco*"), *Si Nos Dejan, Tu Recuerdo y Yo, Tú y Las Nubes, Vámonos, Virgencita de Zapopan*, and many more (Cancioneros.com, 2022). Some of the best-known singing artists who have interpreted his songs include: Jorge Negrete, Pedro Infante, Miguel Acevez Mejia, Pedro Vargas, Antonio Aguilar, Luis Aguilar, Javier Solís, Amalia Mendoza (*La Tariácuri*), Lola Beltrán, Lucha Villa, Vicente Fernandez, known to many as *El Rey de la Música Ranchera* [The King of *Ranchera* Music], Selena, Vicki Carr, Thalia, Estela Nuñez, Ana Gabriel, Alejandro Fernandez, Pedro Fernandez, Luis Miguel, Julio Iglesias, Juan Gabriel, and many more Mexican and internationally recognized, as well as locally known artists, who paid and continue to pay homage to the music of José Alfredo Jiménez.

12. Arellano, 2013.
13. Pearlman, 1984, p. 2.
14. Boleros were popularized by trios, with their own unique sound of voices and instrumentation, in Mexico at least since the early 1900s. The instruments associated with trios vary according to regional folkloric traditions, such as the *son jarocho* (from Veracruz). A basic Jarocho group includes the three primary instruments and their players: a, *jarana* (a type of guitar with baroque roots and shared with the Yucatecan tradition), the *requinto jarocho* (aka guitarra de son), and the *arpa de son jarocho* (regional version of the diatonic harp). A *Jarocho* band would also include the *pandero* (similar to a tambourine), the *quijada* (a jawbone rattle) and depending on the group's size and expertise, also the *cajón* (a wooden box drum with a hole cut on one side), and the double bass (a stringed instrument that is usually plucked) (Levy, 2010).

    Sones, Huapangos, and *Jarabes* each have their own regional as well as musical style variations. For example, three variants of the *Huapango* include *Huasteco* (also known as *son huasteco*), *Norteño*, and *Mariachi* (Huapango-Wikipedia, la enciclopedia libre., 2020). The *son huasteco* comes from a geo-cultural region that includes parts of Tamaulipas, Veracruz, Puebla, Hidalgo, San Luis Potosí, Querétaro and Guanajuato. Among the most recognizable songs of this region is *Cielito Lindo*, written in 1882 by the Mexican composer Quirino Mendoza y Cortés, which some reviewers have dubbed as Mexico's anthem folk song, at least within the *huapango* genre (en.wikipedia.org, Mexico Lindo y Querido, 2022).
15. *Jarabes* and *sones* represent the indigenous, African and Mestizo musical sounds of Mexico's history and rhythms identified with regional Mexican groups and their stylistic folk dances and songs, as do other genres. *Jarabes* and *sones* have several regional versions. An example is the region of the Isthmus of Tehuantepec, with its characteristic instrument, the *marimba*, and its emblematical song, *La Zandunga*. The *huapango* is a form of *son* identified with the *huasteco* indigenous group covering parts of five Mexican states. Among the most famous *huapango* is *Cucurrucucú Paloma*, which was composed by Tomás Méndez, and interpreted with mariachi by the celebrated Lola Beltrán, among many other artists worldwide.
16. Peña, 1985.
17. Tatar, 2015; Herrera-Sobek, 1990; Tatar suggests that like Anglo-American ballads, Mexican American corridos began to contest gender in corridos.

18. Vargas, 2008.
19. Kurland, 2013.
20. Henriques, 2011.
21. Loza, 1993.
22. Gardner, 2017, p. VII.
23. Henriques, 2011.
24. The conferences have taken place over four days and include workshops on mariachi musicianship for hundreds of young students and adults, concerts that showcase new and established mariachi groups, and mariachi groups that accompany famous Mexican and Mexican American singing celebrities such as, in past years, Pedro Fernandez.

References

Arellano, G. (2013, March 29). *The 20 Best Ranchera Singers of All Time*. Retrieved from OCWeekly.com: https://www.ocweekly.com/the-20-greatest-ranchera-singers-of-all-time-the-complete-list-6600601/

Cancioneros: Diario Digital de Musica de Autor (2022). https://www.cancioneros.com/ca/113/0/cancionero-de-jose-alfredo-jimenez

Gardner, D. (2017). Foreword. In D. Phillips (Ed.), *What Is This Thing Called Soul: Conversations on Black Culture and Jazz Education* (pp. vii–IX). New York: Peter Lang.

Henriques, D. (2011). Mariachi Reimaginings: Encounters with Technology, Aesthetics, and Identity. In A. L. Madrid (Ed.), *Transnational Encounters: Music and Performance at the U.S.-Mexico Border* (pp. 85–110). New York: Oxford University Press.

Herrera-Sobek, M. (1990). *The Mexican Corrido: A Feminist Analysis*. Bloomington: Indiana University Press.

Kurland, C. L. (2013). *Hotel Mariachi: Urban Space and Cultural Heritage in Los Angeles*. Albuquerque: University of New Mexico Press.

Levy, D. (2010). *Celso Duarte-son jarocho-Global Encounters: Music of Mexico*. Carnegie Hall-Well Music Institute. https://www.carnegiehall.org/-/media/CarnegieHall/Files/PDFs/Education/Educators/Toolbox/Grade-5/Global-Encounters-Music-of-Mexico/Celso-Duarte-son-jarocho-music-and-Mexico.pdf?la=en&hash=E05F47FAC9D3733F34E885ADA2AC14DC

Loza, S. (1993). *Barrio Rhythm: Mexican American Music in Los Angeles*. Urbana and Chicago: University of Illinois Press.

Museum, M. I. (2021, July n/a). *Guitarron*. ... Retrieved from Musical Instruments Museum: http://www.mim.be/guitarron

Paredes, A. (1993). The Concept of the Emotional Core Applied to the Mexican Corrido "Benjamín Argumendo." In Bauman, R. (Ed.), *Folklore and Culture on the Texas-Mexican Border* (pp. 143–176). Austin: University of Texas, Center for Mexican American Studies.

Pearlman, S. R. (1984). Standarization and Innovation in Mariachi Music Performance in Los Angeles. *Pacific Review of Ethnomusicology, 1,* 1–12.

Peña, M. (1985). *The Texas-Mexican Conjunto.* Austin: University of Texas.

Sheehy. (2006). *Mariachi Music in America: Experiencing Music, Expressing Culture.* New York: Oxford University Press.

Stevenson. (1952). *Music in Mexico: The Only Complete History of Mexican Music from Aztec to Modern Times.* New York: Thomas Y. Crowell Company.

Tatar, B. (2015, March). Destroying Patriarchy: Struggle for Sexual Equality in Mexican-American Corridos and Anglo-American Ballads. *The Journal of American Culture, 38*(1), 4–15.

Vargas, D. (2008). Borderlands Bolerista: The Lycentious Lyricism of Chelo Silva. *Feminist Studies , 34*(1/2), 178–197.

Wikipedia. (2021, March 22). *Guitarrón mexicano.* Retrieved from Wikipedia-the free encyclopedia: https://en.wikipedia.org/wiki/Guitarrón_mexicano

Wikipedia. (2022). Mexico Lindo y Querido. https://en.wikipedia.org/wiki/M%C3%A9xico_Lindo_y_Querido

CHAPTER EIGHT

My Participation in Mariachi Las Generalas: En Primera Voz

[Dated February 11, 2016][1]

Desde 1979 hasta 1986

Querida hija,

Preferí escribirte lo poco que yo recuerdo de mi participación con el Mariachi 'Las Generalas.'

En aquel tiempo estaba yo todavía muy joven, a pesar de mi edad. Yo creo que tendría yo aproximadamente 41 años de edad (¡a eso le llamo joven!)

Para Entonces ya vivía yo con Nick Pastrano y en 1979 mas o menos, contraje matrimonio con él.

Afortunadamente yo permanecía todavía ignorante de lo que la vida me esperaba.

Un día llegó a mi residencia una mujer (no recuerdo cual)–Adela. Me dijo que se estaba formando un grupo de mujeres que supieran tocar instrumentos.

Aparentemente ella me había escuchado cantar con mi guitarra en una fiesta particular–y de allí surgió la encomienda que ella tenía para recabar el grupo necesitado.

Sin preguntarle a Nick y a sabiendas que iba a decir 'no'– yo acepté.

Ese día indicado para ensayos era cerca de donde yo vivía. En la Iglesia 'San Gabriel.'

Así comencé mi viaje, con la música 'Mariachera.'

Eran dos las que se habían unido para formar el 'Mariachi Las Generalas.' El nombre del Mariachi Las Generalas—lo escogió Ma. Elena Muñoz. La segunda era Adela, que estaba casada con un señor que pertenecía a otro 'Mariachi group.'

No recuerdo nombres. Adela tocaba guitarra. Ma Elena no sabia tocar ningún instrumento pero tenía mucha conociencia de lo que era El Mariachi, puesto que ella tenía a un hijo Mariachero. Ella y Adela se conocían a traves de los parientes que estaban en grupos de 'Mariachis.'

Asi empezé mi camino a la musica de Mariachi.

Aunque a Nick no le gustaba, tan solo porque andaba yo de noche por donde quiera con el Mariachi.

Ademas la musica atrae mucha atención Masculina. Era entonces natural que a él le inspiraba celo.

Pero yo no pensaba de esa manera.

A mi la musica era y ha sido para mi—una cosa inexplicable 'Alegria-Tristeza-Sentimiento,' y mucho más que uno encierra adentro de sus pensamientos y sentimientos.

Pasaron los años y yo y todas las compañeras creíamos saber mucho mas de lo que habiamos aprendido con un Mariachi profesor, que nos enseñó a tocar los instrumentos nuevos.

Yo escogí el guitarrón por ser similar a la guitarra.

Otras escogieron el Violín y así por lo consiguiente.

Ma. Elena la directora—no sabía tocar ningún instrumento y escogió la 'vihuela.' Desgraciadamente para ella era difícil tocar la vihuela si no estaba frente a la guitarrista, que era Adela.

Por lo consiguiente todas eramos nuevas con los instrumentos que escogimos.

El amor a la musica Mexicana y en total a toda nota musical-era tanta que aprendimos a acompañarnos nuestras propias canciones.

Nos salieron trabajos para fiestas particulares—para campañas electorales en 'Lincoln Park' y etc.

Fuimos a acomapañar a algunos artistas. Acompañamos a Pepe Infante (hermano de Pedro) pero como no sabíamos todavía todos los tonos, salimos perdiendo en el norte de California. Allí se armó una revolución, con Maria Elena y el que nos contrató.

Regresamos a casa sin pago pero de buen humor, pues esa 'experiencia' no nos quebró.

Seguimos adelante.

La música ya la traíamos por dentro. Nada nos hacía decistir.

Pero desgraciadamente en la musica hay mucho celo entre los propios componentes.

Yo tenía problemas con Adela. Ella no quería que yo cantara, solo ella.

Pero las violinistas, Lupe Rodriguez y Marta Guerra, eran mis amigas fieles y ellas si me acompañaban con gusto.

Al fín, Comenzaron las desavenencias.

Ma Elena comenzó a estafar cuando cobraba en las fiestas[2]

Entonces Lupe Rodriguez (Violinista) se salió primero.

Como eramos muy amigas, Ma. Elena me botó a mí.

Sin saber que yo no tenía ninguna culpa en todo lo que estaba pasando–Lupe creyó que yo todavía andaba con ellas.

Un día le llamé a Lupe y se aclaró todo.

Entonces ella y yo nos unimos como dueto y comenzamos a trabajar con un maestro de música que nos preparó como dueto.

El Maestro Alberto Larios nos preparó y triunfamos ella y yo, y el Maestro nos acompañaba en el órgano. A pesar de todo nada nos detuvo para seguir propagando la música mas querida de ayer y ahora.

Siguen dentro de nosotras esas melodías que aún tenemos prendidas en nuestras gargantas, y mentalmente tarariámos a diario.

Yo con mi edad y con la voz que mi Dios me quiso dar, a pesar de no haber tenido mucha educación musical– Pero muchas interrupciones–por parte de mis propios seres queridos (que no creyeron en mi) he seguido usando esa voz con el mismo sentimiento y gusto, como al principio lo hice.

Yo no sé cual es el destino que se me trazó. Yo siento un gran consuelo y tristeza cuando aun canto Acompañada de esas guitarras o violines o lo que sea.

Para mí todos los instrumentos son música.

Nadamás falta quien los haga sonar bonito y vibrar.

Asi es la musica del 'Mariachi' mucha Alegria, mucho sentimiento, muchos recuerdos y cada uno que lo compone se siente como en la gloria.

Es la musica mas guapachosa y buyanguera, Pero como Alegría nadie le gana.

'Viva El Mariachi'

Es y sera siendo numero 'Uno' para la música Mexicana.

Una vez que se mete en el Corazón es difícil sacarla.

[From 1979 until 1986

Dear Daughter,

I chose to write you the little that I remember about my participation in the mariachi group, *Las Generalas*.

At that time, I was still very young, in spite of my age, I was approximately 41 (and I call that young!). At the time I was already living with Nick Pastrano. I married him about 1979.

Fortunately, I did not yet know what awaited me in life.

One day, a woman came to my house–(I don't remember her name)–Adela. She told me she was forming a group of women who could play instruments.

Apparently, she had heard me sing with my guitar at a private celebration and from there she carried out the task of recruiting women needed for the group.

Without asking Nick, and knowing that he would say 'No,' I accepted.

The day that rehearsal was held, it was near where I lived, at the 'San Gabriel [Mission] Church.'

That's how I began my journey with *'mariachiera'* music.

Two women had decided together to form the Mariachi *Las Generalas*.

It was Maria Elena Munoz's idea to call it *'Las Generalas.'* The other woman was Adela. Her husband was a member of another mariachi group, I don't remember names. Adela played the guitar. Maria Elena didn't play any instrument, but she knew a lot about the mariachi business because she had a son who was a Mariachi. The two women knew each other through family members who were mariachis.

So that's how I started my path into the Mariachi world.

Nick didn't like it because I would go everywhere and had to be out until late at night.

Also, music attracts a lot of masculine attention, so it was natural that it would inspire jealousy in him.

But I didn't think of it that way.

For me, music is and has been an inexplicable thing 'Happiness-Sadness-Sentiment,' and much more that we lock up inside our deepest thoughts and feelings.

As the years passed, my colleagues in the group and I believed that we knew much more than what we had learned from a Mariachi teacher, who had shown us how to play the new instruments.

I chose the *guitarrón* for its similarity to the guitar.

The other members of the group chose the Violin, and so forth.

Maria Elena, the director-didn't know how to play an instrument, and she chose the '*vihuela.*' Unfortunately for her, it was difficult to play the *vihuela* if she was not in front of the guitarist, who was Adela.

To continue, we were all new to the instruments we each chose.

The love of Mexican music and in general to any musical note-was so much that we learned to accompany ourselves with our songs.

We got playing engagements for private parties–at election campaigns, in 'Lincoln Park'[3] and etc.

We went to accompany a few artists. We accompanied Pepe Infante (brother of Pedro) but because we had not yet known all the tones, we ended up losing in northern California. There was quite a revolution there with Maria Elena and the one who contracted us to play. We went home without pay, but yet in good spirits, because that 'experience' didn't break us.

We kept on ahead.

We already carried music in our hearts. Nothing would make us desist.

Unfortunately, there is much jealousy in music amidst musicians.

I had problems with Adela. She didn't want me to sing, just her.

But the violinists, Lupe Rodriguez and Marta Guerra, were my loyal friends and they did accompany me, gladly.

In the end-disagreements began to ensue.

Some about Maria Elena's mishandling of the money earned from our playing engagements.

Then Lupe Rodriguez (violinist) was the first to leave.

As we [Lupe and I] were very good friends, Maria Elena threw me out.

Lupe didn't know that I was not at fault, and she thought I was still with the group.

One day I called Lupe, and everything got cleared up.

Then she and I got together and began working with a music maestro who groomed us to be a duo.

The Maestro Alberto Larios groomed us, and we succeeded, she and I, and the maestro would accompany us on the organ. In spite of everything, nothing stopped us from propagating our beloved music of today and yesteryear.

Inside of the two of us are those melodies that are still caught in our throats, and mentally we sing them daily.

As for me, at my age and with the voice God donned on me—in spite of not having had much musical education—but with many interruptions—due to my own loved ones (who didn't believe in me) I have been using that voice with the same love and joy—as I did from the start.

I don't know what twisted fate for me. I feel a great comfort and sadness when I still sing accompanied by those guitars or violins or whatever.

To me, all instruments are music.

It's only a matter of who can make them sound beautiful and vibrant.

That's how the 'Mariachi' music is a lot of happiness, a lot of feeling, many memories and each one who composes them feels like they're in heaven.

It's the most beautiful and animated music, as for happy music, no one can beat it.

'Viva the Mariachi'

It is and will always be number 'One' as Mexican Music goes.

Once it gets into your heart, it is difficult to get it out.]

After Aurora and Lupe left *Las Generalas*, the group continued to exist for approximately two more years. According to Reifler Flores (2015), it evolved into a coed group and continued to gain popularity, becoming one of the most competitive groups in the East Los Angeles area.

Dueto Las Golondrinas

My mother is proud, even boastful at times, about having been taught by Maestro Larios, whose musical acumen and dedication she always admired. She related to me how she and Lupe became his pupils (see Photo 8.1a, b)

> *Él tocaba el piano y el órgano. Nos puso a que le cantáramos. Cuando nos oyó, nos dijo que yo tenía buena voz, pero Lupe necesitaba desarrollarla más. ¡Uh! ¡Pues me fayé!*[4] *Pero pronto me puso en mi lugar a mí también. Pero aprendimos mucho con él.*

[He was a pianist and organist. He had us sing for him. When he heard us, he told us that I had a good voice, but that Lupe needed to develop hers further. Oh! Well, I just got all cocky! But soon he put me in my place too. But we learned a lot from him.] (Photo 8.2).

Photo 8.1a: Aurora Prado Pastrano, when performing as part of duo *Las Golondrinas*. At Azteca Restaurant, Los Angeles, c1985.

Photo 8.1b: Aurora Pastrano and Lupe Rodriguez, performing with their teacher, Maestro Larios, 1988.

Alicia: *Usted me platicó que había un lugar donde se reunían artistas que usted conoció.* [You once told me of a place where artists gathered, artists you got to know.] (Photo 8.3a, b).

>Aurora: *Oh, eso fue en La Costa[5] en Montebello, donde íbamos a cenar Lupe y yo con el maestro Larios. Allí entraban muchos artistas que venían de México, como María Padilla, allí la conocí y canté con ella. Ella era cantante profesional y muy reconocida en México, Las Hermanas Padilla. Ya se había muerto la hermana, y cuando ella vino a Los Ángeles, ya venía casada con el esposo de ella, Guillermo. Y entonces cuando se murió el maestro Larios también canté con ella. Eso fue cuando Lupe y yo cantábamos con el Maestro Larios. Él había estado tocando en el Restaurant La Costa, pero luego se fue para El Azteca, en San Gabriel. Y allí fue cuando nos metió a Lupe y a mí para cantar en dueto. Un día, estaba el tiempo muy feo, y llovió mucho, y el parking lot donde él estacionaba su carro estaba inundado. Entonces él se bajó de su carro y se fue a tocar el órgano al restaurant, y esa mojada le hizo mucho daño y le pegó pulmonía. Era viernes. El sábado y el domingo tocó. El lunes ya estaba muy malo. El martes se murió. Así que el maestro Larios fue el que nos introdujo a Lupe y a mí como un dueto, pero muchos años después de que yo ya andaba cantando.*

[Oh, that was at La Costa in Montebello, where Lupe and I used to go to dinner with Maestro Larios. Many artists visiting from Mexico used to go in there, such as Maria

Photo 8.2 a, b: (a): Aurora Pastrano with Saulo Sedan (requintista), Los Diamantes. La Costa Restaurant. March 6,1988. (b): Aurora Pastrano with Eduardo Novelo (lead vocals), Trio Montejo. La Costa Restaurant. March 06,1988.

Photo 8.3: Aurora Pastrano and Lupe Rodriguez, performing as duo Las Golondrinas, La Costa Restaurant. May 1988.

Padilla, who I met there, and I sang with her there. She was a professional singer and very famous in Mexico, Las Hermanas Padilla. Her sister had died and when she came to Los Angeles, she was already married to her husband, Guillermo. And when the maestro Larios died, I also sang with her. That was when Lupe and I were singing with him. He had been playing at La Costa Restaurant, but he left and went to El Azteca, in San Gabriel, and that's when he formed Lupe and me into a duo. One day, the weather was very bad, and it rained a lot, and the parking lot where he would park his car was flooded. Then he got out of his car and he went int to play the organ at the restaurant, and that drenching caused him to get sick and he caught pneumonia. It was a Friday. He played on Saturday and Sunday. On Monday he was very sick. On Tuesday he died. So, it was the maestro Larios who introduced Lupe and me as a duo, but that was many years after I began to sing in public.]

Notes

1. The following is reproduced from a letter as it was written to me by my mother.
2. My mother later clarified that her use of the word "*estafar*" in reference to Maria Elena's mishandling of money was an implication hurled among the group, not a proven fact. It was part

of the discord that strained the group, causing the eventual disbanding of the original group as some of the original members left or were asked to leave, including Lupe and my mother.
3. The "Lincoln Park" she refers to here was renamed "Plaza de la Raza" and is located in Lincoln Heights.
4. Her use of this word indicates "to get cocky" or "self-congratulatory"; it is not the same as *fallé*, which means to fail or to let someone down.
5. This particular conversation took place on November 5, 2020, over thirty years after she stopped performing in the duo with Lupe. It is possible that the specific instance(s) she recalls may have taken place at one or more of the restaurants at which they performed in and/or frequented after a performance and which she told me about in previous conversations, which included La Costa in Montebello, El Azteca in San Gabriel, and Lalo's in Los Angeles.

References

Reifler Flores, C. (2015). Las Generalas: Origins of Women's Participation in Mariachi and the Cultural and Transnational Implications. *Karpa, 8*, n.p.

CHAPTER NINE

Mariachi Las Generalas

The pioneer all-female Mariachi group *Las Generalas* (Photo 9.1) began as an idea. It came from a woman who would not let tradition, ridicule, or lack of training dictate what she and other women could or could not be or do, and the seven women she recruited, who believed they could be mariachis and still honor the mariachi tradition, and had the resolve to make it happen. *Las Generalas* confronted layers of patriarchy in order to trailblaze, as women and for women, the path to their place in what had been traditionally a male-only cultural and artistic space. They endured public humiliation and rejection for transgressing against the heterosexual maleness that mariachi performance symbolized. From outside the group came attacks on their musical abilities, stoking internal group tensions as the women challenged each other's leadership and artistic quality. Being pioneer women mariachis also brought some of them spousal disapproval, even disdain. Together, the women of *Las Generalas* navigated danger, humiliation, rejection, discord and more, and as members of their group, together shared experiences such as fear, embarrassment, humor, and camaraderie. Ultimately, as pioneer women mariachis, they uniquely conveyed these human emotions, drawing an empathy from their audiences in ways unparalleled by male mariachis, becoming relatable to their audiences, which is the essence of Mariachi showmanship.

Photo 9.1: Mariachi Las Generalas, late 1970s. From the author's private photo collection.

The Women and the Times[1]

Maria Elena Munóz began singing in public as a child, in her Mexican home town of Vista Hermosa, Michoacán. At nine years old she won an *aficionados* radio contest that earned her a singing tour with a young Pedro Infante. She was a childhood friend of, and sometimes performed at school with, Amalia Mendoza, who would grow to be a national icon of the *ranchera* song, and who, along with her brothers Juan and José, would become known as *Los Tariácuris*. In the United States, in Los Angeles, Maria Elena's uncles made history when they started the first Mexican radio program there, *Los Madrugadores* (The Early Risers),[2] which was on at four o'clock in the morning, the reason for its name. Singing to her uncles' guitar accompaniment, Maria Elena was among the live entertainment featured on the show. She also performed with her father and brothers until she left the stage to become a wife and mother, as tradition and family expectations dictated, and would not return to it until years later, as a widow, and as the leader of a mariachi group.[3]

The idea to form an all-female mariachi group came from Maria Elena Munóz. It was the late 1970s, a time of change caused by the Women's Movement and the Chicano Movement, but socio-political Movements were not what motivated her. Maria Elena wanted to change the elitist bias that delegitimized mariachi music so close to her family's heart, and the male-only ideology that prevented women from participating in it. Her adult son, José Matías, was a mariachi in a group named *Los Vaqueros*, led by Fructoso Valdez. Like other mariachis, Fructoso considered Maria Elena's idea of a women's mariachi group as a degradation to the mariachi tradition, and women's involvement in mariachi music as a cultural deterioration. Other mariachis scoffed at *Las Generalas*, viewing it as ridiculous because they were women, and because they were not young.[4] According to Lupe Rodriguez, then a member of *Las Generalas*,[5] a male mariachi member of the group called Mariachi Martinez, told Maria Elena that she had no ear for music and should not waste her time forming the group. Maria Elena retorted with the assertiveness and determination that were her cornerstone in founding the group: *¡Usted no me va a decir lo que yo puedo y no puedo hacer!* [You are not going to tell me what I can and cannot do!] and forged ahead. She asked her son, José Matías, to help provide mariachi musical training to the group, and Fructoso's wife, Adela, to be co-founder of *Las Generalas*. The original group was composed of Juanita (trumpet), Adela Valdez (guitar), Maria Elena Muñoz (vihuela), Lupe Rodriguez and Marta (violins) Aurora Prado Pastrano (guitarrón), Elvira, and Maria Del Refugio (Photo 9.2).[6]

Adela Valdez loved to sing *rancheras* since she was a child. She would enter radio amateur contests, *aficionados*, supported by her mother but hiding from her father, who objected to having artists in his house. She grew up loving to sing with mariachis, which she would do whenever a group allowed her to join them

Photo 9.2: Mariachi Las Generalas, with instruments, c1970s. From the author's private photo collection.

in a song, but not having a mariachi mentor. When she was still a child her family moved to the United States, where she married a mariachi at the age of fourteen. She and her husband, Fructoso, formed a duo and performed throughout the southwest until they moved to Los Angeles, where he formed *Mariachi Los Vaqueros*. Although Adela continued to sing, Fructoso did not support her artistic pursuits after they began to have children.[7]

Years after Las Generalas disbanded, I interviewed Lupe Rodriguez. She told me that she had begun performing in a duo with her sister when they were young children. They called themselves *Dueto Hermanas Rodriguez*. Although they showed great artistic ability, their parents did not support the girls' pursuits in show business like they did the boys' in the family. As adults, Lupe and her sister performed at local events and venues in southern California, including the rodeo in Riverside, the Azteca Theater, and events in San Fernando, where they were offered contracts to continue performing. They also recorded together in 1971; however, their husbands were afraid that continuing would interfere with caring for their families so the sister act left the stage; Lupe would return to it a few years later, when she joined *Las Generalas*.

Lupe Rodriguez joined *Las Generalas* in November 1980. She had learned only the guitar prior to joining, but she became the violin player in the group, and like all the others, was also a vocalist. She always wore a white flower in her hair as her trademark. She recounts how she became part of the group:

> *Yo estaba muy activa en la iglesia y yo no sé como sabían de mí, cuando llegaron ellas muy encompetadas, Maria Elena y Adela. Llegaron muy pintadas, y dice Maria Elena, 'Buenas noches, venimos a buscar a una señora que nos dicen que canta muy bonito.' Una señora, dije yo, y siguió viniendo y viniendo a la casa y me dijo, 'Yo soy compositora.' Yo nomás le seguía la corriente, y venia y venia, y pense, [gestures with index finger circling around temple]. Empezé con Maria Elena en diferentes restaurantes y lugares y luego me decía, 'Quiero empezar un mariachi de mujeres.'*

> [I was very active in church and I don't know how they found out about me, when they came by, in big hairdos, Maria Elena and Adela, faces all made up, and Maria Elena says, 'Good evening, we are here looking for a lady who they tell us sings very pretty.' A lady, I thought, and she kept coming by and coming by to the house, and she told me, 'I am a composer. I want to start an all-women's mariachi group.' I just went along with her, but she kept coming over and coming over, and I thought ... [gestures with index finger circling temple]. I started with Maria Elena in restaurants and different venues.]

Lupe's account concurs with some of Reifler-Flores's description of how the women became participants in *Las Generalas*:

... the women were recruited from the local church choirs. María Elena went from church to church listening to the voices of the women who sang in the choir. When she heard a voice that she thought would complement the group she was trying to form, she would wait outside after the service and approach them with her project. If the woman were interested and she was married, María Elena would speak to the husband, requesting his permission for his wife to participate ... .Of each woman she [Maria Elena] asked what instrument they would like to play, each responded, 'Whatever you think.' None of the women had prior musical experience, except in the church choir. None played an instrument or had musicians in their families. Maria Elena purchased second hand instruments for the group using her own funds. The women didn't have extra funds to invest. They were all housewives. None of them worked outside the home. All had children. Two were single, the rest were married. They were all Mexican nationals.[8]

Reifler-Flores errs on some key descriptions of the women. In the case of Aurora Prado Pastrano, she was never in a choir nor active in church outside of attending Mass. Aurora believes that Adela or Maria Elena may have heard her sing and play her guitar at some event and that was how they contacted her about joining the group; however, it is likely that her stage reputation as *La Estrella de la Canción Romántica* somehow led to her recruitment into the group. She initially played the *guitarrón* provided by Maria Elena but later purchased and played her own for most of the time she was a member of the group. Her relationship with her husband, Nick, was such that she made her own decision to join, never needing or making use of Maria Elena's mediation. Most importantly, my mother was not a Mexican national; she was an American citizen by birth, a critical point because, as I have argued in this book, this made her mariachi performance especially meaningful as an expression of her cultural *Mexicanidad* and her Mexican American ethnic identity.

Grassroots Musicians, Street-Level Musical Education

Las Generalas as a group did lack formal musical training, something unsurprising as they were grassroots artists, and not unusual among mariachis, who traditionally did not learn the art through an academic education. As the music of the people, mariachi musicianship was learned informally, through apprenticeship; the apprentice learned it from a musician who learned it the same way, and the fundamental lesson was that its performance should be all about demonstrating the music's relevance to and relationship with the audience. This culturally based way of guiding and learning artistic performance in mariachi tradition is similar to the "street level education" associated with jazz musicianship, as Phillips describes it:

> 'Street Level' education is an informal phrase used colloquially amongst jazz musicians. It indicates the process of learning jazz through the act of performing the music in real world settings (or on the bandstand) and indicates a definitive separation from the process of learning jazz in an academic setting. Street level jazz education includes apprenticeships with older/established jazz musicians, learning the etiquette and performance of the music in the act of doing from/with those who are doing it, and gleaning the needed relationship between the music and listener from practical experience.[9]

What *was* unusual for mariachi *Las Generalas* was that the members lacked the essential apprenticeship typically afforded to prospective male mariachis at an early age. Traditionally, only boys were tutored because mariachi was an all-male domain; hence, unlike, or more than girls, boys had access to the tutor-apprentice relationship through their father, male relative, or other male mariachi musician. Boys also had access to the informal contexts of mariachi in which indoctrination takes place, such as mariachi hang outs or rehearsal sessions. The members of *Las Generalas* received only limited training in mariachi performance, from a single individual (some from José Matías; some from a member of Mariachi Martinez) and for a relatively short amount of time, and only after having formed or joined the group. Thus, they learned as a group rather than as individual apprentices. Also, the art of mariachi performance requires that every group member be able to perform vocals and play a mariachi instrument. Only four of the eight *Generalas* had previous public singing experience (Maria Elena, Adela, Aurora, and Lupe). Adela's knowledge of a few chords, Aurora's beginning guitar skills with different styles of Mexican music, and Lupe's home-taught guitar accompaniment provided a pool of talent with the guitar, but neither Aurora or Lupe knew how to play the instrument they each took on (guitarrón and violin, respectively) when the group formed, and none of the other four members had any experience playing an instrument at all.

The Test and the Lesson

By the time the group obtained their first contract to play at a major event, which was accompanying an internationally famous celebrity, *Las Generalas* truly were still amateurs. Either through misjudgment or overconfidence on the part of their leader, committing the group for an engagement of such magnitude was precipitous and perhaps foolhardy. On the other hand, it was Maria Elena's audacity to see this as an opportunity, to seize it, to take the risk and accept the challenge, that pushed this group of intrepid women to begin making history as an all-female mariachi group (Photo 9.3). Unfortunately, this came at a heavy price. According to my mother:

> *No eramos profesionales; eramos principiantes. Los instrumentos andaban por todos rumbos. Cuando vino Pepe Infante, el hermano de Pedro Infante, aquí a California, venía a presentarse en diferentes teatros. Y nosotras, porque eramos baratas. No sabíamos, los instrumentos andaban por ningun rumbo. Él quería que lo acompañaramos y no sabíamos ningún tono. Así que nos apedraron, nos tiraron con tomates y todo, allí en Bakersfield.*

[We were not professionals; we were beginners. The instruments were going all over the place. When Pepe Infante, the brother of Pedro Infante, came here to California, he was coming to appear at different theaters. And us, because we were inexpensive. We didn't know. The instruments were going in every direction. He wanted us to accompany him and we didn't know any [tones, pitches]. So, they stoned us, they threw tomatoes and everything at us, there in Bakersfield.]

Photo 9.3: Poster of event in Bakersfield in which Las Generalas were to accompany famous singer Pepe Infante. November 19, 1982. From the private archives of Aurora Prado Pastrano.

The devastation they went through for their performance at that event was not all they experienced that day. Lupe was also sexually harassed in a situation bordering on assault, as she explained to me years later:

> *No nos pagaron. Luego se oyó el comentario que, si hubiéramos sido más condescendientes con los viejos, los organizadores, hubiéramos ido mas adelante, pero no. A mi se me hace que era de narco mafiosos. Andábamos en mucho peligro. Uno de ellos, de los cantantes, quería que los acompañáramos y no quisimos. Yo fui la primera que dijo que no. No podíamos. Cuando terminamos de tocar nos íbamos a subir al van, cuando él me jaloneó para que me subiera en el carro con él, en un carro lleno de hombres y yo diciéndoles no, no, y nadie me ayudó y brinqué adentro del van. Es que la música nos gusta tanto. Y regresamos sin dinero.*

> [They didn't pay us. Then someone said that if we had been more accommodating with those men, the organizers, we might've done better, but no. I believe that it was a narco-mafia. We were in much danger. One of them, one of the singers, wanted us to accompany them [with the song] and we didn't want to. I was the first one to say no. We couldn't. When we finished playing and we were getting in the van, he pulled me to get me to go in the car with him, in a car full of men, and me telling them no, no, and no one would help me, and I managed to jump inside the van. It's just that we love the music so much. And we returned without any money.]

For grassroots artists with a street-level education, experiencing public rejection and humiliation most likely are not uncommon in the artist's early career, an important difference from an academically trained musical artist. The artist with a musical education may learn to perform a written musical piece adequately, regardless of its cultural origin, by reading the sheet music, but a street-level musician like a mariachi or jazz musician without academic musical training, draws strictly from their apprenticeship, their empirical, subjective knowledge and creativity. The need to demonstrate a keen musical ear and a robust knowledge of cultural music, maintain the cultural symbolism in any musical innovation, relate to the audience through musical interpretation, and do so without the guidance of sheet music or conductor, places the artistic burden solely on the performer who is serious about the art. In turn, the audience of a street-level musician measures its appreciation for the performance with the same criteria. While artistic innovation and creativity are expected by the audience, it bases its degree of approval on the performer's ability to honor the cultural significance of the music in the performance. Succeeding at this in mariachi musicianship takes apprenticeship and/or a live performing experience that involves trial and error. Failure is not an end-all for the beginning street-level or grassroots musician who has no fame to damage. Failing to impress an audience may be common at the start, but how the performer handles that failure may determine whether there will be a future artistic career. Damani Phillips shows this as he describes his own experience with failure and humiliation:

> One of my more memorable incidents happened at Baker's Keyboard Lounge, one of Detroit's most established jazz clubs … I was called up by Teddy [Harris] to play on a song one night, and after being asked if I would be okay with the tune I replied 'yes.' In reality, I did not know the chord changes to the tune and was a bit overconfident in my abilities to use my ears to "hear" my way through the song. The song began and my performance of the melody was abysmal, at best. As the solo section of the tune began, I easily missed 80% of the chord changes during the first 2 choruses–but kept playing as if I was somehow going to *make* what I was playing fit the chord progression. As we got a few measures into the 3rd chorus, Teddy stopped playing, stopped the rest of the band, slowly turned to me and said, 'Young man, get the fuck off the stage!' The most embarrassing musical moment of my life had just transpired in front of a packed house at the top jazz club in town.
>
> … After a few days of licking my wounds, I made it my mission to reclaim my respect! … I went back to Baker's … This time around, however, I played it like I owned it. From that day forward, Teddy and the rest of the cats in the band were very welcoming, open, and generous with their tutelage. I didn't understand at first, but this whole ordeal was simultaneously a lesson and a test. The lesson was that, if you don't know a tune well enough to play it competently, don't say that you do. It's both dishonest and disrespectful to the music and musicians you're playing with. The test was to see how I would rebound from the events of the prior week. Would I fold up shop and never return, or would I come back stronger as a result? In the eyes of these giants of Detroit jazz, returning well-prepared earned their respect, and conversely, their willingness to take me under their wing.[10]

The humiliation that *Las Generalas* went through at the Bakersfield, California event, so similar to Phillips's experience, was equally unforgettable but pivotal for the group. After traveling for hours, they returned home unpaid and disgraced. But this did not make them desist. The experience fueled their determination to continue to grow artistically to become a true professional mariachi group, because to do so offered the chance to express their love of the music. It would take far more learning, practice, commitment, and experience on their part; and this it did. Rehearsals intensified, along with the courage and determination, the *ganas*, to become mariachis. According to my mother:

> *Practicábamos– dos veces por semana. Me acuerdo que eran los miércoles y no me acuerdo que otro día. Durábamos horas practicando una sola canción. A Nick no le gustaba que yo fuera. Salía de la casa a estas horas, y no llegaba hasta de noche.*

[We practiced–twice a week. I remember it was on Wednesdays and I don't recall what other day. We would be practicing for hours for just a single song. Nick didn't like that I went. I would leave the house about this time in the afternoon, and I didn't get home until nighttime.][11]

Rising to the Challenge: Becoming Professionals

Las Generalas overcame the humiliation they suffered on the Bakersfield stage, to become a respected professional group. Their professional status was evidenced by their repertory, musical form, performance contexts,[12] instrumentation,[13] mariachi performance dress,[14] and paid playing engagements (Photo 9.4). They wore matching embellished mariachi *trajes* with long skirts, except for sombreros, in uniform colors such as brown, maroon, cream, and the traditional black. The eight

Photo 9.4: Promotional poster of event featuring Mariachi Las Generalas. c1983. From the private archive collection of Aurora Prado Pastrano.

members fulfilled the number of musicians that would define a fully equipped mariachi group, and their instruments included a vihuela, two violins, two guitars, two trumpets, and a guitarrón. Their repertory was typical for mariachis, including *rancheras, corridos, sones, boleros,* and of course, the Sunday Mass music (See Appendix A).

San Gabriel Mission church, itself an historic landmark, is also historic as the very site where *Las Generalas* formed their pioneer all-female mariachi group. Sunday Mass at that church became their standing weekly engagement. As amateurs and later as professionals, *Las Generalas* played for the Mass every Sunday, for free. Otherwise, their paid engagements included *chambas (gigs) de planta*, (playing at private and public events and venues) and shows. They were also a featured act at political campaigns in the Mexican American community, including one event held at Plaza de la Raza (formerly called Lincoln Park) in Lincoln Heights, in support of governor Jerry Brown, and another for assemblywoman, Gloria Molina.

Through their son and husband who were mariachis, Maria Elena and Adela respectively, knew Mariachi etiquette and professionalism and they used this knowledge to set rules of comportment for the group. Mariachis should not consort with members of the audience at any time they are working. The audience is encouraged to interact with the mariachi performers, but this is done within specific cultural limits, when the audience is invited by the mariachi group to demonstrate its enjoyment of the music and its approval of the performance by joining in the performance itself with yells, cheers, and singing along with the chorus of specific songs. Outside this form of interaction, mariachis in *traje* maintain a line of physical and social distance from the audience during breaks. This is considered part of the respect paid to the Mariachi tradition represented in the *traje*.

Their adopted rules of etiquette went even farther for *Las Generalas*, who recognized they were setting a precedent for the participation of women artists in a traditionally male musical world. As women mariachis, *Las Generalas* dealt with certain safety concerns, as in the sexual harassment Lupe experienced in Bakersfield, and felt the need to ensure safeguards in their work. To help prevent problems, they refused bookings at bars and avoided engagements that would keep them late in the evening, or that could "get out of hand."[15]

Las Generalas also dealt with internal tensions and conflict affecting the group. In one case, Marta, one of the violinists in the group, broke the rules by drinking at the bar and dancing with an event guest while in her *traje*. Her actions provoked disapproval from the other group members, who saw it as inviting disrespect to themselves as women, and a reprimand from Maria Elena, leading to an argument. In a different situation, Maria Elena, who provided rides to the women to and from their homes, supposedly to help them avoid problems with their husbands and to offer them transportation, created a strain for Lupe:

> *Yo no manejaba. María Elena me llevaba y me traía, y ustedes creían que yo era la consentida de ella. Me sentía muy manipulada por ella. Me sentía yo manipulada, absorbida por ella y no podía obedecer a mi esposo, como que yo no tenía vida propia. Cuando me liberé de ella, dije Gracias a Dios.*

> [I didn't drive. Maria Elena would pick me up and bring me back and you all thought that I was her favorite. I felt very manipulated by her. I felt manipulated. I couldn't obey my husband, as if I had no life of my own. When I freed myself of her, I thought, Thank God.][16]

Discord in general is not unusual among mariachi groups. With the frequent interactions among the members demanded by rehearsals and engagements, tensions are prone to rise and misunderstandings and disagreements to occur, especially when the members are unfamiliar with all the nuances involved in being a mariachi, as would be particularly true among an all-female group:

> Because women's presence in mariachi challenges some of the basic conceptions of who should perform this music and how it should be done, the tensions revealed expose key conceptualizations of traditionalism, nationalism, ethnicity, race, and gender in their active, performative usage.[17]

As Las Generalas learned their lesson and passed the very stringent test that challenged their survival as a group, rebounding after their worst performance, part of their reward was gaining the respect and acceptance of other mariachi groups. According to Lupe Rodriguez:

> *Cómo tocamos en Iglesias nosotras. En Santa Cecilia, dijo el padre, ¿'Quien es la vocalista?' y dice Adela, 'todas somos, todas cantamos.' Y luego, estaban unos mariachis y ¡Híjole! Unos mariachis de a de veras, y dijeron ellos, 'Nosotros las seguimos' y luego, salimos bien y después salimos todos de la misa y tocamos todos La Negra y otras más. ¡Una cosa tan bonita! Y me acuerdo en una boda, un Mariachi de jovencitos y nos dijeron, 'Ustedes nos enseñan las canciones' porque no sabían cantar, y ellos nos enseñaban a tocar.*

> [How we played in churches. At Santa Cecilia, the priest asked us, 'Who is the vocalist?' and Adela says, 'we are, we all sing.' And then, there was a Mariachi group, Gees! They were a true Mariachi group, and they said, 'we'll follow you' and we did well, so afterward, we all came out of Mass and we all played *La Negra* and some other songs together. What a beautiful thing! And I remember at a wedding, a youth Mariachi group, and they said to us, 'You show us the songs' because they didn't know how to sing, and they showed *us* how to play.][18]

Their main reward was winning the empathy and praise of their audiences. Their hard work showed in their artistic ability, though it may have never reached a quality worthy of national fame. As my mother recently recalled, *Fíjate, ¡Cuando empezamos ninguna sabia tocar el instrumento y todas aprendimos!* [Just think, when we started none of us knew how to play the instrument, and we all learned!] and as Maria Elena reportedly said, "We never were very good, but we worked a lot" (Photo 9.5).[19]

Perhaps the most historically important part of *Las Generalas*, is that as pioneer women mariachis, they turned the significance of their gender from a barrier into a unique form of connection with their audience through their performance, to the point that it earned them privileges not afforded to male mariachis. As Lupe recalled:

> *Nosotras tenemos tantas cosas chistosas de contar. Unos novios nos dijeron 'que nos toquen 'El Cochinilla',' era gente de Mexicali y así le dicen, 'pues ándale.' Llegó la boda. María Elena y yo la íbamos a cantar. María Elena se llevó la letra, pero no se ve bien que estemos leyendo y cantando, y no podía leer sin lentes y traía la letra en la mano, leyéndola de lejos, y se la acercó–estaba al revés. ¡Y una risa! Toda la gente riéndose, y Aurora y Marta y las demás muy serias, seguían toque y toque y nosotras riéndonos más, y la gente toda riéndose. Le dije a María Elena, 'no nos van a pagar,' pero cuando acabamos, hasta nos sentaron en una mesa.*

Photo 9.5: Promotional poster of event featuring *Mariachi Las Generalas* as guests of honor. January 28, 1983. From the private archive collection of Aurora Prado Pastrano.

La demás gente se sirvió sola, y a nosotras nos sirvieron, 'Ándenle, Muchachas' y nos pusieron cajas de cervezas. Después el señor ... [an unnamed mariachi] *nos dijo, 'porque son mujeres. Si hubiéramos sido nosotros los hombres, no nos hubieran dejado salirnos con eso.'*

[We have so many funny things to relate. A bride and groom-to-be asked us to play at their wedding, and to play the song, *El Cochinilla*, which is a popular song among people from Mexicali, like them. Well, sure. The wedding day arrived. Maria Elena and I were going to sing it. Maria Elena had taken along the written lyrics, but it doesn't look good for us to be reading while singing the song, and she couldn't read without her glasses and she had the written song in her hand, reading it from a distance, and when she brought it up close, it was upside down. How we laughed! All the people laughing, and Aurora and Marta and the rest of them, very serious, they kept on playing and playing while we were just laughing, and the people all were laughing. I told Maria Elena, 'they're not going to pay us' but when we finished, they even seated us at a table. The rest of the people (guests) had to serve themselves but we were served, 'Come on, girls' and they put boxes of beer at our table. Later, Mr. ... (an unnamed mariachi) told us, 'It's because you are women. If it had been us men, they wouldn't have let us get away with something like that.']

The Finale, Aurora and Lupe Rodriguez

On a Sunday afternoon, years after the disbanding of *Las Generalas*, my mother and I sit with Lupe and her husband, Sylvestre, and their numerous children, children's spouses, and grandchildren in the backyard of their family's home. They are celebrating one of their daughters' birthday and I ask permission to use our conversation as an interview with Lupe for the book. I receive a unanimous approval, as one of her adult children says it would give everyone a chance to hear about their mom's life as a mariachi:

Alicia: *Quien le enseñó a cantar?* [Who taught you to sing?]
Lupe: *De nacimiento, desde muy chiquita.* [From birth, since I was very young.]
Alicia: *Quien le enseñó a tocar la guitarra?* [Who taught you to play guitar?]
Lupe: *Mi papá. Somos doce hermanos. Un hermano agarraba la guitarra, el otro el peine, y todos cantaban. Todos tocaban nomás de oído. Mi mamá y papá cantaban mucho. Había mucha alegría en la casa.*

[My father. We are twelve siblings. One sibling would take the guitar, another the comb, and everyone sang. Everyone played only by ear. There was a lot of joyfulness at home.]

Sylvestre: *Fíjese que Lupe viene de una familia muy numerosa. Son doce, seis y seis, y todos una voz, pero [kisses his fingers], pero sus papás no la apoyaban; a los hijos si les permitían, pero–Lupe y su hermana–pudieron haber hecho bastante pero nunca les dieron permiso.*

[You know, Lupe comes from a very numerous family. There are twelve, six and six, and they all have such a voice [kissing his fingers, indicating he's referring to something very fine], but her parents didn't give her any support. They did permit the sons, but – Lupe and her sister could have done very much, but they never gave them permission.]

Lupe: *Mi hermana y yo nos presentamos en el Teatro Azteca en vestido de lentejuela y se presentó por primera vez, Felipe Arriaga. Nosotras casadas y con hijos, pos–no pudimos mucho, pero para el jaripeo en Riverside–Pero luego llegaron los contratos y se asustaron los maridos, 'Ay Lupe, ¿y luego los hijos?'*
Hicimos un disco, mi hermana y yo en 1971, y fue cuando nos contrataron en San Fernando y luego nos querían contratar– Sylvestre hasta quería divorciarse de mi.

[My sister and I performed at Teatro Azteca, in sequined dress, in an event that featured the first public appearance of Felipe Arriaga. We were each married and with children, well, we couldn't do much, but we did the rodeo in Riverside–but then the contracts started coming and that scared our husbands, 'Ay, Lupe, and what about the children?' We recorded, my sister and I, in 1971, and it was then that we got contracted in San Fernando and they wanted to contract us–but Sylvestre even wanted to divorce me.]

I bring up Lupe's participation in the mariachi group and ask her and Sylvestre how it affected their relationship at home:

Sylvestre: *Trabajaban viernes, sábado y domingo.* [They worked Friday, Saturday and Sunday.]
Alicia: *¿Y como se sentia usted de eso?* [And how did you feel about that?]
Sylvestre *¡O, pues muy orgulloso! A pesar de estar en el mariachi, nunca desatendió a los muchachos, y mucho menos a mí.*

[Oh, well, very proud! In spite of being in the mariachi group, she never neglected the children, and much less me.]

Lupe: *A veces andaba con tremendo dolor de cabeza. Salía yo apurada porque no tenía tiempo con tanta familia y nomás oía la música y me sentía bien. Llegaba a la casa y me sentía mal otra vez. A veces salía yo pintándome las uñas porque con tanta familia no tenía tiempo.*

[At times I would have a tremendous headache. I would leave (the house) in a hurry because I never had time with such a big family and as soon as I would hear the music

I would feel well. I would return home and would feel ill again. Sometimes I would be polishing my nails as I was leaving because with such a big family, I didn't have time.]

As the mother of ten, managing traditional cultural expectations as mother and wife along with the demands of being a mariachi, Lupe unknowingly became a role model for other women:

Una vez fuimos con la Asociación de Cantantes y Compositores, y Rubén y María Elena, y el presidente de la Asociación, al Canal 46. Allí mismo me maquillaron. Yo no sabía, pero era para preguntarme que como le hacía para atender a mis hijos, y María Elena se metía y contestaba, y se metía a contestar, y entonces le dijeron, 'por favor, déjela a ella que conteste.' Me dijeron, 'La entrevistamos a usted para que las mujeres vean que pueden hacer muchas cosas.' Es que la mujer Mexicana cree que se casó y allí esta pisada.

[We once went with The Association of Singers and Composers and Ruben and Maria Elena and the President of the Association, to Channel 46. They put make up on me right there (at the station). I didn't know but it was to ask me how I managed to tend to my kids, and Maria Elena kept answering, getting in and answering, and then they told her, 'Please, let her answer.' They told me, 'We wanted to interview you so that women are able to see that they can do many things.' It's because a Mexican woman believes that once she is married, that's it, she is pinned down.]

With obvious pride in her voice and looking around the yard at her children's smiling faces she added that her kids are all good kids.

Someone brings out her guitar and hands it to her. The cacophony of voices speaking in Spanish and English suddenly quiets down. Lupe and my mom choose a song to sing, one by Cuco Sánchez, *Que Manera de Perder*. When they finish singing it, Lupe's daughter, Griselda, comments: *¡Mom, no ha pasado ni un dia desde la ultima vez que cantaron!* [Mom, not a day has gone by since the last time you two sang!]

The paired voices of the two former mariachi women do sound beautiful. Lupe takes out the capo, adjusting it on the guitar as she and my mom decide on another song. Griselda says she remembers when the group used to play *Cruz de Olvido* and asks them to play it, adding:

I remember going to their practices, above the bakery in San Gabriel. My dad would always take us, and he'd drive to the park while my mom practiced (with the group). *¿Qué año, Mom?* [What year, Mom? 81?] I was ten. We spent a lot of days in my dad's car waiting for my mom.]

Griselda's siblings chime in their agreement. Then Lupe and my mom begin singing from their mariachi and duo repertory: *De Que Manera Te Olvido*,[20] as

Photo 9.6: Aurora Prado Pastrano, in Mariachi *traje*, 1994. From the private photo collection of the author.

everyone lets out "oohs" and "ahhs," *No Señor, Yo No Me Casaré, Piquetes de Hormiga*, (Lupe's other daughter, Delia, joins in this song), and *Hay Unos Ojos*. They then do a song each. Lupe sings *La Malagueña*, with a beautiful vibrato; then my mom sings one of my favorites, *Cancionero*. This would be the last opportunity to meet with Lupe and her family, as we lost contact with them over the years, but as the evening closes in, the two women do their finale, *Hay Que Saber Perder*, making it very difficult for the rest of us to leave (Photo 9.6).

Notes

1. The first-hand interview information that I was able to obtain, other than from my mother, was from Lupe Rodriguez, another original member of the group. The passing of time and lost ties left me unable to locate and include the other group members who were close with my mother.
2. Loza, 1993.
3. Reifler-Flores, 2015.
4. Reifler-Flores, 2015.
5. All the information from Lupe Rodriguez that I include here I obtained on one occasion, during a visit to her family home circa May 2010.
6. Both Aurora and Elvira were to be the guitarrón players, but according to Lupe, Elvira did not succeed because she wouldn't study or practice "Es que no estudiaba." Elvira did not remain long

with the group. Also, at some point during the group's startup time, they used the assistance of a male trumpetist, Manuel Lopez.
7. Reifler-Flores, 2015
8. Reifler-Flores, 2015, p. n.
9. Phillips, 2017, p. 18.
10. Phillips, 2017, p. 5.
11. Aurora Prado Pastrano, interview May 11, 2020.
12. Pearlman, 1984.
13. Sheehy, 2006.
14. Perez, 2016.
15. Reifler-Flores, 2015, p. n.
16. From the interview with Lupe, circa May, 2010.
17. Jáquez, 2002, p. 168.
18. Ibid.
19. Reifler-Flores, 2015, p. n.
20. Federico Mendez Tejeda, composer; popularized by Vicente Fernandez.

References

Jáquez, C. F. (2002). Meeting la Cantante Through Verse, Song, and Performance. In N. C. Najera-Ramirez (Ed.), *Chicana Traditions: Continuity and Change* (pp. 167–182). Urbana and Chicago: University of Illinois.

Loza, S. (1993). *Barrio Rhythm: Mexican American Music in Los Angeles.* Urbana and Chicago: University of Illinois.

Muñoz, N. (2007–2020). Mujeres en el Mariachi. https://www.mujeresenelmariachi.com

Pearlman, S. R. (1984). Standarization and Innovation in Mariachi Music Performance in Los Angeles. *Pacific Review of Ethnomusicology, 1*, 1–12.

Perez, X. (2016, August 11). Women Transcend Traditional Roles – of Mariachi, Share in Spotlight. *The San Diego Union Tribune*, p. 14.

Phillips, D. (2017). *What Is This Thing Called Soul: Conversations on Black Culture and Jazz Education.* New York: Peter Lang.

Reifler Flores, C. (2015). Las Generalas: Origins of Women's Participation in Mariachi and the Cultural and Transnational Implications. *Karpa, 8*, n.p.

Sheehy. (2006). *Mariachi Music in America: Experiencing Music, Expressing Culture.* New York: Oxford University Press.

EPILOGUE

Fallaste, Corazón: Legacies, Closures, and Failings of the Heart

From the Montclair Canyon east of Los Angeles, blare the sounds of Chicano music. The year is 2021 and the pandemic cannot stop the music makers or the music lovers; it only forces their adaptation to the public health conditions. It's a drive-in concert, pay-per-car, people sitting to watch and listen in their vehicles. Hard to do because the music moves you. The headliner that evening is Suavé The Band. It is tagged as a "Latin" showband. They have a strong horn section and are known for their cover of bands like Earth, Wind and Fire, Tower of Power, and Chicago, and for playing Jazz, R&B, Rock, Top 40, Swing, *Cumbias, Merengues, Cha-Cha-Chá,* and *Boleros.* It's the kind of music and the kind of band that plays at clubs all over L. A. and its environs, catering to Mexican American, white and diverse audiences. Like similar bands, "Suavé" also does casuals, gigs at *quinceañeras,* weddings, and corporate events and also like similar bands, they are featured at Disneyland, on Baja cruise ships to Ensenada, and the Battle of the Bands. On weekends, usually Sundays, at the Santa Fe Springs Swap Meet, a predominance of Mexican American people stroll along to shop, eat *elotes* and *tacos al carbón,* drink *Horchata* and *Jamaica,* and listen and dance to Suavé The Band or similar bands, their kids busy being kids, acculturated to the English language and its mainstream musical sounds of today, yet all the while their ears and eyes absorbing the legacy of their Chicano music history.

Eddie Chavira and Suavé The Band

Rene Burguan (band leader, trumpet) formed Suavé The Band in 1998. The other members include, Danny Balancio (trombone), Eddie Chavira (sax, flute and backup vocals), Tony Shogren (drums), Carlo Tanori (bass guitar), Javier Marquez (guitar), Christian Boyd (keyboard), and Veronica Carrillo (vocals).[1] As is characteristic of grassroots bands in Los Angeles, the members have day jobs, but as their webpage suggests, they play in the band because they are good at making music, and/or because they love doing it.

Playing the saxophone was not really a result of Eddie's proclivity for it nor did he originally intend to develop it into a particular musical style. His second grade teacher noticed his musical ability and convinced his parents that it should be nurtured. They followed her recommendation, although within their financial limitations. He explained how he came to study the saxophone:

> Mom and dad went to a thrift store. It happened to have a sax and because it was on sale, it was the cheapest instrument there, so dad said, 'that's what you're going to play.'[2]

Nevertheless, playing the sax, he gravitated toward a Latin musical style.

Eddie has been with Suavé The Band for about fifteen years. He has been playing in bands since about 1973, at almost seventeen, when he started with a band called Fantasy, which he describes as "versatile." Fantasy played "ballads, Mexican music, and some Top 40, mostly casual." In the 1980s, he joined The Mob, which also played what he calls "Latin tunes" and did casual engagements like *quinceañeras* and high school dances. He eventually joined Powerhouse, the band he played with the longest before joining Sangria. Both bands were known for their musical repertories, instrumentations with a horn section, and great vocals with female leads. Powerhouse had two trumpets, a trombone, and the sax. Both bands were unforgettable with the music they produced onstage. Tables at events or clubs were usually empty because people got up to dance as soon as Sangria started playing. Powerhouse was more of a show band; their audiences listened and watched more than they danced. It was also a racially mixed group: white, black, Chinese American, Mexican American. They played mostly Top 40, as well as *boleros*, including what to Mexican American audiences in Los Angeles, is the requisite, *Sabor a Mi*.

Like many people who grew up in East Los Angeles, Eddie Chavira is a *pocho*. He is like many other Mexican American descendants of at least one immigrant parent, a member of the second and subsequent generation continuum that muddies any attempt to define or describe Mexican Americans and other Latinos as a single social identity. He is bilingual, though his understanding of Spanish is greater and quicker than his ability to speak it, or to speak it comfortably with a native Spanish speaker. He exemplifies the diversity that characterizes Mexican Americans in such ways as our spoken languages (Spanish, English, Indigenous, others), how assimilated and acculturated we are to United States mainstream culture, how much we identify with our Mexican cultural roots, how much knowledge and understanding we each have about our Mexican/Chicano/Latino history, and how we differ in the musical styles we experience or prefer.

Eddie grew up hearing various genres of Mexican music, black soul, jazz, Motown, R&B oldies, other styles, and mainstream music, the pop hits that filled the airwaves and music scenes. The *rancheras* and *boleros* that he heard were those most listened to among young Mexican Americans in L.A. He also knows mariachi music because it is part of his cultural music, because he is a musician (though not himself a mariachi), and because it is almost impossible to live in Los Angeles, especially East L.A., not having heard or seen a mariachi band, but also because he grew up having a mariachi aunt, named Aurora Prado Pastrano.

David Chanes

David Chanes grew up in East Los Angeles, where he was a local musician of Mexican music since he was a teenager, in the 1950s. His musical mentor was his older brother, a *requinto* player and a perfectionist when it came to playing music. His brother could detect the slightest imperfection in David's playing, and would quickly bring it to his attention. David admired his brother's musical ability so much, that he would spend days re-learning the part he missed until he perfected it. While still in high school, his own dedication to the music made him prefer to go home and practice the guitar and the *requinto* rather than participate in extracurricular school activities. He became a master *requintista* and credited his mentor for his own skill, but, as he told me, "I was never as good as my brother."

According to David, in the 1970s, he was playing with a group named Los Brillantes. They were popular throughout southern California and were featured at Disneyland and other notable venues and events throughout the region, but one performance was especially memorable to him: A concert held at the Santa Anita Racetrack. Natividad Cano's Mariachi Los Camperos were the star group, with the special appearance of the great Amalia Mendoza. Los Brillantes were supposed to be the opening act, but as David explained to me:

> I got there very early because I was so excited that we were going to be in the same show with Amalia Mendoza. I got there very early. I was in the trailer, I was the first one there, when pretty soon, Amalia Mendoza came in. She had come early too. *Y le dije, 'Un placer conocerla, Señorita Mendoza' y me dijo, 'Por favor no me llame Señorita Mendoza. Mi nombre es Amalia. Llámame Amalia.' Era muy amable.* [It is a pleasure to meet you, Miss Mendoza, and she said, 'Please don't call me Miss Mendoza. My name is Amalia. Please call me Amalia.' She was so friendly, so kind.]
>
> We talked for a long time, and then she asked if she could sing with my group, in the opening of the show. I was very honored. That was not how the program was supposed to go, my group was just the opening act, so Nati Cano got very upset with me, but it was Amalia Mendoza's idea to sing with my group.

I met David circa 2007, when the trio he was part of, Sol Y Luna, was appearing at the Del Mar Restaurant (formerly named "Asaderos") in Yucaipa, California, east of Los Angeles. David (*requinto*), and Eddie Farias (guitar) the core of the trio, along with the third member, who varied (guitar or violin), were the entertainment offered by *la casa* there every Friday, from five to nine p.m. As a traditional trio, they played and sang mostly *boleros,* but they also played other traditional Mexican music, including *rancheras* and *corridos*. They played from table to table, and I never knew them to fail to meet the clientele's requests. David, in particular, seemed to know the lyrics and music to every old Mexican song. When the other trio members were unsure of the song, or of the full lyrics, they were able to please the audience by following his lead, as the focus was usually on him, because the requinto player embellishes the song.[3] They also fulfilled requests for English songs, including country, rock, oldies, and songs by specific artists like Johnny Cash, Patsy Cline, Nat King Cole, The Eagles, Credence, and The Beatles, among others. The trio also brought liveliness to the evening by interacting with the clientele with their friendly salutations and good-natured humor, something that is more typical of Mariachis working *al talón* or *de planta*, than of trios. It was also a demonstration of the love the trio had for their music and its performance.

Legacies

Grassroot groups like Suave the Band, Fantasy, The Mob, Sangria, Powerhouse, and Sol y Luna, like the multitude of other music artists and groups that abound in the region, are links in the chain of musical performers who have kept the West Coast East Side Sound alive. They are the legacies of the earlier artists who connected us to our musical heritage represented in the many original genres of music and song. The current East Side Sound is today's evolved version, with artists that reflect their own subjectivities in their musical innovations, yet still honor our musical heritage in new productions of our cultural music. The many culturally, racially, ethnically and gender-mixed bands and the variety of performing groups, including bandas, conjuntos, trios, mariachis, rock bands, and other traditional, contemporary and hybrid music groups and individual artists that abound, are all a thriving, robust demonstration of today's diverse and inclusive East Side Sound that yet continues to mark and celebrate the music that defines us culturally, our *Latinismo*.

Through her mentorship, her dedication to performance, and her wholehearted love of music, Aurora Prado Pastrano connected new generations to our musical past, creating cultural bridges that would help us to continue to build our cultural history represented in our music, just like Aparicio noted about the Latina salsa music icon[4]:

> ... Celia Cruz's vocality and song repertoire literally create a hemispheric community of Latino and Latin American listeners that crosses generations, national borders and cultural divides. It serves as a vehicle of cultural memory that unifies Latinos, at least temporarily, across age and national borders.

As *La Estrella de la Canción Romántica*, Aurora Prado's musical performances were trans-racial, trans-class, trans-generational, trans-national and gender-inclusive; and as one of *Las Generalas*, Aurora Prado Pastrano's legacy as a mariachi pioneer was to mark the affirmation of women's contribution to the production and circulation of Mexican songs and styles from the history and collective memory and experience of Mexico to the Mexican diaspora.

Closures

The passing of years and her stage in life have not slowed Aurora Prado Pastrano's love of music and her desire to perform it. At age 94, her memory refuses to let go of those old lyrics and melodies that always filled her life (Photo E.1). Until recently, when her hands finally refused to obey her will, she would accompany herself with the guitar at home, in private, and at every family gathering. To my knowledge, her last stage performance as a recognized local artist was for a Cinco de Mayo pageant celebration sponsored by San Bernardino City College, in San Bernardino, California, where she sang, *Cuando Dos Almas*, accompanying herself with the guitar. Now unable to play the guitar, she still plays songs like Perfidia and Begin the Beguine on the piano, at home (Photo E.2). Her hearing is almost gone without the boost of a hearing aid, but she still is happiest when she sings. She and I spend our times together singing, especially our favorite *boleros*, such as *La Hiedra*, and *rancheras*, like *Grítenme Piedras Del Campo*. She taught her grandson,

Photo E.1: Aurora Prado Pastrano, examining her guitarrón. December, 2020. From the private photo collection of the author.

Photo E.2: Aurora Prado Pastrano, up late playing the piano. December 2020. From the private photo collection of the author.

Patrick, to strum *huapangos*, *rancheras*, and other Mexican musical rhythms on the guitar and he accompanies his nana singing songs of yesteryear. In the last decade or so, she became a fan of Freddy Fender and the love songs he sang in his *Tejano* musical style. She loves to listen to his recordings, though the *conjunto Tejano* music still does not inspire her generally. Her skill at narrative and prose keep her actively writing her life stories and constructing new song lyrics, through which she continues to relate her life's story and her world view.

While preparing this book, I went looking through the collection of photos and other memorabilia she has collected through the years (Photo E.3). The memories she holds in these items showed a never-ending effort to learn and celebrate music. She collected old *cancioneros*, books with song lyrics, of songs popularized by her favorite artists, in Spanish and English.

Aurora Prado Pastrano celebrated her 90th birthday with one of her usual impromptu performances, singing one of her favorite soft *ranchera* songs, *Guitarras de Media Noche*, with her friends, David Chanes, Eddie Farias, and Negro, the Trio Sol Y Luna, at Del Mar Restaurant (https://www.youtube.com/watch?v=3ByZOq3GCe4). She was still shameless when she asked to sing a song or two with them, and her audaciousness still provoked in me that old mix of embarrassment and pride I felt as a six-year-old child. To my continued relief, most of the people there seemed impressed. Perhaps some listened as a show of respect, presumably due to her age, and still others showed indifference or perhaps annoyance at the interruption to their dining or conversation, making me cringe at the thought. It is as if time stood still since my earliest childhood memories of my mother singing on that stage at the church fair.

Photo E.3: Some of the Cancioneros in Aurora Prado Pastrano's private collection.

While spending an evening together listening to some of my mother's favorite music, as usual, she began to recall old songs, and sang one that she said reminds her of her grandmother, *El Hijo Desobediente*. Then, the song, *"Fallaste Corazón"* began to play. It was 2021 and ten months into the COVID-19 Pandemic. Drawing silent and pensive, she said to me:

> Esa fue la última canción que canté con el trío allí en Asaderos.[5] Esa noche había mucha gente. El lugar estaba más lleno que nunca, y cuando la empecé a cantar, se entusiasmó la gente. Fue la última noche que estuve allí. Después de esa noche cerraron. Todo se cerró, ahorita parece un ghost town.

> [That was the last song that I sang with the trio there at Asaderos. That night there were a lot of people. The place was more filled than ever, and when I started singing, the people became quite enthused by it. It was the last night that I was there. After that night, they closed down. Everything closed down. Right now, it looks like a ghost town.]

The pandemic lent a tragically poetic context to the end of my mother's public performance. It would take only something this extreme to make her stop doing what she loves most, with the artist friends who always welcomed her to join them in their performance, and who she grew to appreciate the most among her music colleagues. On that Friday evening, it was by chance that Negro happened to fill in as the third member of the trio Sol y Luna in that restaurant. It seemed almost ordained that it should be her last performance with him, the person who, fifty years earlier, jump-started her performing career when he invited her onto the stage to sing *Mucho Corazón* with his Conjunto Papaloápan in that nightclub in East Los Angeles. Many years later, in her old age, my mother would look forward to Friday evenings, when she could go to that restaurant in Yucaipa, California to listen to the trio and join them in a song or two, and they kindly welcoming her, enhancing her singing with their masterful sounds of requinto, guitars, and unforgettable voices.

David Chanes, Eddie Farias, Negro, and Aurora Prado Pastrano each were local artists whose fame reached geographic and temporal limits. As Mexican American artists, they had in common a vast knowledge and a love of their Mexican cultural music, which they truly enjoyed sharing with their listeners (Photo E.4). That David and Aurora should say goodbye to performance and to each other that way, forced by the pandemic, the retirement and subsequent passing of David, and simultaneous relocation of my mother, was truly elegiac.

Failings of the Heart

The final song that my mother performed in public also marked a closure to the biggest adversity in her life. Martin had been out of her life for more than fifty

Photo E.4: Aurora Prado Pastrano with David Chanes, in Yucaipa, CA. May 12, 2017. From the private photo collection of the author.

years, since she left him behind in Juárez. A few years later, he asked her for a reconciliation, something that caused him humiliation with his own family when she derided the very idea and flatly refused him. She shrugs now wondering if he is dead or alive but admits that what he took from her life remains a painful memory. Yet, as always, she shows that through her music, she rose above it, as told by the song she wrote with him in mind, *Debes Pensarlo Bien*, and another song, a popular old *ranchera* that she sang that final night at the restaurant. Fittingly, the song's title would allude to Martin's failure to contain, dominate or define her, and I feel sure that when she performed the lyrics to *Fallaste Corazón*, she did so *con mucho corazón*, with all her heart:

> *Y tu que te creías*
> *el rey de todo el mundo*
> *Y tu que nunca fuiste*
> *capaz de perdonar/*
> *Y cruel y despiadado*
> *de todos te reías*
> *hoy imploras cariño, aunque sea por piedad/*
> *¿A dónde está tu orgullo,*
> *a donde esta el coraje?*

¿Porqué hoy que estás vencido,
mendigas caridad? /
Ya ves que no es lo mismo
amar que ser amado
hoy que estás acabado
que lástima me das/
Maldito corazón,
me alegro que ahora sufras
y llores y te humilles
ante este gran amor/
La vida es la ruleta
en que apostamos todos
y a ti te había tocado nomás la de ganar/
Pero hoy tu buena suerte
la espalda te ha volteado
fallaste Corazón,
no vuelvas a apostar.[6]

[And you, who thought yourself
the king of the whole world
and you, who were never
capable of forgiving/
And cruel and merciless
you laughed at everyone
Today you beg for love
even if it's only from pity/
Where is your pride,
where is the fury?
Why, now that you're defeated,
do you beg for charity? /
You see now?
It's not the same to love as to be loved
and now that you are finished
you are pitiful to me/
Damned Heart,
I am glad that now you suffer
and you cry and you are humbled
in the presence of this great love/
Life is the roulette where everybody bets
and you always had winning on your side
but today Lady Luck has turned her back on you
now that you are finished, don't ever bet again.] (Translation my own)
(see Photo E.5).

Photo E.5: Aurora Prado Pastrano, May 14, 2015. From the private photo collection of the author.

Notes

1. Per the website, Suave The Band, http://mobile.suavetheband.com/meettheband.html. Information, such as band membership, may differ since then.
2. I paraphrase his statement to the best of my recollection because he said it decades ago.
3. Arcos, 2019.
4. Aparicio, 1999, p. 228.
5. Asaderos was renamed Del Mar, but she still continues to refer to it by its former name.
6. Song title, *Fallaste Corazón*, Cuco Sánchez, composer; as recorded by artist singer, Amalia Mendoza.

References

Aparicio, F. (1999). The Blackness of Sugar: Celia Cruz and the Performance of (Trans) Nationalism. *Cultural Studies, 13*(2), 223–236.

Arcos, B. (2019, April 16). *These LA Musicians Are Reviving Bolero Music*. Retrieved from LAist: https://laist.com/news/entertainment/these-la-musicians-are-reviving-bolero-music

APPENDIX A

Misa Panamericana/Order of Mass for Mariachi

(As Played by Mariachi Las Generalas)

1. Canto De Entrada I
2. Canto De Entrada II
3. Canto Penitencial
4. Gloria
5. Canto De Preparación
6. Entre Tus Manos
7. Aclamación Del Prefacio
8. Amen
9. Padre Nuestro
10. Fracción Del Pan
11. Pescador De Hombres
12. Canto De Salida
13. De Colores

MISA EN HONOR DE LA VIRGEN DE GUADALUPE (*RANCHERA*)

14. Viva La Virgen Ranchera

15. Señor Ten Piedad
16. Gloria
17. Aleluya
18. Danza Del Ofertorio
19. Santo, Santo
20. Padre Nuestro
21. Cordero De Dios
22. Canto Final
23. Noche De Paz

APPENDIX B

Aurora Prado Pastrano's Collection of Old Popular Song Titles

A Cambio de Qué
A La Luz Del Día
A Pesar de Todo
A Stranger in my Arms
A Un Paso Del Abismo (de: Cuco Sánchez)
Adiós Ranchero
Adiós, Adiós, Adiós
Adiós, Mariquita Linda
Adonde Andará
Aguanta Corazón
Alborada
All The Way
Alma De Acero
Alma De Cristal
Amanecí Otra Vez (aka Amanecí En Tus Brazos)
Amapola
Amargura
Amazing Grace
Ambición de Quererte
Amigo Organillero

Amigos Nada Mas
Amor De La Calle (Fernando Z. Maldonado)
Amor Eterno/Eternal Love (de Juan Gabriel Translated to English by Aurora Pastrano)
Amor Gitano
Amor Mío (Javier Solís)
Amor Perdido
Amor Por Gotitas
Amorcito Corazón (as sung by Pedro Infante)
Ando Que Me Lleva La Tristeza
Anillo De Compromiso
Anoche Soñé
Aprendiste a Volar
Arandas
Arnulfo González
Atotonilco
Aunque Tengas Razón
Aventurera (de Agustín Lara)
Ayúdame Dios Mío
Barandales
Barquita de Madera
Before the Last Tear Drop Falls
Bésame y Olvídame
Besando
Besando La Cruz
Birthday to Miguela
Blanca Navidad
Caballo Prieto Azabache
Cama De Piedra
Caminemos
Camino de Guanajuato
Caminos De La Vida
Canción Del Alma
Canta Guitarra Canta
Canta, Canta, Canta
Cantarás Conmigo (Javier Solís)
Carabela
Carta a Ester
Carta Abierta

Carta Fatal
Carta Jugada
Cartas Marcadas
Celoso
Cenizas
Cerca Del Mar
Cerezo Rosa
Cheque al Portador
Chotis Madrid (de Agustín Lara)
Cielo de Sonora
Cien Años
Como Dijo Cristo (Javier Solís)
Compadécete Mujer
Compréndeme
Confusión
Conozco A Los Dos
Contigo
Contigo (cantan Los Panchos)
Contigo En La Distancia
Corrido De Chiquis
Cruz De Olvido
Cuando Abras Los Ojos
Cuando Calienta El Sol
Cuando Dos Almas
Cuando Nadie Te Quiera (L. Y M. José A. Jimenez)
Cuando No Hay Amor
Cuatro Cirios
Cuatro Vidas
Cuentas Claras
Cuesta Abajo (tango)
Cuquita
De Que Manera Te Olvido
De Que Tamaño Me Quieres
De Un Rancho A Otro
Déjame Llorar
Desdén (Bolero)
Desesperanza
Desolación
Despedida Con Mariachi

Despreciado
Destino
Destrozado el Corazón
Devuélveme el Corazón
Día de Reyes
Día de San Juan
Dicen Que Los Hombres No Deben Llorar
Diez Años
Dilema
Dime Que Si Me Quieres
Dios No Lo Quiera
Dos Amores
Dos Arbolitos
Dos Hojas Sin Rumbo
Dos Mentiras
Dos Seres
El Adiós Del Soldado
El Asesino
El Ausente
El Becerro
El Caballo Blanco
El Cielo De Chihuahua
El Cofrecito
El Crucifijo de Piedra
El Día Que Me Quieras
El Mal Querido
El Pecador
El Perro Negro (J.A. Jiménez)
El Plebeyo
El Redentor (tango?)
El Rey
El Sinaloense
El Vicio
Ella
En El Ultimo Trago (de J.A. Jimenez)
En Mi Viejo San Juan
Entre Suspiro Y Suspiro
Es Mejor Querer
Espérame En El Cielo

Está Sellado Por El Destino
Esta Tarde Vi Llover
Eternamente
Fallaste, Corazón
Falsa
Felicidades
Feria De Las Flores
Finca de Adobe
Flor De Azalea
Flor De Un Día
Flores Negras
Golondrina Mensajera
Golpes De Pecho
Grítenme Piedras Del Campo
Guadalajara
Guitarras De Medianoche
Hay Que Saber Perder
Hay Unos Ojos
He Sabido Que Te Amaba
Hermoso Cariño
Huella De Mis Besos
I Can't Stop Loving You
I Will Never Love Again (song by Juan Gabriel; translation by Aurora Pastrano)
Imposible
Incertidumbre
Inocente Pobre Amiga
Inquietud
La Barca
La Barca de Guaymas
La Basurita
La Brisa Del Mar
La Calandria
La Consentida
La Corriente
La Despedida
La Diferencia
La Entrega
La Farsante

La Gloria Eres Tu (Los Diamantes)
La Hiedra
La Hija De Nadie
La Huella de Mis Besos
La Lámpara
La Ley Del Monte
La Mal Pagadora
La Mancornadora
La Mentira
La Novia Pobre (Los Dandys)
La Número Cien
La Pajarera (cantan hnos. Zaizar)
La Paloma (Los Panchos)
La Paloma Blanca (Julio Iglesias)
La Traicionera
La Ultima Copa
La Única Estrella
La Vida Es Un Sueño
La Zopilota
Lagrimas De Amor (De Raúl Shaw Moreno)
Lagrimas Del Alma
Lámpara Sin Luz
Las Mañanitas
Las Noches Las Hago Días
Las Palmeras
Le Falta Un Clavo A Mi Cruz
Libro Abierto
Llévame Todas Las Tardes
Llorando A Mares
Llorando A Solas
Llorar
Llorarás, Llorarás
Loca Pasión (bolero de Edmundo Domínguez)
Los Barandales
Los Dos
Los Hombres No Lloran
Los Laureles
Los Mil Besos
Los Zapatitos De Charol

Luto en el Alma
Malagueña
Mano a Mano
Marcha Nupcial
María Bonita
Maria Elena (bolero) (as sung by Nat King Cole)
Marinero de Mazatlán
Me Piden
Me Recordarás
Me Sobra Corazón (Los Delfines)
Mejor Me Voy
Mentirosa
Mi Amor Se Ha Ido
Mi Amor Se Me Fué
Mi Rival
Miénteme
Mil Cadenas
Mil Noches
Morenita
Motivos
Mucho Corazón
Nacimos Para Amarnos
Nada Contigo
Nadie
Negra Consentida
Ni en Defensa Propia
Ni Princesa Ni Esclava No Digas Nada
No Discutamos
No Me Calienta Ni El Sol
No Me Quieras Tanto
No Me Vuelvo A Enamorar
No Vale La Pena
No Vengo a Pedirte Amores
No Volveré
Noche De Reyes
Noche Tenebrosa y Fría
Nochecita
Nosotros (canción clásica; cantan varios tríos)
Ojos De Juventud

Pa' Que Me Sirve La Vida (ranchera)
Pa' Que Te Acuerdes De Mi
Página Blanca
Pajarillo Barranqueño
Palabra De Rey
Palabras De Mujer
Paloma Errante
Paloma Que Atravesando
Para Que Volver
Parece Que Fue Ayer
Paso Del Norte (corrido)
Perdida
Pídele A Dios (bolero)
Piensa En Mi
Piquetes De Hormiga
Pobre Corazón
Pobre Del Pobre
Podría Volver
Por Ningún Motivo
Por Tu Culpa (Julia Palma)
Por Tu Culpa Nomas
Por Un Amor
Por Voluntad De Dios
Porque te Querré Tanto[1]
Preciosa
Preciosa (bolero; canta Virginia López, de Rafael Hernández)
Presentimiento
Prieta Linda
Primero Dios Mañana
Que Bonito Amor
Que me Vean Llorando
Que Nos Entierren Juntos
Que Raro
Que Seas Feliz
Que Suerte La Mia
Que Te Importa
Que Va
Que Voy a Hacer Sin Ti
Quiéreme Mucho (de María Grever)

Rancho Alegre
Reconciliación
Regálame Esta Noche
Reina Mia
Rezaré
Rival
Rosa (de Agustín Lara)
Ruega Por Nosotros (Miguel Aceves Mejía)
Ruleta
Sábelo Bien
Sabor A Mi
Sabrás Que Te Quiero (Javier Solís)
San Juan Del Rio
Se Me Olvido Otra Vez
Seguimos Pecando
Si Acaso Vuelves (Lola Beltrán)
Si Dios Me Quita La Vida
Si Me Tuvieras Confianza
Si Nos Dejan
Siempre Viva
Siento (Feelings)
Sigamos Pecando
Silverio (de Agustín Lara)
Sin Sangre En Las Venas
Sin Ti
Soberbia
Solamente La Mano De Dios
Solamente Una Vez
Solo Tu y Nadie Mas
Sonora Querida
Sortilegio
Stop the World
Sucedió
Sufro Tu Ausencia
Tabernero (tango)
Tango Negro
Te Fuiste
Te Quiero
Te Quiero Con La Vida

Te Vas Ángel Mío
Te Vas O Te Quedas
Te Voy a Olvidar
Tennessee Waltz
Tiburón, Tiburón
Tienen Tus Ojos
Todo Tiene Su Razón (bolero)
Tómate Una Copa
Traigo un Amor
Tres Días
Tres Recuerdos
Tres Regalos
Tu Dirás Lo Que Hacemos
Tu Me Acostumbraste
Tu No Comprendes
Tu No Me Comprendes
Tu Solo Tu
Tu Y Yo
Últimos Días
Un Mundo Raro
Un Sueño de Tantos
Una Carta
Una Eternidad
Una Imploración
Una Noche Me Embriagué
Una Noche Tenebrosa Y Fría
Una Pura Y Dos Con Sal
Vagabundo
Vereda Tropical
Virgencita de Talpa
Viva mi Desgracia
Volver A Empezar (Begin The Beguine)
Volveré
Voy A Dejarte
Voy De Gallo (Los Calaveras)
Voy Gritando Por La Calle
Vuelve Gaviota
Y Ahora Como Le Hago
Y Todo Acabó

Ya Me Voy (canción ranchera)
Yesterday When I Was Young
Your Cheating Heart

Note

1. According to her notation, the song title does not include "Yo", but it is likely the song sung by Los Bondadosos, which is titled, "Porque te Querré Yo Tanto."

APPENDIX C

Selected Song Lyrics

Adiós Muchachos (*tango*; Julio Cesar Sanders and Cesar Vedani, composers)

Adiós, muchachos, compañeros de mi vida,
barra querida de aquellos tiempos.
Me toca a mí hoy emprender la retirada,
debo alejarme de mi buena muchachada/
Adiós, muchachos. Ya me voy y me resigno
Contra el destino nadie la talla
Se terminaron para mí todas las farras,
mi cuerpo enfermo no resiste más/
Acuden a mi mente recuerdos de otros tiempos,
de los bellos momentos que antaño disfruté
cerquita de mi madre, santa viejita,
y de mi noviecita que tanto idolatré/
¿Se acuerdan que era hermosa, más bella que una diosa
y que ebrio yo de amor, le di mi corazón,
mas el Señor, celoso de sus encantos,
hundiéndome en el llanto me la llevó?/
Es Dios el juez supremo. No hay quien se le resista
ya estoy acostumbrado su ley a respetar,
pues mi vida deshizo con sus mandatos
al robarme a mi madre y a mi novia también/

Dos lágrimas sinceras derramo en mi partida
por la barra querida que nunca me olvidó
y al darles, mis amigos, mi adiós postrero,
les doy con toda mi alma mi bendición.
[Goodbye, young friends, companions of my life,
Beloved gang of those times
It is my turn to start the departure
I must leave my dear young friends behind/
Goodbye, young friends, I leave now, I am resigned
Against fate no one can measure up
For me, the binges have ended
My sickened body can resist no more/
Memories of other times come into my mind,
of the wonderful moments of yesteryear that I enjoyed
close to my saintly old mother
And my betrothed, whom I so idolized/
Do you recall that she was stunning, more beautiful than a goddess?
And I, inebriated with love, gave her my heart?
But the Lord, jealous of her charms,
Engulfing me in tears, took her from me/
God is the supreme judge, who no one can resist
I am now accustomed His law to respect
For, my life He undid with his mandates
When he stole my mother, and my betrothed as well/
Two sincere tears I cry at my departure
For the beloved gang, that never forgot me
And as I leave you, friends, my final goodbye
I give with all my soul, my blessing to you.] (Translation mine)

Amor Chiquito (polka; Fernando López, composer)[1]

Amor chiquito, acabado de nacer,
Eres mi encanto, eres todo mi querer/
Ven a mis brazos, te amaré con ilusión,
Porque te quiero y te doy todo mi amor/
Yo solo vivo por ti, sufro por ti,
Muero por ti, espero me hagas feliz
Como yo a ti, porque te quiero
Y te doy todo mi amor/
Amor chiquito, acabado de nacer
Eres mi encanto, eres todo mi querer/
Instrumental
Amor chiquito, acabado de nacer,

Eres mi encanto, eres todo mi querer/
Ven a mis brazos, te amaré con ilusión,
Porque te quiero y te doy todo mi amor/
Yo solo vivo por ti, sufro por ti,
Muero por ti, espero me hagas feliz
Como yo a ti, porque te quiero
Y te doy todo mi amor/
Amor chiquito, acabado de nacer,
Eres mi encanto, eres todo mi querer/
[Little Love, just a newborn
You are my charm, you are everything I love
Come to my arms, you will be my hopes and dreams
Because I love you, and I give you all my heart/
I only live for you, suffer for you,
Die for you, I hope you make me happy
As I do you, because I love you
And I give you all my love/
Little Love, just a newborn
You are my charm, you are all that I love/
Instrumental
(Repeat All) (Translation my own)

Amor de la Calle (bolero; Fernando Z. Maldonado, composer) (Letradecancion.com, 2010–2021)

Amor de la calle
que vendes tus besos a cambio de amor
aunque tú le quieres
aunque tú le esperes el tarda en llegar/
no olvidas tu pena
bailando y tomando, fingiendo reír
y el frío de la noche
castiga tu alma y pierdes la fé/
Amor de la calle
que buscando vas cariño
con tu carita pintada
con tu carita pintada
con el corazón herido/
Si tuvieras un cariño
un cariño verdadero
tú serías tal vez distinta
como o igual a otras mujeres
pero te han mentido tanto/

Cuando ya has bebido mucho
vas llorando por la calle
y si el mundo te comprendiera
pero no saben tu pena/
Amor de la calle
que buscando vas cariño
con tu carita pintada
con tu carita pintada
con el corazón herido/
Cuando ya has bebido mucho
vas llorando por la calle ....
[Street Love
you sell your kisses in exchange for love
although you love him
although you wait for him, he arrives late/
You cannot forget your sorrow
dancing and drinking, pretending to smile
and the cold of night
punishes your soul and you lose faith/
Street Love
you seek affection
with your little face painted
with your little face painted
and your heart wounded/
If you had a love
a true love
you might have been different
such as or the same as other women
but you have been lied to so/
When you have been drinking much
you go crying through the streets
if the world would understand you
but they do not know your sorrow/
Street Love
you go seeking affection
with your little face painted
with your little face painted
and your heart wounded.] (Translation my own)

Aquellos Ojos Verdes (bolero; Nilo Menéndez and Adolfo Utrera)

Fueron tus ojos
Los que me dieron

El tema dulce de mi canción
Tus ojos verdes, claros, serenos
Ojos que han sido mi inspiración/
Aquellos ojos verdes
de mirada serena
dejaron en mi alma
eterna fe de amar/
Anhelos de caricias
de besos y ternuras
de todas las dulzuras
que sabían brindar/
Aquellos ojos verdes
serenos como un lago
en cuyas quietas aguas
un día me miré/
No saben la tristeza
que a mi alma le dejaron
aquellos ojos verdes
que ya nunca besaré.
No saben la tristeza
que a mi alma le dejaron
aquellos ojos verdes
que yo nunca besaré (Strachwitz, 2021) (Enterprises, 2016).
[It was your eyes
that gave me
the sweet theme of my song/
Those green eyes, clear, serene
eyes that have been my inspiration/
Those green eyes
that cast a serene gaze
have left in my soul
eternal faith in love/
A longing for caresses
for tenderness and kisses
and for all of the sweetness
that they knew how to give/
Those green eyes
serene as a lake
in whose quiet waters
my reflection I once saw/
They know not the sadness
that they left in my soul
those green eyes
that I shall never kiss again. (Translation my own)

Camino de Guanajuato *(ranchera;* José Alfredo Jimenez*)* (Wall, 2016)

No vale nada la vida
la vida no vale nada
comienza siempre llorando
y así llorando se acaba
por eso es que en este mundo
la vida no vale nada/
Bonito León, Guanajuato
la feria con su jugada
allí se apuesta la vida
y se respeta al que gana
allá en mi León, Guanajuato
la vida no vale nada/
Camino de Guanajuato
que pasas por tanto pueblo
no pases por Salamanca
que allí me hiere el recuerdo
vete rodeando veredas
no pases porque me muero/
El Cristo de tu montaña
el cerro del Cubilete
consuelo de los que sufren
adoración de la gente
el Cristo de tu montaña
del cerro del Cubilete/
Camino de Santa Rosa
la sierra de Guanajuato
allí nomás tras lomita
se ve Dolores Hidalgo
yo allí me quedo, paisano
allí es mi pueblo adorado.
[It is worth nothing, life
life is worth nothing
it starts out always crying
and likewise, it ends crying
that's why in this world
life is worth nothing/
Pretty Leon, Guanajuato
its fair, with its move
life is a bet there
and winners are respected
there, in my Leon, Guanajuato

life is worth nothing/
The way to Guanajuato
you pass through so many towns
don't pass through Salamanca
for there the memory pains me
circle around its side ways
don't pass there because I'll die/
The Christ on its mountain
on the hill El Cubilete
comfort of the sufferers
worship of the people
the Christ of its mountain
on the hill of El Cubilete/
The way to Santa Rosa
the sierra of Guanajuato
there, behind the small hill
is a view of Dolores Hidalgo
there I will stay, my fellow
there, in my beloved town. (Translation mine)

Cancionero (*bolero*; Alvaro Carrillo, composer; as recorded by Los Panchos) (zacrorp, 2017)

Yo soy un humilde cancionero
y cantarte quiero
una historia humana
pues sé que te ama
quien misó ese ruego/
Si la ves,
cancionero, dile tú que soy felíz,
que por ella muchas veces te pedí
una canción para brindar por su alegría/
Si la ves,
cancionero, dile claro en tu canción
que en mis ojos amanece su ilusión
como una nueva primavera, cada día/
No le digas,
que me viste muy triste y muy cansado,
no le digas
que sin ella me siento destrozado/
Si la ves
cancionero vuelve pronto a mi rincón,
y aunque mientas haz felíz mi corazón,

vuelve a decirme que me quiere todavía/
No le digas
Que me viste ...
[I am a humble singer
wishing to sing for you
a human story,
for I know that he loves you,
he, who sent this begging missive/
If you see her,
singer, tell her that I am happy
that for her, many times I asked you
for a song to toast to her happiness/
If you see her,
singer, tell her clearly in your song
that the hope for her in my eyes dawns
like a springtime, every day/
Do not tell her
that you saw me so tired, so sad,
do not tell her
that without her I feel destroyed/
If you see her
singer, run back to my hiding place
if you must lie, make my heart happy again
and tell me that she loves me still/
Do not tell her
that you saw me so sad, ...] (Translation mine)

Compréndeme (*bolero;* Maria Alma, composer; as sung and recorded by the composer.) (Aguado Snider, 2010) (SACM, 2019)

Yo quiero
que comprendas
vida mía
que tu amor y mi amor
no pueden ser/
que quiso ser sincera
el alma mía
y por no herirte a ti
todo callé/
Te tuve una vez
muy dentro de mi corazón
y no se porqué
me fui alejando de ti/

Perdona, mi bien,
si digo toda la verdad
la vida es así
y debes de comprenderme/
No volverás
a escuchar mis palabras de amor
ya no tendrás
el sabor de mis besos/
Y quiero desearte hoy
que me alejo de ti
que encuentres al fin
quien comprenda tu cariño (se repite.)
[I hope
that you understand
dear one of my life
that our love
cannot be/
That my soul
wished to be sincere
but kept silent
to avoid hurting you/
I once held you
deep within my heart
and I don't know why
my love departed from you/
Forgive me, my dear,
for speaking the truth
but life is like this
and you have to understand me/
You will never again
hear words of love from me
you will not have
the taste of my kisses/
And I want to wish you
now that I depart from you
that you find at last
someone who understands your love.] (Translation mine)

Consentida (*bolero*; Alfredo Nuñez de Borbón, composer; as recorded by Los Tres Diamantes)

Llevo tantas penas, en el alma,
que al mirarte a ti, nunca pensé,

que pudiera al fin, otra vez poner,
en un nuevo amor, mi fe/
Aunque lo pague, con el precio de mi vida;
aunque comprenda, lo que tengo que sufrir
puedo jurar, que tu serás, mi consentida
y que, a nadie, quiero tanto, como a ti/
Has que contigo, mi calvario, se haga santo
ya no me importa, lo que digan, los demás
mi corazón, se ha de quedar, entre tus brazos
cuando al fin este, cansado ya, de tanto amar.
[I carry such suffering in my soul
that, as I look at you, I never thought
that at last, I could, once again,
place faith in a new love/
Even if the price I pay is my life
even if I know what I must suffer
I can swear that you will be my chosen one
that I'll love no one as much as I love you/
Make my Calvary a holy one
I don't care what people will say
my heart will remain in your embrace
when at last it is tired of having loved.

Desvelo de Amor (*bolero*; Rafael Hernandez, composer; as recorded by Los Dandys) (YouTube, 2014).

Sufro mucho tu ausencia, no te lo niego
Ya, no puedo vivir, si a mi lado no estás/
Dicen, que soy cobarde, que tengo miedo
de perder tu cariño, de tus besos perder/
Yo comprendo, que es mucho, lo que te quiero
no, no puedo remediarlo, que voy a hacer/
Te juro que dormir, casi no puedo,
mi vida es un martirio, sin cesar
mirando tu retrato, me consuelo,
vuelvo a dormir y vuelvo, a despertar/
Dejo el lecho y me asomo, a la ventana,
contemplo de la noche, su esplendor
me sorprende la luz, de la mañana,
ay! en mi loco desvelo, por tu amor/
[I suffer greatly from your absence, I don't deny it
I cannot live, if you are not by my side/
They say that I am a coward, that I am afraid

of losing your love, of losing your kisses/
I understand, my love for you is too great
I cannot help that, what can I do?/
I swear to you, I can barely sleep
my life is an unceasing misery
looking at your picture gives me comfort
I sleep and then I wake again/
I leave my bed and look out the window
I contemplate the night's splendor
the morning light catches me by surprise
oh, in my insane sleeplessness over your love.] (Translation mine)

El Hijo Desobediente (corrido; Helio Gerardo Anastarón, composer) (Herrera, 1986, pp. 255–256)

Un domingo estando herrando
se encontraron dos mancebos,
metiendo mano a sus fierros,
como queriendo pelear/
Cuando se estaban peleando
pues llego su padre de uno,
"Hijo de mi corazón,
ya no pelees con ninguno"/
Quítese de aquí mi padre
que estoy más bravo que un león,
no valla a sacar mi espada y le traspase el corazón/
El padre muy sorprendido
rompio su semblante tierno,
al oir que con su ascento,
su hijo retaba al eterno:/
Hijo de mi corazon
por lo que acabas de hablar,
antes de que raye el sol
la vida te han de quitar/
Lo que le encargo a mi padre
que no me entierre en sagrado,
que me entierre en tierra bruta
donde me trille el ganado/
Con una mano de fuera
y un papel sobre-dorado,
con un letrero que diga:
"Felipe fue desgraciado"/
El caballo colorado hace un año que nació,
ahí se lo dejo a mi padre

por la crianza que me dio/
De tres caballos que tengo
ahi se los dejo a los pobres,
para que si quiera digan "
Felipe, Dios te perdone"/
Bajaron al toro prieto
que nunca lo habian bajado,
pero ahora si ya bajo
revuelto con el ganado/
Cuando el coraje se agolpa
en la mente de la gente,
muchas veces nos obliga
a faltar a un inocente/
Ya con esta me despido
con la estrella del Oriente
esto le puede pasaral
hijo desobediente.
[One Sunday, while two young farriers
were busy working the metal
they got into a heated quarrel
and each one reached for the barrel/
Once the fight had begun
arrived the father of one
pleading, "my beloved son,
you must retire your gun"/
Father, you best get away
because I'm mad as a lion,
my sword could just find its way through your heart,
and I'm not lyin'/
And upon hearing his son,
the boy challenge the Almighty,
the father, tenderness gone,
said to his son, quite rightly:/
"My boy, my beloved son,
for what you have just now spoken
before the light of the dawn
your life will sure have been taken"/
I only ask of you, dad
don't bury me in sacred ground
bury me in the crude dirt
where the cattle hooves do pound/
With one hand outside the coffin
holding a paper, gold-leafed
and on it a sign that reads:

"Felipe's no-good life lived"/
The young, the sorrel horse,
that was born a year ago
to my father, I leave, of course
as thanks for raising me so/
And as for the other horses
to the poor, I wish to give
for prayer they may be sources:
"Felipe's soul God forgive"/
The black bull they just brought down
was never brought down before,
but now that he is around
he's not special anymore/
When people lose their temper
their minds often get so lost
and they often don't remember
the innocent lives they caused/
So, with the star of the East
my friends, I here now depart
the errant son's story, at least
I hope you've taken to heart. (Translation mine)

Eternamente (*bolero-ranchera*; Alberto Dominguez, composer; as recorded by Javier Solis) (Genius.com, 2021)

Pensar que todo tengo
y nada puedo yo tener
la vida me da flores
el sol me da su luz/
Pensar que todo tengo
y nada puedo yo tener
porque lo tengo todo
pero me faltas tu/
Dime vida
si tu sufres
por mi amor?
Si una duda llega a tu alma
a atormentar? /
Comprende
que como nadie yo te quiero
y tu vivirás
en mi corazón
una eternidad/

Tu bien sabes
Que los años pasarán
pero nunca
que yo te olvide
lograrán/
Pues tuyo
será mi amor eternamente
y para los dos
la felicidad
tendrá que brillar
y para los dos
la felicidad
tendrá que brillar/
Pues tuyo ... (se repite)
[To think that I have everything
and yet, I have nothing
life gives me flowers
the sun gives me its light/
To think that I have everything
and yet, I have nothing
for, I have everything
but I do not have you/
Tell me, my dear
do you suffer for my love?/
Does a doubt
torment your soul?
please know, dear
that I love you like no other could
and you shall live
within my heart
for an eternity/
You do know
that the years will pass
but they will never
cause me to forget you
because yours
will be my love eternally
and for us both
happiness will have to shine./
(Repeats from: You do know ...) (Translation mine)

Grítenme Piedras del Campo (*ranchera*; composed and recorded by Cuco Sánchez) (letradecancion.com, 2010–2021)

*Soy como el viento que corre
alrededor de este mundo
anda entre muchos placeres
anda entre muchos placeres
pero no es suyo ninguno/
Soy como el pájaro en jaula
preso y hundido en tu amor
y aunque la jaula sea de oro
y aunque la jaula sea de oro
no deja de ser prisión/
Háblenme montes y valles
grítenme piedras del campo
¿Cuándo habían visto en la vida
querer como estoy queriendo,
llorar como estoy llorando,
morir como estoy muriendo? /
A veces me siento un sol
y el mundo me importa nada
luego despierto y me río
luego despierto y me río
soy mucho menos que nada/
En fin, soy en este mundo
como la pluma en el aire
sin rumbo voy por la vida
sin rumbo voy por la vida
y de eso tú eres culpable/
Háblenme montes y valles
grítenme piedras del campo
¿Cuándo habían visto en la vida
querer como estoy queriendo,
llorar como estoy llorando,
morir como estoy muriendo?*
[I'm like the wind that runs
throughout this world
it is among many pleasures
it is among many pleasures
but it owns not one of them/
I'm like the bird in a cage
prisoner drowned in your love
and even if the cage is golden

and even if the cage is golden
it does not stop being a prison/
Talk to me, hills and valleys
yell to me, rocks of the countryside
when in your life have you seen
loving as I am loving
crying as I am crying
dying as I am dying? /
At times I feel that I am the sun
and the world is meaningless to me
then I wake up and laugh
then I wake up and laugh
I am much less than nothing/
In all, I am in this world
like a plume in the air
aimlessly I go through life
aimlessly I go through life
and of that, you are the cause/
Talk to me, hills and valleys
yell to me, rocks of the countryside
when in your life have you seen
loving as I am loving
crying as I am crying
dying as I am dying?] (Translation my own)

Hay Que Saber Perder (*bolero*; Abel Dominguez, composer) (Foundation, 2021)

Cuando un amor se va
que desesperación
cuando un cariño vuela
nada consuela mi corazón/
Dan ganas de llorar
no es fácil olvidar
al querer que nos deja
y que se aleja sin compasión/
No puedo comprender
que cosa es el amor
si lo que más quería
el alma mía me abandonó/
Pero no hay que llorar
hay que saber perder
lo mismo pierde un hombre
que una mujer.

[When a love departs
what desperation!
When a love flies [away]
nothing consoles the heart/
It feels like crying
it's not easy to forget
the love that departs
and leaves us, mercilessly/
I cannot understand
what this thing is, called love
if what I most loved,
my very soul, abandoned me/
But no point in crying
we must learn to lose
a man loses the same
as a woman does. [Translation my own]

Juan Charrasqueado (*corrido*; Víctor Cordero, composer)

*Voy a contarles un corrido muy mentado,
lo que ha pasado allá en la Hacienda de la Flor;
la triste historia de un ranchero enamorado,
que fue borracho, parrandero y jugador/
Juan se llamaba y lo apodaban "Charrasqueado"
era valiente y arriesgado en el amor
a las mujeres más bonitas se llevaba,
de aquellos campos no quedaba ni una flor/
Un día domingo que se andaba emborrachando,
a la cantina le corrieron a avisar
"cuídate Juan, que ya por ahí te andan buscando,
son muchos hombres no te vayan a matar"/
No tuvo tiempo de montar en su caballo,
pistola en mano se le echaron de a montón.
"Estoy borracho— les gritaba— y soy buen gallo,"
cuando una bala atravesó su corazón/
Creció la milpa con la lluvia en el potrero
y las palomas van volando al pedregal;
bonitos toros llevan hoy al matadero,
que buen caballo va montando el caporal/
Ya las campanas del santuario están doblando
todos los fieles se dirigen a rezar,
y por el cerro los rancheros van bajando,
a un hombre muerto que lo llevan a enterrar/*

En una choza muy humilde llora un niño,
y las mujeres se aconsejan y se van,
solo su madre lo consuela con cariño,
mirando al cielo, llora y reza por su Juan/
Y aquí termino de cantar este corrido,
de Juan ranchero, "Charrasqueado" y burlador;
que se creyó de las mujeres consentido,
y fue borracho, parrandero y jugador. (McKinley, 2005)
[I will now sing you a well-known ballad
of what once happened in the Hacienda of the Flower
the sad story of a love-struck rancher
who was a drinker, a carouser and a gambler/
Juan he was called and nicknamed "Scarface."
he was brave and daring in love
he went after the prettiest girls
in those fields, he didn't leave a single flower/
One Sunday, he was drinking
and having fun into the saloon,
they ran in to say, "Be careful, Juan, they're looking for you
many men are coming and they plan to kill you"/
No time to jump on his horse
with a pistol in his hand, his shots rang out
"I may be drunk, but I'm a brave man!", he cried
when a bullet ripped through his heart/
The cornfields grow with the rain near the corral
and the doves fly to the rocky heights
pretty bulls are taken to the slaughterhouse
the foreman rides about on a pretty stallion/
The church bells are now ringing
the faithful wend their way to pray
and from the mountains the ranchers come down
the dead man they carry off to bury/
In a humble dwelling, a baby boy cries
and women come to comfort and then they leave
 only his mother, with love, cradles him
looking to the heavens, crying and praying for her Juan/
And here I finish singing this ballad
of Juan, the rancher, the scar faced prankster
he believed himself the darling of the pampered ladies
who was a drinker, a carouser and gambler] (McKinley, 2005).

La Feria de las Flores (*ranchera*; Chucho Monge, composer)

Me Gusta Cantarle Al Viento
porque vuelan mis Cantares

y digo lo que yo siento
por toditos los lugares/
Aquí vine porque vine
a la feria de las flores
no hay cerro que se me empine
ni cuaco que se me atore/
En mi caballo retinto
He venido de muy lejos
Y traigo pistola al cinto
Y con ella doy consejos/
Atravesé la montaña
Pa' venir a ver las flores
Aquí hay una rosa huraña
Qu'es la flor de mis amores/
Y aunque otro quiera cortarla
Yo la divisé primero
Y juro que he de cortarla
Aunque tenga jardinero/
Yo la he de ver trasplantada
en el huerto de mi casa
y si sale el jardinero
pues a ver, a ver que pasa.
[I like to sing to the wind
because my singing flies
and I say what I feel
in every single place/
I came here because I came
to the fair of the flowers
there's no hill too steep for me
and no horse that will leave me stuck/
In my dark horse
I have come from afar
and I carry a pistol at my belt
and with it I give advice/
I crossed the mountain
just to come and see the flowers
there's a shy flower here
who's the flower of my [many] love[s]/
And even if another [man] wants to cut [that flower]
I set my sights on her first
and I swear that I will cut [that flower]
even if she has a gardener/
I will see her transplanted

in the orchard of my house
and if her gardener steps out
well, we'll just see what happens.] (Translation my own)

La Hiedra[2] (*bolero*; composers: Saverio Seracini and Vincenzo D'Aquisto, Ben Molar)

Pasaron desde aquel ayer
ya tantos años,
dejaron en su gris correr
mil desengaños/
Mas cuando quiero recordar
nuestro pasado,
te siento cual la hiedra
ligada a mí,
y así hasta la eternidad
te sentiré/
Yo sé que estoy ligado a ti
más fuerte que la hiedra
porque tus ojos de mis sueños
no pueden separarse jamás/
Donde quiera que estés
mi voz escucharás
llamándote con ansiedad,
por la pena ya sin final
de sentirte en mi soledad/
Jamás la hiedra y la pared
podrían apretarse más,
igual tus ojos de mis ojos,
no pueden separarse jamás/
Donde quiera que estés
mi voz escucharás,
llamándote con mi canción;
más fuerte que el dolor
se aferra nuestro amor
como la hiedra, como la hiedra.
[It has been, since that yesterday
so many years
and in their shades of gray,
a thousand disappointments/
Yet when I want to recall
our past,
I feel you as the ivy

bound to me
and so, until eternity
I shall feel you/
I know that I am bound to you
more tightly than the ivy
because your eyes from my dreams
cannot be separated, ever/
Wherever you may be
my voice you will hear
calling you anxiously/
for the sorrow, now without end
of feeling you in my loneliness/
Never could the ivy and the wall
be more tightly bound together
similarly, your eyes from my eyes
cannot be separated, ever/
Wherever you may be
my voice you will hear
calling you with my song
much stronger than the sorrow
our love tightly holds on
just like the ivy, just like the ivy. (Translation my own)

Marta (*bolero*; classical; composer: Moises Simons)

Linda flor de alborada
Que brotaste del suelo
Cuando la luz del cielo
Tu capullo besaba/
De las rosas encanto
El pensil te ama tanto
Que ya loco de amor
Siente celos del aire, y del agua y del sol/
Marta,
Capullito de rosas
Marta,
Del jardín linda flor
Dime, que feliz mariposa
En tu cáliz se posa
A libar tu dulzor/
Marta,
En tus claras pupilas
Brilla una aurora de amor/

Marta,
en tus ojos azules
De inefable candor
Veo en ellos a Dios.
[Beautiful flower of the arboretum
who sprouted from the ground
when the light of the sky
kissed your rosebud/
Of the flowers, you are enchantment
the palette loves you so much
that so crazed with love
it feels jealous of the water, the air, and the sun/
Marta,
little bud of roses
Marta
of the garden, beautiful flower
tell me, what happy butterfly
in your pistil it lands
to imbibe your sweetness/
Marta
in your clear pupils
shines a dawn of love
of ineffable candor
I see God in them.] (Translation my own)

Muñequita Linda (aka Te Quiero Dijiste) (bolero; Maria Grever, composer)

Te quiero, dijiste
tomando mis manos
entre tus manitas
de blanco marfil/
Y sentí en mi pecho
un fuerte latido
después un suspiro
y luego el chasquido
de un beso febril/
Muñequita linda
de cabellos de oro
de dientes de perla
labios de rubí/
Dime si me quieres
como yo te adoro
si de mi te acuerdas

como yo de ti/
A veces escucho
un eco divino
que envuelto en la brisa
parece decir:/
Si te quiero mucho
mucho, mucho, mucho
tanto como entonces
siempre, hasta morir.
[I love you, you said,
taking my hands
into your small hands
of white marble/
I felt in my heart
a strong beat
and then a sigh
and then the click
of a feverish kiss/
Beautiful little doll
of golden hair,
of teeth of pearls,
lips of ruby/
Tell me if you love me
as I adore you,
if you think about me
as I, about you?/
At times I can hear
a divine echo
that, enshrouded by dew,
seems to say:/
I do love you so,
so very, very, much,
as much as I did then,
always until death. (Translation mine)

Nochecita (*bolero*; Victor Huesca, composer; as interpreted by Trio Los Jaibos)

Cómo, se podrá olvidar
noche, mi testigo fiel,
dime, tú que sabes bien
si lo que canto yo
ya no puede ser/
Nochecita que de ensueño

fue mi vida,
cuando tu amor
sin mi cariño
se quedó/
Con el alma en mil pedazos,
yo te digo,
que he sufrido
la mas triste decepción/
Porque sabes
que adorarte es mi delirio,
tú te burlas
y no tienes compasión/
Yo te quiero, y en silencio
he de adorarte,
en las noches
cuando escuches
mi canción/
Porque sabes
que adorarte es mi delirio ...
[How could anyone forget
Night, my faithful witness
tell me, you who knows so well,
what I now sing,
can no longer be/
Little Night, that in my dreams
was my life
when your love
without my love was left/
With my soul in pieces
I now tell you
that I have suffered
the saddest disappointment/
Because you know
that adoring you is my delirium
you mock me,
and you have no compassion/
I love you, and in silence
I shall adore you,
in the nighttime,
when you listen, to my song/
Because you know
that adoring you is my delirium ... (Translation my own)

Nochecita (bolero; Victor Huesca, composer; as interpreted by Eydie Gorme and Los Panchos)

Nochecita que en ensueño fue mi vida
cuando su amor y su cariño me olvido
con el alma en mil pedazos yo te digo
lo que he sufrido al sentir tu decepción/
Aunque sabes que el amarte es mi delirio
Tu te burlas y no tienes compasión
Yo te quiero y en silencio he de adorarte
cuando escuches en las noches mi canción.
[Little Night, who in dreams was my life
when his love and his affection forgot me
with my soul in a thousand pieces, I tell you
how I have suffered, feeling your disappointment/
Though you know, that to love you is my delirium
you mock me, you have no compassion
I love you and in silence I shall adore you
In the nighttime, when you listen to my song.] (Translation mine)

Pecadora: (*bolero*; Agustin Lara, composer; as interpreted by Libertad Lamarque)

Divina claridad
la de tus ojos
diáfanas como gotas de cristal
uvas que se humedecen con sollozos
sangre y sonrisas juntas al mirar
sangre y sonrisas juntas al mirar/
Porqué te hizo el destino pecadora
si no sabes vender el corazón
porqué pretende odiarte quien te adora
porqué vuelve a quererte quien te odió/
Si cada noche tuya es una aurora
si cada nueva lagrima es el sol
¿porqué te hizo el destino pecadora?
si no sabes vender el corazón/
instrumental ...
Si cada noche tuya
Es una aurora ... (as interpreted by Libertad Lamarque) (unsiglodelibertad, 2009).
[Divine clarity
in your eyes
transparent like crystal droplets
grapes being moistened by sobs

blood and smiles together in a look
blood and smiles together in a look/
Why did destiny make you a sinner
when you know not how to sell your heart?
Why does the one who adores you, hopes to hate you?
Why does the one who hates you, love you again? /
If every one of your nights is a dawn
if every new tear is the sun
Why did destiny make you a sinner?
When you know not how to sell your heart/
Instrumental …
If every one of your nights is a dawn
if every new tear is the sun … (Translation my own)

Perdida (*bolero;* Chucho Navarro, composer; as recorded by Trio Los Panchos) (cancioneros.com/letras, 2021)

Perdida
te ha llamado la gente
sin saber que has sufrido
con desesperación/
Vencida
quedaste tu en la vida
por no tener cariño
que te diera ilusión/
Perdida
por que al fango rodaste
después que destrozaron
tu virtud y tu honor/
No importa que te llamen perdida
yo le daré a tu vida
que destrozo el engaño
la verdad de mi amor
[se repite toda]
[Perdida, a nickname you have been given,
no morals and a sinner,
that's what most people say/
Defeated, now your life is so uncertain
your confidence is missing
and happiness delayed/
Weary, the scorn has never ended
so low have you descended,
harming your hope and your faith/

Regardless, if they call you Perdida,
your courage and rejection
have won my deep affection,
my love for you always.] [All repeats.] (Translation by Aurora P. Pastrano, January 2007.)

Piquetes de Hormiga (*ranchera*; Magdaleno Oliva, composer; as sung by Conjunto Michoacan)

Dices que ya no me quieres
que tienes nuevos amores
cuando te sientas perdida
chiquita nomas no llores/
Si ya no me quieres ver
para que lo andas contando
no te vayas a quedar
como campana sonando/
En medio de un hormiguero
te voy a dejar sentada
a ver que carita pones
cuando estés bien picoteada/
Me hiciste llorar
me hiciste sufrir
piquetes de hormiga
tendrás que sentir/
Que desgraciada es mi suerte
y que poca es mi fortuna
cada vez que vengo a verte
hay un pato en la laguna/
Debajo de un huizachito
hizo su nido un conejo
quisiste jugar conmigo
y te puse el aparejo/
En medio de un hormiguero
te voy a dejar sentada
a ver que carita pones
cuando estés bien picoteada/
Me hiciste llorar
me hiciste sufrir
piquetes de hormiga tendrás que sentir. (Google, n/a)
[You say you no longer love me
you say that you have new loving
when you're feeling lost without me

baby just don't come crying/
If you no longer want to see me
why go around to tell?
you know that you might end up
just like the ringing bell/
In the middle of an ant's nest
I'm going to leave you sitting
let's see what face you put on
when you are totally bitten/
You hurt me, you know
I cried for you so
and now all those ant bites
you will feel somehow/
How unfortunate I am
how miserable is my luck
each time that I come to see you
I find in the pond, a duck/
Under a huizachito
a rabbit has made its nest
and you tried to play with me
but instead I got your best/
In the middle of an ant's nest
I'm going to leave you sitting
let's see what face you put on
when you are totally bitten. (Translation mine)

Perdón (*bolero*; Pedro Flores, composer; as interpreted by Los Tres Caballeros)

Perdón
vida de mi vida
perdón
si es que te he faltado
perdón
cariñito amado, ángel adorado
dame tu perdón/
Jamás habrá quien separe
amor de tu amor el mío
porque si adorarte ansió
es que el amor mío
sufre por tu amor/
Si tu sabes que te quiero
con todo el corazón/
que tu eres el anhelo

que tu eres mi esperanza
de mi única ilusión/
ven y calma mis angustias
con un poco de amor/
Que es todo lo que ansia
que es todo lo que ansia
cuando ama mi pobre corazón (Mess, 2021)
[Forgive me,
life of my life,
forgive me,
if I have failed you
forgive me,
little love of mine
my adored angel,
grant me your forgiveness/
Never, will anyone separate
love, yours from mine;
why, if I yearn to adore you
is it that my love
suffers for your love? /
If you know that I love you
with all of my heart
that you are my dream
that you are my hope
my only dream/
Come and calm my anguish
with a little love
that is all that is wished
that is all that is wished
by my poor heart.] (Translation mine)

Perjura (*classical*; Miguel Lerdo de Tejada, composer; as recorded by Jorge Negrete)

No se me olvida
cuando en tus brazos
al darte un beso
mi alma te di/
Cuando a tu lado
de amor gozando
¡ay! delirando
morir creí/
Cuando mis labios
en tu albo cuello

con fiebre loca
mi bien posé/
Y en los transportes
de amor excelso
no sé hasta dónde
mi alma se fue/
¿Por qué no fueron
aquellas horas como soñé?
¿Por qué ¡ay! huyeron
y no han podido nunca volver?/
¿Por qué no he muerto
cuando eras mía y yo tu dios?
¿Cómo es que vivo
si éramos uno y hoy somos dos? (Cancioneros, 2021)
[I do not forget
when in your arms
when in a kiss
my soul I gave you/
When, at your side
joyful in love
oh! Delirious
I thought I'd die/
When my lips
on your fair neck
crazed with feverish love
I posed my love/
And while transporting
my love exalted
I know not to where
My soul took flight/
Why were they not,
those hours as I dreamed?
Why did they, oh! Flee
never able to return? /
Why did I not die
when you were mine, and I your God?
how is it that I live
if once we were one, and now we are two?] (Translation mine)

Que te Quiero (*bolero*; Agustin Lara, composer; as recorded by Elvira Quintana)

Cuando puedan mis labios hablarte
y logren decirte lo que eres en mí
qué de cosas irán a contarte

cuántas otras sabrás tú de mí/
Que te quiero, sabrás que te quiero
cariño como este jamás existió
que mis ojos jamás han llorado
como aquella tarde que te dije adiós/
Que deseo volver a tu lado
tenerte conmigo vivir nuestro amor
que te quiero, sabrás que te quiero
porque eres mi vida, mi cielo y mi Dios/
Que deseo volver a tu lado
tenerte conmigo vivir nuestro amor
que te quiero, sabrás que te quiero
porque eres mi vida, mi cielo y mi Dios.
[When my lips are able to speak to you
and are able to tell you what you are in me
what things they will tell you!
what more you will know about me! /
That I love you,
you'll know that I love you
love like this
never existed before/
That my eyes
never have cried
as much as they did that night
that I said goodbye/
That I wish
to return to your side
have you near me
live our love/
That I love you,
you must know
that I love you
for, you are my life, my heaven, and my God.] (Translation mine)

Quizás, Quizás, Quizás (*bolero*; Osvaldo Farrés, composer) (Wikipedia, 2021).

Siempre que te pregunto
que cuándo, cómo y dónde
tú siempre me respondes
quizás, quizás, quizás/
Y así pasan los días
y yo, desesperando
y tú, tú contestando

quizás, quizás, quizás/
Estas perdiendo el tiempo
pensando, pensando
por lo que mas tu quieras
hasta cuando, hasta cuando?/
Y asi pasan los dias
y yo desesperando
y tu tu contestando
quizas, quizas, quizas.
[You won't admit you love me
and so, how am I ever
to know, you always tell me,
perhaps, perhaps, perhaps/
A million times I ask you
and then, I ask you over
again, and then you answer,
perhaps, perhaps, perhaps/
If you can't make your mind up
we'll never get started
and I don't want to wind up
being parted, brokenhearted/
So, if you really love me
say "yes" but if you don't, dear
confess, and please don't tell me
perhaps, perhaps, perhaps/
If you can't make your mind up
we'll never get started …. (Translation as recorded by Doris Day) (SAS, 2018)

Notes

1. Although one source (Cancion.com.mx, 2010–2021), credits this song to the Chilean Juan S. Garrido, a commentator on the website notes that is erroneous and that it was composed by Cuban songwriter Fernando Lopez and was recorded by Las Hermanas Aguila, with Juan S. Garrido's orchestra in 1939. This is corroborated (though the date of the recording is not provided) by the Strachwitz's Arhoolie Collection, (Strachwitz, 2021; Frontera, 2018).
2. The Italian ballad *L'edera*, composed in 1958 by Saverio Seracini and Vincenzo D'Aquisto, was re-titled as *La Hiedra* when it was transformed into a *bolero* and recorded by Mexican trios Los Tres Reyes, Los Panchos, and renowned *bolero-ranchero* soloist, Javier Solís (triosclas, 2018). The Argentinean composer Ben Molar is credited for re-writing *La Hiedra's* lyrics in Spanish (Castro Gomez, 2013).

Index

A

Academic musical training 152
Adiós Muchachos 189–190
Affirmative Action 86
African American Diaspora
    Movement 69, 85
African Blacks 68
Afro-Cuban cultural production 64
Afro-Cuban rumba dancers 64
Age
    in Mariachi music and
        performance 121–123
All-female mariachi group 151
Alma, M. 95
Amor Chiquito 190–191
Amor de la Calle 191–192
Angelitos Negros 63, 68
Anti-War Movement 79
Anzaldúa, G. 107
Apodaca-Williams families 25
Aquellos Ojos Verdes 192–193
Arellano, G. 121

Armendáriz, P. 62
Association of Artists and Singers 97, 99,
    100, 111
Association of Singers and Composers 160

B

Balancio, D. 164
Barrioization 14
Batalla de Puebla 58
Begin the Beguine 28
Beltrán, L. 7
Black Civil Rights Movement 79
Black immigrants 68
Black Lives Matter Movement 25, 85
Blackness and Mexican racial
    contradictions 63
Black or Black-mixed racial categories 68
Black soul 165
Blanco, A. E.
    Píntame Angelitos Negros 69
Bolerista Tejana 3, 106

Boleros 3, 7, 10, 27, 64–65, 77, 86, 91, 165
   Mexican music lovers and performers 91
   musical revolution 106
Boyd, C. 164
Bravado vocalization 107
Bravías 107
Brillantes, L. 165
Brown Berets 81
Burguan, R. 164

C

Camino de Guanajuato 194–195
Cancionero 195–196
Cannibal and the Headhunters 88
Cantándole a Veracruz 103
Carpas 61
Carranza, V. 59
Carrillo, V. 164
Castro, S. 81
Catholicism 15, 18, 84
Chanes, D. 165–166
   closures 167–170
   failings of the heart 170–173
   legacies 166–167
Chavira, E. 164–165
Chavira, J. 89, 90
Chicano Civil Rights Movement 10, 81–83
   identity, sadness and resistance 84–86
   philosophical and political divide 83–84
Chicano cultural identity 123
Chicano Cultural Renaissance 86–87
   La Estrella in 91
   Mexican cultural music 86
Chicano liberation 81
Chicano militant group 81
Chicano Movement 4, 146
   Cultural Renaissance 123
Chicano music 2, 87–90, 163
Chicano Renaissance
   Mariachi music and musicianship 123
Christianity 52
Cinco de Mayo 1862, 58
Ciudad Juárez

El Fronterizo 75
life and music in
   emotional survival 42–46
   marriage bond 39–42
   mistress and motherhood 36–39
   models of women's
      independence 46–49
   ¡No Me Quiero Casar!/I Don't Want to
      Get Married!, 33–36
   origins and religious legacies 51–53
   tia Eduvijes 49–51
Civil rights movements 78–80
Classical religious music 107
Coatlícue 52
Compréndeme 108, 196–197
Conjuntos Tejanos 27
Conjunto Papaloápan 102, 103, 170
Consentida 7, 197–198
Copla 64
Corridos 7, 10, 27, 59, 62, 86, 120
Cortázar, E. 28
COVID-19 pandemic 170
Cuban-born artists
   Mexican film genre 64
Cultural identity 120
Cultural music 2, 9, 86, 120, 152, 165, 167, 170
   cultural identity and community 2
Culture
   of Mexican working-class people 20

D

D'Aquisto, V. 220
Davis, E. 88
Debes Pensarlo Bien 171
Delgadillo, T. 69
Desvelo de Amor 198–199
Díaz, P. 58
Diego, J. 51, 52
Discrimination 19–20
   race and class differences 21–25
   racism in education 20–21
Domestic violence
   protection for women against 40

Don Steele, R. 76–77
Dueto Hermanas Rodriguez 148
Dueto Las Golondrinas 139–142

E

East Side Sound of Chicano music 87–90
Education
  racism in 20–21
  street-level musical education 149–150
Eisenstein, S. 66
El Chamizal 16
  economic constraints 21
  guitar 27
  legacies of discrimination 19–20
    born to run 28–29
    race and class differences 21–25
    racism in education 20–21
  music in 25–28
  poverty, economic levels 22
  Prado family 14–19
  Texan Mexican community 27
El Chicano 88
El Derecho de Nacer (The Right to be Born) 63, 69
Elena, M. 138, 142
El Hijo Desobediente 170, 199–201
El Segundo Barrio 16
Enamorada 67
English-language love songs 107
Esperón, M.
  Alma de Veracruz 70
Estrada, T. 95
Eternamente 108, 201–202
Eubanks, B. 76
Euro-centered cultural hegemony 127

F

Fallaste Corazón 11, 170
  legacies, closures, and failings of the heart 163–173
Fantasy 166
Farias, E. 166, 169, 170

Félix, M. 62, 67
Female bolero composers 96
Female mariachis 3, 10
Female Mexican labor 39
Feminist Movement 80
Fender, F. 169
Fernandez, E. 61, 66, 67
Films and music 10
Flores, R. 138
Folk musical styles. *See specific styles*
Freedom of Religion Act 15

G

Gardner, D. 123
Gender
  in Mariachi music and performance 121–123
Genres
  in Mariachi music 120–121
Golden Age of Cinema 9
Gonzalez, J. "Chuy" 89
Gorme, E. 90
Grassroots cultural workers 9
Grassroots musicians 149–150, 152, 166
Great Depression 20, 22
Grever, M. 95, 107
Grítenme Piedras del Campo 203–204
Guerra, M. 137
Guerrero, L. 87
Guitarrón 2–4, 119, 137

H

Hay Que Saber Perder 204–205
Hermanas Padilla 140, 142
Hidalgo y Costilla, M. 57–58
Huesca, A. 64, 70

I

Infante, P. 7, 47, 69, 146
  event in Bakersfield 151

International Mariachi Conference 125
Interpretando el bolero 106
Intérpretes of boleros 106

J

Jarocho music 64–65, 102
Jazz musicianship 123, 149, 165
Jiménez, J. A. 7, 28, 77, 128
Juan Charrasqueado 205–206
Juan, T. 22
Juana Gallo 67
Juanita, A. 14, 25, 28, 33
Juárez
    El Respeto Al Derecho Ajeno Es La Paz
        (Respect for the Rights of Others is
        Peace) 58
    life and music in *see* Ciudad Juárez

K

Kazem, C. 76
Kennedy, B. 84, 101, 102
King, Dr. Martin Luther, Jr. 79

L

*La Asociación de Artistas, Cantantes, y
    Compositores* 84, 97, 101
La Cucaracha 67
La Estrella
    in Chicano Renaissance 91
    promotion of 98
La Estrella De La Canción Romántica 11, 91,
    98, 104, 106, 149, 167
    becoming Aurora Pastrano 110–116
    Bolerista Stage: East Los Angeles
        1960s 96–105
    dissonant diva 106–108
    family attitudes 108–110
La Feria de las Flores 206–208
La Hiedra 208–209
La Hora de los Aficionados 96

La Negra, T. 64
La Opinión 76
La Palestina 17
La Perversa 71
Lara, A. 64, 71
La Raza 81, 83
Larios, M. 139
Las Generalas 2
    becoming professionals 154–158
    Dueto Las Golondrinas 139–142
    the finale, Aurora and
        Rodriguez 158–161
    grassroots musicians 149–150
    with instruments, c1970s 147
    internal tensions 155
    lack in musical training 149
    in late 1970s 146
    Misa Panamericana/Order of Mass for
        Mariachi 175–176
    promotional poster of event 154, 157
    street-level musical education 149–150
    test and lesson 150–154
    women and times 146–149
Latina Women's Movement 85
Latinismo 167
Latin musical style 164
Legacies of discrimination 19–20
    born to run 28–29
    race and class differences 21–25
    racism in education 20–21
Lewis, J. 79, 91
Life and music in El Chamizal 25–28
    legacies of discrimination 19–20
    born to run 28–29
    race and class differences 21–25
    racism in education 20–21
    Prado family 14–19
Life and music in Juárez
    emotional survival 42–46
    marriage bond 39–42
    mistress and motherhood 36–39
    models of women's independence 46–49
    ¡No Me Quiero Casar!/I Don't Want to
        Get Married!, 33–36
    origins and religious legacies 51–53

tia Eduvijes 49–51
Light classics 28, 107
Lincoln Park 143
Little Ray 87, 88
Live performances 28, 106
Llorarás, Llorarás 9, 33–53
Lopez, F. 220
Los Angeles
    grassroots bands 164
    Mexican American audiences 164
Los Angeles County Human Relations Council
    Mexican American youth issues 81
Los Dandys 7
Los Madrugadores (The Early Risers) 146
Los Mil Besos 7
Los Panchos 7
Los Tariácuris 146
Los Tres Aces 7
Los Vaqueros 147

M

Madero, F. I. 58
Magdalene, M. 66, 71
Mainstream music 165
Malagueña Salerosa 121
Male mariachis 145
Male song composers 95
Malo 88
Maria Candelaria 66
Mariachi
    Las Generalas
        becoming professionals 154–158
        Dueto Las Golondrinas 139–142
        the finale, Aurora and Rodriguez 158–161
        grassroots musicians 149–150
        with instruments, c1970s 147
        internal tensions 155
        lack in musical training 149
        in late 1970s 146
        Misa Panamericana/Order of Mass for Mariachi 175–176
        promotional poster of event 154, 157
        street-level musical education 149–150
        test and lesson 150–154
        women and times 146–149
    male musical performance 3
    Mariachi Festival X (10th) Anniversary, June 19 & 20, 1999 126
    music and performance
        defined 119
        gender and age 121–123
        genres in 120–121
        Jarabe Tapatío 121
        Mariachi Vargas de Tecatitlán 119
        Mexican national identity 120
        musicianship 119, 120
        rancheras and *corridos* 120, 121
        Son de la Negra 121
        Spanish colonialism 119
        in the United States 123–128
    rehearsals 156
    "street-level" musical tradition 123
    in *traje* 155
Mariachiera music 136
Mariachi Los Vaqueros 148
Mariachi Reyna de Los Angeles 4
Mariachi showmanship 145
Marquez, J. 164
Marta 28, 209–210
Martindale, W. 76
Marty's 109
Matachines 53
Matías, J. 147
Mejía, M. A. 7
Mendoza, A. 7, 77, 101, 146, 166, 173
Mestizaje 63
Mexican Americans 13, 19, 123
    business sector 22
    community 76, 78, 83, 155
    culture 2
    ethnic identity 2, 149
    mariachi groups 124
    music groups 2, 90
    performing artists 123
    students, vocational classes 82

Mexican Catholicism 53
Mexican cultural identity 10, 60, 76
Mexican cultural music 27, 60, 86, 123, 165, 170
Mexican culture
  institutionalized discrimination 19
Mexicanidad 26
Mexican national identity 9
Mexican nationalism 86, 122
Mexican radio program 146
Mexican railroad workers 14
Mexican Revolution 14, 58, 62, 120
Mexican society
  female composers 95
  Mariachi 120
Mexico
  African Blacks 68
  Basilica of Our Lady of Guadalupe 52
  blackness and Mexican racial contradictions 63
  Bolero music 64–65
  Catholic devotion 53
  Christianity 52
  colonias 53
  Cultural Renaissance 60
  cultural themes 61
  education in 57–60
  film genres 60, 61
  folklore films 64
  folk music and songs 60
  gender 61–62
  Golden Age of Cinema 60–61
  illiteracy 59
  indianness 61–62
  Jarocho music 64–65
  Mexican folklore and the Mexican Revolution 61
  musicals and musical hybrids 64
  national identity 57–65
  politics 61–62
  rumbera films 64, 65
  Rumberas music 64–65
  social justice 61–62
  traditional folk music and songs 27
  traditional music 64
  war of independence 57
Million Dollar Theatre 101
Misa Panamericana/Order of Mass for Mariachi 175–176
Mission San Gabriel church 126
Molar, B. 220
Moreno, M. 61
Morgan, W. R. 76–77
Mucho Corazón 106, 170
  autoethnographic biography 4–9
Mujer Sola 40
Mulatos 63, 69
Muñequita Linda 7, 210–211
Munoz, M. E. 136, 137
  aficionados radio contest 146
  assertiveness and determination 147
  Mariachi Martinez 147
  women's mariachi group 147
Music
  in Ciudad Juárez
    emotional survival 42–46
    marriage bond 39–42
    mistress and motherhood 36–39
    models of women's independence 46–49
    ¡*No Me Quiero Casar!*/I Don't Want to Get Married!, 33–36
    origins and religious legacies 51–53
    tia Eduvijes 49–51
  in El Chamizal 25–28
    born to run 28–29
    legacies of discrimination 19–20
    race and class differences 21–25
    racism in education 20–21
  Prado family 14–19
Música de Orquesta 28
Musical dramas 64
Musical education 138
Musical nightlife 108
Música norteña 27
Music artists
  historical recognition 3
Music lovers 163
Music makers 163
Music of Mexican Americans 8

N

Naa, Na, Na, Na Naa 75–91
Nationalism 120
Negrete, J. 7, 47, 67
Negro 102–104, 169, 170
¡No Me Quiero Casar!/I Don't Want to Get Married! 33–36
Nochecita 28, 211–213
Novelo, E. 141

O

Obregón, A. 66

P

Para Morir Iguales 108
Pascual, D. 43
Pasodobles 27
Pastrano, N. 112, 113, 115, 136
Pecadora 213–214
Pepa, D. 46, 47
Perdida 214–215
Perdón 216–217
Pérez, L. 3
Perfidia 28
Perjura 217–218
Phillips, D.
    failure and humiliation 153
Pioneer women mariachis 145, 157
Piquetes de Hormiga 215–216
Political activism 84
Polkas 27
Porter, C. 28
Powerhouse 166
Prado, A. A. 9
Prado, A. P. 96, 97
    ad hoc performances 5
    Amor Perdido 97
    audience's culture-sensitive conception 107
    avoidance of *plebe* songs and *bravía* styles 107
    Cancioneros in 169
    Catholic upbringing 52
    with Chanes 171
    classical music 28
    collection of old popular song titles 177–187
    Conjunto Papaloápan album 103
    cultural identity and gendered subjectivity 2
    cultural music 106
    dissonant diva 106
    East Los Angeles music scene 97
    emotional survival 42–46
    entrepreneur women 48
    ethnic identity 84
    examining guitarrón 168
    La Estrella de la Canción Romántica/Star of the Romantic Song 2, 4, 5
    level of understanding of Spanish 21
    love of music 167
    mariachi *guitarrón* player 2, 3
    Mariachi *traje* 1994, 161
    melody and vocalization style 107
    Mucho Corazón 6–7
    mujer sola 105
    musical performances 91, 167
    national citizenship 85
    performing as duo *Las Golondrinas*, La Costa Restaurant 142
    performing at State Ballroom 101, 102
    playing the piano 168
    promotional poster of performance program (Thrift Furniture Co.) 111, 112
    promotion of *La Estrella* 98
    public musical performances 2, 106, 170
    ranchera songs 169
    socioeconomic and sociopolitical disadvantages 21
    stages of life 2, 5
    Tex-Mex experience 7
    with Saulo Sedan (requintista) 141

Promociones Serrano 98
Public artists 8
Public schools
    Mexican children 20

Q

Que te Quiero 218–219
Quizás, Quizás, Quizás 219–220

R

Race and class differences 21–25
Racial discrimination 63
Racism
    in education 20–21
Ramírez, A. 28
Ranchera-boleros 107
Rancheras 7, 10, 27, 62, 86, 90, 107, 120, 165
R&B oldies 165
Reifler-Flores, C. 4, 148, 149
Reinoso, O. 81
Requinto 165
Rodriguez, L. 11, 137, 138, 140, 142, 147
    La Malagueña 161
    Las Generalas 148
    participation in mariachi group 159
    role model for women 160
    sexual harassment 155
Rosie and the Originals 88
Rumbera films 64, 65
Rumberas music 64–65, 72

S

Salon Mexico 71
Sánchez, C. 7, 160
Sánchez, S. 109
Sangria 166
Sedan, S. 141
Seracini, S. 220
Sexual harassment 155

Sexual, racial/gender normativity 107
Shogren, T. 164
Silva, C.
    as interpreter of song 106
Simón, M. 28
Sin Un Amor 13–29
Socio-cultural system
    mistress and motherhood 36
Socio-political movements 146
Solís, J. 47, 90, 220
Son Clave de Oro 64, 70
Spanish invaders and missionaries 15
Stevenson, R. 120
Street-level musical education 123, 149–150, 152
Student Movement 85
Suavé The Band 163–166
Sue, C. 63
Sunny and the Sunglows (aka: Sunny and the Sunliners) 88

T

Tampoco cantaba bravías 107
Tangos 7, 107
Tanori, C. 164
Tejano music 2
Texas-Mexican conjunto music 27
Tex-Mex music styles 28
The Big Beats 90
Thee Midniters 88
The Mob 164, 166
The Tejano Jim Crow Experience 19
The Village Callers 87
Tia Eduvijes
    injustices of the *Porfiriato* 49
    spiritual beliefs and practices 50
Tierra 88
Tierra Brava 70
Tizoc: Amor Indio (Indian Love) 66
Tonantzín 52
Tosti, T. 87
Trio Calaveras 67–68
Trio Sol y Luna 104, 166, 169, 170

Trobairitz 96
Trump, D. 9, 85
Tuna, C. 76–77
Tu Olvido 28

U

United Mexican American Students (UMAS) 82
United States
    all-female mariachi 4
    development of the railway system 14
    Mariachi music in 123–128
    Mexican Americans in 13
    Mexican immigrants 14

V

Valdelamar, E. E. 7
Valdelamar, M. E. 95, 96
Valdez, A.
    rancheras 147
Valses 27
Van Dyke, C. 76–77
Vargas, D. 2, 106
Velázquez, C. 95
Veracruz 102
    Historia de un Gran Amor 69
Victoria, M. 96
Viet Nam War 81
Villa, P. 59
Volver, Volver 119–130

W

Wallace, G. 91

West Coast East Side Sound. *See* Chicano musical brand
Williams, H. 79
Williams, J. 25
Women
    bolero singers 105
    entrepreneurship 46
    involvement in mariachi music 147
    in *Las Generalas* 148
    leadership and artistic quality 145
    as music composers 95
    pioneer women mariachis 145
    protection against domestic violence 40
    sexuality 95
    tortillería and *carbonera owners* 46
Women's Movement 80, 146
Working-class Mexicans
    institutionalized discrimination 19
Working-class urban Mexican Communities 22

X

XEJ or XEW radio station 59, 97

Y

Young Citizens for Community Action (YCCA) 81

Z

Zacarías, M. 67
Zapata, E. 59

www.ingramcontent.com/pod-product-compliance
Lightning Source LLC
Chambersburg PA
CBHW072148290426
44111CB00012B/2008